VANCOUVER
TO
CANBERRA
1983-1990

VANCOUVER
TO
CANBERRA
1983-1990

**Report of the Central Committee
of the World Council of Churches
to the Seventh Assembly**

Edited by Thomas F. Best

WCC Publications, Geneva

Also available in French, German and Spanish

Photos: inside front cover and p.ix, WCC/Peter Williams

Cover design: Rob Lucas

ISBN 2-8254-0987-1

© 1990 WCC Publications, World Council of Churches,
150 route de Ferney, 1211 Geneva 2, Switzerland

Printed in Switzerland

Table of Contents

Preface

This book forms the official report on the work of the World Council of Churches (WCC) and the path it has taken since its last assembly in Vancouver in 1983. It is important that assembly delegates from the member churches should acquaint themselves, through this report, with the work which the World Council has done in the years since Vancouver so that they can be prepared for the discussions and debates that await them in Canberra.

The task of an assembly is to examine critically the road so far travelled by the Council, and to take decisions about the Council's future work. In so doing it is important to bear in mind the purposes of the World Council of Churches as laid down in its constitution. Some of these are as follows:

1) to call the churches to the goal of visible unity in one faith and in one eucharistic fellowship expressed in worship and in common life in Christ, and to advance towards that unity in order that the world may believe;

2) to facilitate the common witness of the churches in each place and in all places;

3) to support the churches in their worldwide missionary and evangelistic task;

4) to express the common concern of the churches in the service of human need, the breaking down of barriers between people, and the promotion of one human family in justice and peace;

5) to foster the renewal of the churches in unity, worship, mission and service.

Those participants who are preparing for an assembly for the first time will probably be astonished — and perhaps also confused — by the multitude of tasks which the Council carries out through its various programme units. This makes it all the more important to gain a general picture, and not to let the many individual fields in which the World

Council is active obscure the great, overarching vision which the Council seeks to serve in all the areas of its work. That vision is most clearly expressed in Jesus' prayer for the unity of the church: "that they may all be one. As you, Father, are in me and I am in you, may they also be in us, so that the world may believe that you have sent me" (John 17:21 NRSV).

Dr Willem A. Visser 't Hooft, the first general secretary of the World Council of Churches, used to sum up its task as that of mediating "the whole Gospel for the whole world through the whole church".

I hope that, by their prayers, experiences and decisions, the delegates to the coming assembly in Canberra will help the WCC to fulfill in the years ahead its calling to serve the cause of unity among all Christians, and to promote the common life of all human beings in justice and peace.

HEINZ JOACHIM HELD
Moderator, central committee

Introduction

It seems impossible that only eight years have passed since the last World Council of Churches assembly in Vancouver. History has moved at incredible speed, changes follow upon changes.

Vancouver took for granted a world divided between two powerful blocks in a permanent attitude of cold war. Their security, and the security of the world as a whole, was built on a balance of terror. Today, conversations on disarmament have come to some fruition and there are evidences that further progress will soon be achieved. Perhaps the hottest debate in Vancouver was on the issue of the Soviet troops in Afghanistan. Today, those troops have gone home, the "mistake" has been officially recognized by the Soviet authorities, but peace has not yet come to the Afghan people.

While the apartheid regime is still a tragic reality in South Africa the recent independence of Namibia, and the beginning of conversations between the liberation movements and the South African government have opened the door to the hope that, before too long, the new day of justice and reconciliation will dawn for the whole of Southern Africa.

In 1983 a great number of Latin American countries were suffering under military dictatorships. Today every country in Latin America has a democratically elected government. While this is not the end-solution for the problems of the peoples of Latin America — as shown dramatically by the civil wars going on in Guatemala, El Salvador, Peru and elsewhere, and by hyperinflation in Argentina and Brazil — still the framework of democratic institutions is a far better point of departure for the search for social justice and national reconciliation than dictatorships.

At the Nairobi assembly in 1975, debate centred on questions of human rights in socialist countries, especially in Eastern Europe. Today, in most of these countries democratic elections are being held and a multi-party system established. Church buildings which had been taken away are being given back by the thousands, and religion, especially Christian religion, is recognized as one of the main partners in this shaping of a new society. Of course this process is not without tensions, as manifested by the ethnic conflicts within the Soviet Union and in the Balkan countries, and the uncertainties over the borders established after the second world war.

But there have been negative developments as well: drug consumption, especially in rich countries, and international trade and banking operations related to that despicable traffic, pose problems of the first magnitude. It is estimated that today the drug trade comes second only to that in weapons!

The steady increase in the general contamination of the atmosphere and in the desertification taking place in Africa and Latin America is a growing threat for the present and the future of humanity. While there is a new awareness of such problems, the political will and the radical courage needed to control them are lacking. In Vancouver the delegations from the Pacific challenged us with their plight of being a testing ground for atomic weapons, and the possibility that they will become a "garbage dump" for the rich nations of the earth. We will hear again in Canberra their *cri de coeur* asking for international solidarity to preserve the beauty of their islands and the purity of the Pacific Ocean — not only for themselves, but for the glory of God and the benefit of humankind.

New challenges confront us today. Developments in modern science, especially genetic science, enhancing the capacity of humankind to expand its control over its own life and future, are full of promise. The WCC central committee addressed this issue at its meeting in Moscow and the report produced on that occasion is worth reading and pondering. Technology, translating science into products which are intended for the benefit of humankind, is also transforming our habitat and human communications. The debate over the patenting of new forms of life — that is, whether they should become commercial commodities — not only challenges cherished values, but also raises profound social and economic issues touching the relations between human beings, and between humankind and nature.

There is a recognized need to engage in the search for a new model of society built upon the experience achieved in the long years of confrontation between capitalism and socialism. The fact remains that the world economic system is not able to cope with the problem of international debt. Poverty is increasing by leaps and bounds in countries of the South, while the concentration of riches in the industrialized nations goes beyond any previous imagining. How can we develop the economy, while

preserving human solidarity? Or, to put the human factor first, how can
we build societies of reciprocal, sustainable support which are able to
cope with the needs of the majority of the people of the world?

Population growth continues unabated. Since Vancouver the population of our planet has increased by nearly five hundred million people.
While Christians (and people of other convictions) may disagree on the
means and ways to control this population growth, they cannot disagree
on the need for a responsible approach to parenthood for the sake of both
the present and future generations.

The new "awakening" of religion around the world deserves special
consideration. It reflects a new thirst for meaning, for eternity; it reflects a
new desire for values which are perceived to be more permanent than the
changing fashions of the day. It is an invitation to evangelism, to
announce the good news of God in Jesus Christ to a generation which,
like the people in Athens, is basically "very religious" (Acts 17:22).
While this new reality gives a welcome opening to the mystery of faith
and to the search for meaning and values in society, it is also true that the
religious awakening today often assumes forms of fanatical fundamentalism, or includes ethnic claims which make of religion a dangerous force
in society. Here too we have a new challenge before us, and the "dialogue
with people of other faiths" becomes existential: the life and death
obligation to learn how to live together, how to build pluralistic societies
committed to truly human values.

It is in *this* world that the WCC has been trying, since Vancouver, to
live out its ecumenical vision. In this it is challenged by these words from
the assembly:

> The theme of the assembly — "Jesus Christ — the Life of the World" —
> expresses this vision. Life is the gift we receive. But unless we continue to
> grow, the vision of one faith and one humanity will not achieve maturity
> (*Gathered for Life*, p.250).

As this book as a whole is a report on the WCC since its previous
assembly, I will not pretend to be exhaustive but will give only some
indications, following the Vancouver guidelines, as to where I perceive
the cutting edge of that growth — in the life of the churches or in the life
of the WCC.

1. Growing towards unity

During this period we inherited the document on *Baptism, Eucharist
and Ministry* (BEM) and engaged in the process of its reception. The

many official responses sent to us by the churches are being fully documented. The main doctrinal challenge before us, as I see it, is to develop a common understanding of the ministry. Within this context the issue of the ordination of women has been vigorously debated during this period, and statements from the holy see in Rome and from Orthodox consultations have indicated their difficulties in this regard. There are traditions, canons, theological convictions which make it difficult even to enter into a consideration of it. However, two things should be mentioned:

a) There have been many positive dimensions to the response from the churches. For example, the Orthodox churches have responded with a new affirmation of the old tradition concerning the ordination of deaconesses.

b) It has become clear that it is unfair to claim that the ordination of women is *the* — or even one of the main — obstacles to the unity of the church! We had been disunited, after all, for many centuries before this topic was even raised! It is simply a consequence of the wider problem, namely our lack of reciprocal recognition of ministries. Once we have attained this goal we can then reflect together whether the denial, by some churches, of ordination to women is in fact "discrimination". Meanwhile, of course, nothing impedes a consideration of the issue of ordination of women within every Christian family, and this is taking place already.

New councils of churches have emerged. In several of them the Roman Catholic Church has become a full member. The number of member churches of the WCC has increased, but we recognize that there are still many churches which do not feel inclined to participate in any conciliar structure.

But perhaps the main point of concentration in our search for unity has been found in our work towards a common commitment, expressed through concrete actions in which we hope to see not only the fruits of our faith, but the full manifestation of our being the church of Jesus Christ. Thus, a meeting on the ecumenical sharing of resources held in El Escorial, Spain, developed "Guidelines for Sharing" which were proposed to the churches as common fundamental affirmations. Later the San Antonio conference on world mission and evangelism developed "Acts of Commitment" which extended an invitation to the participants, and through them to their churches, to assume before God the responsibility for actions of solidarity in response to the concrete situations and problems of today.

The convocation on "Justice, Peace and the Integrity of Creation" (JPIC) held in Seoul, Korea, in March 1990 marked the culmination of this search so far, and set the terms of the debate which is still before us. The dream had been to develop a conciliar process through which the churches would express the unity which they have achieved, and which would enable them to grow further in that unity by working together in the fields of justice, peace and the integrity of creation. We discovered very soon that the expression "conciliar fellowship" created problems for churches with certain dogmatic understandings of the term "conciliar". So, in practice, the process concentrated on the search for a covenant — an alliance — for justice, peace and the integrity of creation. The use of the word "covenant" is deeply intentional, indicating that, in our sharing together in the search for solutions to the problems, we are partners in the covenant which God has established with all of humankind in the promise made to Noah and in the cross and resurrection of Jesus Christ. The churches are now invited to reflect and pray about this covenant, and to enable their delegates to take further steps towards covenanting in the context of the Canberra assembly.

We recognize increasingly that the unity of the church is a sacrament of the peace and reconciliation which God desires for the whole of creation. In consequence, we see the search for our internal unity as a symbol of God's purpose for the whole of creation. At the same time we would like to see the ecumenical movement, and the unity we seek, as an instrument also of the wider reconciliation and renewal of humankind as a whole. The search for a covenant which brings our common responsibility for God's creation into the spiritual framework of God's overall love for the world, is not without biblical foundations and theological rationale. We want to grow into unity, and we perceive this growth as involving all aspects of our being the church of Jesus Christ. The search for a common confession of the apostolic faith, the common worship of the Triune God, and the common affirmation of our love for God is demonstrated in our love for our neighbour in justice, in peace, and in our care of creation.

2. Growing towards justice and peace

> Growth towards full ecclesial, spiritual, and political commitment to this expression by all member churches, in all their dimensions, should be one of the purposes of all programmes of the WCC. Justice, peace and the well-being of the whole creation are inseparable (*Gathered for Life*, p.251).

The many sections in this book will enable one to follow the WCC's engagement in expressions of solidarity with people struggling for justice in many parts of the world. The Programme to Combat Racism (PCR), especially through its Special Fund, addresses the injustice of racism. The Human Rights Resource Office for Latin America (HRROLA) has played a significant role and one which is widely recognized in that continent. The Urban Rural Mission (URM) ministry of the Commission on World Mission and Evangelism (CWME), announcing the name of Jesus Christ within ongoing historical struggles, has been an inspiration for many. Something similar can be said of the work of the Commission on the Churches' Participation in Development (CCPD), the Christian Medical Commission (CMC), and other programmes. The work of the Churches' Commission on International Affairs (CCIA) has assumed a particular importance in the fulfilment of our peace ministry, and in our attempt to facilitate solutions to local conflicts in many parts of the world. The bringing together of delegations of Christians from North and South Korea was a humble attempt to open up lines of communication between the people from both parts of that divided peninsula; their participation in the WCC central committee meeting in Moscow was a sign of hope.

The central committee in Buenos Aires was welcomed by those who had been victims of the former military dictatorship and who were celebrating their country's newly obtained freedom. They expressed their gratitude to the ecumenical movement, and to the WCC in particular, for the support which they had received during many difficult years. Listening to the mothers of the Plaza de Mayo as they expressed their gratitude to the World Council was a moving experience, one which will long remain in our memory.

The attempt to grow towards justice and peace focused during this period on the search for a covenant on justice, peace and the integrity of creation. Other sections of the WCC, such as CCPD, were working on the widespread economic crisis, especially in the many countries which carry the heavy burden of foreign debt. Church and Society focused on developing a theology of creation. All these efforts came to fruition in Seoul with the adoption of basic theological affirmations gathering up our ecumenical convictions on justice, peace and the integrity of creation and in the formulation of four covenants now submitted for consideration and action by the churches — one on the international economic order; a second on the search for alternative models to doctrines of national security; a third on the need to confront the growing danger of the "warming up" of the earth's atmosphere; and the fourth calling for a common stance against the evil of racism.

Because the attention of the central committee was called to the situation in Romania on three different occasions, we must add here a note on that discussion. Both in Hanover and in Moscow the debate centred on how best we may confront the situation of injustice prevailing in that country. In both cases the central committee decided not to make a public statement of condemnation, but rather to keep the lines of communication open with the churches in Romania. By referring to the concerns expressed by different international organizations we made it clear that we recognized the serious-ness of the situation but that, at the same time, we wanted to maintain our contacts which were valued by the people who were suffering. The more recent debate in Geneva centred on how, in this new context, we would judge the actions which we had taken in Hanover and in Moscow, and on our need to face what was perceived by the majority of members as a serious mistake of judgment. History will pass its own judgment on this whole process. But one point is clear: we affirm together our fundamental responsibility for supporting those suffering under oppression, and for strengthening the churches to become the servant body of Jesus Christ, suffering with and struggling for others. Our "political" judgment as to how to achieve these goals in specific situations may not always be unanimous, but the basic aim and the theological presuppositions undergirding our actions remain the same, and on that we are agreed.

3. Growing towards a vital and coherent theology

> A vital theology will incorporate the rich diversity of theological approaches emerging out of the varied experiences of churches throughout the world. A coherent theological approach will incorporate tradition and methods of reflection which represent the concrete needs and call of each and all members of the ecumenical movement towards unity of life and faith (*Gathered for Life*, p.251).

The forum character of the WCC, the way in which we *are* a council of churches, does not allow us to have an "official" theology. We are a permanent "laboratory" where the testimonies of different traditions, of different cultural expressions of the gospel, are in dialogue with each other; but at the same time, as we become a community of faith, we try to express the convictions which seem to be common to all of us. Faith and Order has attempted this in BEM and continues to work towards the "Common Expression of the Apostolic Faith", while relating the search for church unity to issues of human renewal in "The Unity of the Church and the Renewal of Human Community". The elements brought together in the basis of the WCC — confessing the Triune God, the person of Jesus Christ, the authority of the Bible, and the "fellowship character" of our life as a council — are all basic components of our vision. There is a "cutting edge" of common ecumenical convictions, summarized most recently in the affirmations of faith agreed upon in Seoul. But clearly, in a living organism such as the WCC, new challenges emerge continually to test both the vitality of our theology and our ability to grow towards a more coherent common expression of our faith.

The new challenges before us are complex, and often controversial. For example, feminist theology questions the way in which we speak about God and the symbols we use for God, obliging us to undertake serious research and debate. The executive committee agreed that this issue calls for a concentrated theological analysis to be developed after Canberra.

Several publications during this period were devoted to the search for a vital and coherent theology. It seems that the vitality of a common missionary theology *is* present in as much as we recognize ourselves in the documents of El Escorial, San Antonio or Seoul. At the same time it is obvious that the relationship between social ethics and ecclesiology remains a major challenge, one to which we need to devote our best intellectual effort. Seoul was an illustration of the possibilities — and difficulties — of a world ecumenical conversation. The preparatory document submitted for the consideration of the participants was attacked from all angles and was finally accepted only as a "working document" to help the churches in the study of the topic; it did not bear the official approval of the convocation itself. In Seoul we found it easier to spell out our common missionary obedience than to articulate together the theological foundations of that mission and that obedience. When we add to that the difficulty of understanding JPIC as a conciliar process, and the difficulty in relating our covenanting on specific issues to the fundamental covenant which God has established in Jesus Christ, we see that we still have much work to do in this field.

The celebration of the millennium of the evangelization of Russia, attended by many ecumenical visitors, and the meeting of the central committee in Moscow, were two occasions for Protestants to be immersed in the classical expressions of Orthodox life. This was a discovery for many, not only in the sense of coming to know something new, but also in the sense of discovering the depth of our common convictions, the reality of our belonging to a common, growing tradition which has its roots in the biblical revelation and which is manifest today in the common confession of the whole people of God. Perhaps the apparently provocative expression from the Programme of Theological Education (PTE) — "theology by the people" — is not unrelated to that sense of tradition, of coherence in the life of the churches as a whole which should be a permanent part of our ecumenical existence.

4. Growing towards new dimensions of the churches' self-understanding

This challenge is one which we will continue to explore together. At the last meeting of the central committee a proposal was approved to enter into a process of reflection, "searching for a common understanding of the World Council of Churches". In this process unavoidable questions will be raised about the developing self-understanding of each of the member churches: How far has the fact of belonging to the fellowship of the WCC had a real impact on the ongoing life of the church? What have the churches learned through their participation in the ecumenical movement? For it is evident that there is a creative interaction among the member churches, manifested by reciprocal visits, increased solidarity, and the sharing of liturgical elements among various traditions.

The executive committee held two of its meetings in two very diverse situations. In 1986 in Kinshasa, Zaïre, we were hosted by the Kimbanguist Church and experienced a warm spirituality which was born in Africa and has been nurtured over the past fifty years, a sense of discipline, and an awareness of evangelistic and missionary responsibility. In 1988 the committee met in Istanbul, Turkey, the home of the Ecumenical Patriarchate. Here we were right at the heart of Orthodoxy, letting our imagination roam through the centuries to embrace the many missionary services which this church has rendered to the world church. With these two experiences, so different from each other, we were able to experience something of the plenitude of the ecumenical movement, and of the diverse Christian values to be shared in this reciprocal encounter.

The future study mentioned above will test the degree to which the ecumenical dimension of the churches' self-understanding is a reality. In the meantime we continue to pray for the day when this ecumenical dimension will be a normal component of our being the church of Jesus Christ: we need to grow until our ecumenical belonging is recognized as a constitutive element of our being a church. We look forward to the day when the intercession for the unity of the church, for the ecumenical movement, for the World Council of Churches, becomes a normal part of our churches' Sunday liturgies.

5. Growing towards a community of confessing and learning

> The gospel must be proclaimed in order to be believed. Unity must be experienced in common life and thus also be learned. Spirituality must be formed in order to be lived. All three must be at the centre of the life of all churches for the sake of the world; all three must be embodied in worship and work. The full engagement of the laity is crucial to this embodiment. Children and youth can elicit and contribute new vitality to this engagement, invigorating the vision and deepening the commitment of adults (*Gathered for Life*, p.252).

To confess Jesus Christ is integral to our being an ecumenical family. To proclaim the gospel, to evangelize, belongs to our very essence. There is no church without mission; there is no mission without the name of Jesus Christ. Several programmes of the World Council are serving this vocation of the ecumenical family. But the witness of the World Council of Churches as a whole is conceived as proclamation. The whole process of JPIC seeks to be a witness to the love of God manifested in Jesus Christ; PCR is not a "programme" of social action, but a testimony rendered to the power of the gospel to break all chains of oppression. The gospel must be proclaimed in order to be believed, and San Antonio reminded us that this proclamation is made from within the wholeness of the life of the church.

This proclamation can only be enhanced by the increased participation, in the life of the churches, of all their members. The period under review has seen the launching of the "Ecumenical Decade of the Churches in Solidarity with Women". This is an invitation to churches to affirm their solidarity with women as they struggle to overcome injustice in society, and seek to use all their God-given gifts in the service of the whole church. This ecumenical decade is becoming, in itself, a proclamation of the power of Jesus Christ to create a community wherein all of God's gifts are able to come to real fruition.

Our attention should also be called to the development of an ecumenical youth network which will culminate in 1992 with the holding of a world youth gathering. The WCC Sub-unit on Youth, together with other ecumenical organizations, is fully engaged in this process, which should further enrich the ecumenical movement through increased youth participation. This process will be a visible contribution to the growth of our ecumenical community, both in the quality of its present work and in the forming of a new generation of ecumenical leaders.

The creation of the Visser 't Hooft Endowment Fund has precisely the same aim: to provide opportunities for training present and future generations of ecumenical leaders. We hope that this fund will become fully operational at about the time of the assembly.

Spirituality, especially its expression in worship, has become central in the life of the WCC. The memory of the worship held in the tent at Vancouver has become a permanent inspiration, permeating all ecumenical encounters. The theme of the Canberra assembly — "Come, Holy Spirit — Renew the Whole Creation" — is particularly suited to help us relive, and further emphasize, this dimension of spirituality, of transcendence, of adoration. The aim is the ecumenical formation of the people of God: shaping the awareness, locally, of the richness of the global church, and the awareness, when we face global issues, that they are lived out in the worship life and concrete commitment of children, men and women in particular places facing specific situations. Ecumenical formation means an integration into the abiding tradition of the church, where gratitude for the many gifts given by God to God's church over the centuries is an invitation to common commitment to faithfulness today. Many WCC materials have been produced in forms suitable for use at the congregational level. The Bible study resources produced in preparation for the great meetings of Larnaca, El Escorial, San Antonio, Seoul and the assembly have been particularly important. We have tried through the life of the Council as a whole to stimulate the churches to grow into the community of learning and proclamation to which we are called in the discipleship of Jesus Christ.

An important tool for building up this ecumenical consciousness is the ecumenical dictionary now under production. A treasury of "ecumenical memory", it can significantly contribute to ecumenical formation in the years to come.

Towards the future

1. The World Council of Churches is, by its nature, a manifestation of the life of the churches in the service of the central message of the gospel: we announce the name of Jesus Christ and, in his name, we affirm a spiritual reality, a personal relationship with God which is the fullest manifestation of our human freedom, of our being made in the image of God. The name of Jesus Christ, the focal point of the Bible story, is at the centre of the ecumenical movement as well, and will remain so. In a world where humankind is becoming increasingly capable of understand-

ing the bewildering intricacies of the created world, we need to proclaim that the hidden meaning of that creation has been revealed to us in Jesus Christ and that that meaning is love, is freedom, is solidarity. We need to regain the vision of the kingdom of God, and to see the mission of the church at the service of that vision. The theme of our assembly ideally expresses this vision: "Come, Holy Spirit — Renew the Whole Creation".

2. We need the courage to organize, in order to respond more effectively to the needs of the world and to God's challenges. The need for a closer relationship with our member churches, with the whole Christian family, and with people of other religions or philosophical convictions, is clear. We need to increase our capacity to respond to the local situations where, for the churches and people, the global issues become concrete realities of pain and hope. The Holy Spirit, active in the church through word and sacrament, is also active and present in the world through all manifestations of creative love. The presence of the Spirit in God's creation is an invitation to take risks, to go forward, to enter into encounters, dialogue and collaboration in the most diverse situations — and all with the assurance that God is already there at work. Our testimony to Jesus Christ demands that we be present, that we respond, in a way far beyond our present institutional possibilities.

3. Two main events are waiting for us beyond the assembly: in 1992 the global youth event, and in 1993 the Faith and Order world conference on the unity we seek. It is significant that those two events come in rapid succession: the first to bring, with the passion of youth, the sense of urgency for the fulfilment of our mission; the second — inspired by the challenge and strengthened by the participation of young people — inviting the churches to recover once again the vision of the una sancta, and to commit ourselves anew to that unity which will be the response given by the Father to the prayer of the Son.

Many other activities and programmes are already present in anticipation, and many will take shape during the assembly and immediately after. In fact we are already eager to start planning for the years ahead, but the assembly theme, "Come, Holy Spirit — Renew the Whole Creation", invites us to pray and to wait for our personal renewal, the renewal of our churches, and the renewal of the whole ecumenical movement.

EMILIO CASTRO
General secretary
World Council of Churches

Vancouver to Canberra:
a Reader's Guide

Calvin Coolidge, the mid-1920s president of the United States, was reputed to have been so taciturn that once when he opened his mouth a moth flew out. The same would never be said of those of us who are privileged to toil in the ecumenical vineyard. Words — words of inspiration, presentation, explanation, clarification — are the tools through which we interpret our vision of the unity of the church, and its programmatic consequences, to the churches and to the world at large. The following comments are offered to help the reader make his or her way through the words of this book and, perhaps, to see beyond them to the commitment and excitement which lies behind many of the facts, figures and programmes reported here.

Formally speaking, *Vancouver to Canberra* is the official report of the central committee of the World Council of Churches' seventh assembly in Canberra, Australia, 7-20 February 1991. Its purpose is to present, in a form which although condensed is as complete as possible, the aims and activities of the WCC since its sixth assembly in Vancouver, Canada, 24 July-10 August 1983. This book is, then, the World Council, in the "person" of its focal body of oversight, being accountable to the churches — in a special way, of course, to its own member churches, but more generally to all the churches and Christian groups, and to the public at large.

Logically speaking, *Vancouver to Canberra* is organized according to the major divisions of the WCC itself, with accounts from the General Secretariat and each of the three programme units. (The report from the finance committee is included immediately after that on the General Secretariat.) Three appendices give up-to-date information on the Council: a selected list of the publications which it has produced since Vancouver, the members of its central committee, and its member churches. A fourth appendix lists the abbreviations and acronyms which have been used.

With respect to its preparation, *Vancouver to Canberra* is the result of a participatory process, begun in early 1989, which aimed at enabling each WCC programme division to describe as it wished its own goals, organization and work since the previous assembly. The accounts produced by each sub-unit and programme division were then reviewed and co-ordinated at the unit level, and after initial editing these texts were submitted for discussion and review to the WCC central committee meeting in Geneva in March 1990. (This is, then, with the exceptions noted below, the effective "cut-off" date for information included in the text.) Finally central committee in plenary approved the text "as its report to the Canberra assembly, with the understanding that appropriate revision will take place in light of the discussions which have occurred in the respective committees" (*Minutes*, central committee, 1990).

A careful and detailed process of "appropriate revision" has since sought to incorporate the central committee's comments, which ranged from the helpfully precise (factual corrections of dates, or a reminder of a programme emphasis which had been omitted) to the hopefully general ("Please make this section more lively and accessible to the average reader!"). Virtually every portion of the text has undergone some changes; one sub-unit account has been substantially revised (CWME, reworked by sub-unit staff at the strong suggestion of the Unit I committee). Some items have, of necessity, been added (or earlier texts reworked) only later. This includes the account of the "Justice, Peace and Integrity of Creation" process, whose world gathering in Seoul finished only on the eve of the central committee meeting, and the results of the long efforts towards programmatic re-organization, which were decided only at the central committee meeting itself.

For the sake of clarity, readability and consistency a few changes in the presentation of material have been made. The discussion of the ecumenical sharing of resources process has been consolidated and set within the chapter on the General Secretariat (where it has been lodged administratively since before the Vancouver assembly). With one or two (self-authenticating, I think) exceptions, we have avoided mentioning staff by name; and long lists of meetings have been avoided, as have footnotes (bibliographical information on cited texts published since Vancouver is available in appendix 1).

The abbreviations which litter the international institutional landscape — in our case CICARWS, CWME, PCR, PTE, JPIC, ECPG and many more — try the patience even of the "initiated" (one observer, who knew better theologically, exclaimed in a sublime moment of ecumenical exasperation that our "alphabet soup" would have been unintelligible even at Pentecost). To minimize confusion we have used the full name of each organization or programme (followed by the acronym in parentheses) for the first reference in each chapter.

Stylistically speaking, *Vancouver to Canberra* reflects the work of many contributors surveying seven years of work carried on by between two and three hundred staff from between fifty and sixty different nations and speaking some 40 languages as mother tongue (readers are left to speculate on the relationship of literary style to subject-matter and work style). It need hardly be said that, in preparing such a work, the editor's task has been more managerial than literary, and that the very nature of the work has precluded the search for a particular, much less a particularly elegant, prose style.

There is, inevitably, a certain amount of specialized "bureaucratic" language. David Johnson, the distinguished editor of *Uppsala to Nairobi*, was bold to say in his introduction to that book that "jargon and ecumenical short-hand are maddening diseases to those newly exposed to them". Fifteen years later, the disease shows no signs of remission. (What is not clear is whether the disease is itself a symptom, namely of a certain routinization of the charismatic, or perhaps simply a hardening of the intellectual arteries — and really only history can tell us this, though it is the duty of the Canberra assembly to make a preliminary diagnosis.)

Humanly speaking, *Vancouver to Canberra* represents many hours of work by staff from every part of the WCC. Here we can mention only those responsible for organizing the contributions from each major division: for the General Secretariat, Jean Stromberg; for Finance, Midge Béguin-Austin; for Unit I, the editor; for Unit II, Beth Ferris; and for Unit III, Clifford Payne. On behalf of the central committee, I extend sincere thanks to all these persons, to all who have written portions of the text, and to all those involved in the many and complicated stages of its production in not less than four languages.

These, then, are our "words", those telling about the WCC's faith, life and work from *Vancouver to Canberra*. The words are important but it is more important to look beyond the words, beyond the programmes and budget details, to the vision which, in varying ways and to varying degrees, animates us all: the calling to work for the visible unity of Christ's church, for its life and renewal, and for its witness, mission and service to the whole human community. These words, and the vision and commitment which lie behind them, are offered to that end.

TOM BEST
Pentecost 1990

General Secretariat

The mandate of the General Secretariat is to promote the wholeness and oneness of the World Council of Churches, enabling its member churches to grow towards a truly ecumenical and conciliar fellowship in fulfilment of their common calling. This requires of the General Secretariat both the co-ordination of Council programmes and the direct development of relationships with member churches and ecumenical bodies around the world.

The General Secretariat comprises the general secretary and his associated staff who are responsible for the programmes, functions and services carried out for the Council as a whole.

This report indicates how the co-ordinating, relationship-building role of the General Secretariat has been carried out since Vancouver.

RELATIONSHIPS WITH MEMBER CHURCHES

Relationships and communication with member churches have been taken very seriously during these years; nevertheless the statement from the Programme Guidelines Committee in Vancouver remains a challenge: "The Council will have to find more imaginative ways and devote more time and resources to being with the member churches and developing more programmes with them." There is a continuing need to find staff time and resources to encourage and co-ordinate two-way communication and relationships between the Council and its member churches.

Visits

There have been extensive team visits involving both staff and members of the central committee during this period, particularly around the meetings of the executive and central committees. In addition commissions and working groups, when holding their meetings in various countries, have frequently made team visits a part of their agenda. The general secretary has been present at important moments of celebration in the lives of the churches, including the 500th anniversary of the birth of Martin Luther in the German Democratic Republic and the millennium of Christianity in Russia, as well as situations where churches were encountering specific challenges in their missionary work, such as Armenia, Istanbul, Belfast, Lebanon, Israel and the occupied territories, Nigeria, Ethiopia, and Uganda. Both Philip Potter and Emilio Castro visited China. WCC staff members have travelled widely in different regions as a part of their programmatic responsibility. Such visits and travel remain a primary means of interpreting the WCC and of increasing contacts, not only with church leadership but with people at every level.

An Eminent Church Persons Group (ECPG) was appointed by the executive committee at its meeting in Atlanta, Georgia, USA, in September 1987 to explain WCC policies and actions relating to Southern Africa, and to promote international action aimed at ending the pain and suffering experienced by the people of South Africa and Namibia. The group visited governments, churches and church-related groups in Switzerland, France, Belgium, United Kingdom, Federal Republic of Germany, Japan, and the USA. The group was also received by the UN secretary-general, Mr Perez de Cuellar, the UN Special Committee on Apartheid, and the European Community in Brussels.

A number of heads of churches and church delegations have visited the WCC headquarters in Geneva, among them Pope John Paul II in 1984 and His All Holiness the Ecumenical Patriarch Dimitrios I in 1987. In addition, several thousand persons visit the Ecumenical Centre each year (there were 3,300 in 1989). Most come as church-related groups specifically to learn about the WCC. These visits provide an important opportunity for ecumenical learning and are a valuable means of contact with church members from many countries.

Orthodox churches

Since the Vancouver assembly the participation of both Eastern and Oriental Orthodox churches in the life of the Council has grown, in the spirit of previous consultations on ecumenical issues. The revision of the rules of debate (XIV.6.b.) regarding voting on matters which concern ecclesiological self-understanding, which was requested by the Orthodox churches, has proved its value. Further efforts have been made to increase Orthodox participation in the WCC central and executive committees, commissions and working groups, and on staff. A more numerous and geographically extended Orthodox representation has been agreed upon for the Canberra assembly; this should be reflected in the membership of the new governing bodies. The nomination of Orthodox staff in all sub-units remains a great challenge. In 1989 the central committee approved the proposal of the general secretary to set aside funds for ecumenical leadership formation, especially with the view of meeting the needs for more Orthodox staff. During the last four years the number of WCC scholarships for Orthodox candidates has gradually increased.

The contribution of representatives of Orthodox churches to WCC programmes, conferences, consultations and workshops has become more dynamic, ecumenically committed and creative. This applies also to Orthodox leadership of committees and ad hoc groups, to the preparation of papers on major issues and documents on important theological/ ecclesiological themes, and to shaping the programmatic reorganization of the WCC. An active role in these areas has been played by the (staff) Orthodox task force. It has organized and sponsored, in co-operation with several sub-units, 15 consultations relating to topics central to the ecumenical agenda: baptism, eucharist and ministry (BEM); the apostolic faith; mission and evangelism; dialogue; spirituality; worship; renewal; education; the role of women; justice, peace and the integrity of creation (JPIC); and the main theme and sub-themes of the Canberra assembly.

Every year, an Orthodox seminar has been organized at the Ecumenical Institute in Bossey. Several WCC meetings, including those of the central and executive committees, commissions and working groups, as well as consultations have been hosted by Orthodox churches.

Issues important to the development of relationships and the removal of obstacles to understanding and co-operation have been the subject of regular correspondence with primates of Orthodox churches and Orthodox members of the central committee.

The WCC has accompanied its Orthodox member churches in jubilee celebrations, during great events of joy and during periods of concern about internal church life and Christian witness. The visits of the general secretary to Orthodox churches have strengthened relations and ecumeni-cal co-operation. The official visits of the patriarchs of Constantinople, Antioch, Georgia, Cilicia and Ethiopia, as well as of other eminent representatives of Orthodox churches, to the Ecumenical Centre have been an affirmation of the Orthodox commitment to the life and work of the WCC. This commitment is reflected also in the decisions of the third preconciliar pan-Orthodox conference (Geneva, 1986), and in other documents, statements and publications. Thus there are new perspectives for greater Orthodox participation at all levels of the life of the WCC.

United and uniting churches

The united and uniting churches, through their commitment to the structural expression of visible unity, their experience in dialogue and their insights on theological/ecclesiological issues, offer a special witness and challenge to the WCC and the ecumenical movement as a whole.

The fifth international consultation of united and uniting churches, held in Potsdam, GDR, 1-8 July 1987, planned and conducted in co-operation with Faith and Order staff and attended by Roman Catholic and Orthodox observers, examined in a fresh way the relationship of unity to the themes of renewal, participation and mission. The focal issues in this discussion included: (a) the spiritual dimension of visible union; (b) the inter-relation of theology and action ("unity in solidarity, in the pursuit of justice and in mission, as well as unity in faith and order need to be related structurally", Potsdam report, para. 66); and (c) the experience of the united and uniting churches with common structures of decision-making and authoritative teaching. It is particularly here that the united churches are contributing to the WCC agenda; the attempts of some united churches to reconcile episcopally-ordered with non-episcopally-ordered church structures are very significant for the whole ecumenical movement.

The continuation committee of the fifth international consultation is continuing to foster the united and uniting churches' reflection on such issues as the nature of the unity we seek, models of Christian unity (including fresh understandings of organic unity), the search for common structures of teaching and decision-making, unity and mission, and the relationship between church unity and the churches' mission, witness and service.

Churches in Eastern European countries

During the post-Vancouver period the WCC followed closely its relationships with churches in the then-socialist countries in Eastern Europe. The general secretary, his deputies, and many programme staff have visited most of the churches in those countries. Personal contacts with church leaders, members of central committee, theological schools and national ecumenical bodies have been strengthened, and the involvement of these churches in WCC programmes has increased. The dialogue on relevant issues, such as *glasnost* and *perestroika*, with their implications for the local churches, church-state relations, human rights and

religious liberty, renewal, unity and common Christian witness in the new
period, has become an important part of the ecumenical agenda. In recent
months the WCC has accompanied its member churches in their participation and response to the dramatic changes in the life of Eastern European
countries.

The WCC meetings hosted in Eastern Europe, particularly the central
committee meeting in the Soviet Union (1989), the jubilee celebrations of
the Russian Orthodox Church and other events have offered propitious
occasions for further encounters on all these topics. The attention of the
central committee has centred twice — at its meetings in Hanover and in
Moscow — on the situation in Romania. With much pain, solidarity with
the member churches was affirmed and shown. Today we rejoice in the
new freedom of the Romanian people and in the renewal taking place in
the churches there.

New member churches

Since Vancouver (and up to the central committee meeting of 1990) 16
churches have become full members, and four have become associate
members of the WCC. Two of the new full members were formerly
associate members; two are the result of unions between member churches in the Lutheran family, four separate churches now being represented by two. The new member and associate member churches are
from Africa (9), the Pacific (2), North America (2), Asia (1), Central
America (1), and Latin America (1). In addition ten councils of churches
have become associate member councils since Vancouver.

The new member and associate member churches (the latter marked *)
are:

Africa

1984 Presbyterian Church in the Sudan

Episcopal Baptist Community in Africa (Zaire)

1985 Igreja Evangélica Congregacional em Angola (Evangelical Congregational Church in Angola)

Ekklesia Yanuwa a Nigeria (Church of the Brethren in Nigeria)

Eglise du Christ au Zaïre — Communauté Baptiste du Zaïre Ouest
(Church of Christ in Zaire — Baptist Community of Western Zaire)

Methodist Church in Zimbabwe

Igreja Evangélica Unida de Angola* (United Evangelical Church of Angola)

Missao Evangélica Pentecostal de Angola* (Evangelical Pentecostal Mission of Angola)

1987 Methodist Church, Ivory Coast

1990 Evangelical Lutheran Church of Zimbabwe

Reformed Church of Zimbabwe

Pacific

1985 Congregational Christian Church in American Samoa

1989 Kiribati Protestant Church

1990 Evangelical Lutheran Church of Papua New Guinea

North America

1985 Evangelical Lutheran Church in Canada (formed by the union of the Evangelical Lutheran Church of Canada and the Lutheran Church in America — Canada Section — both already full members)

1988 Evangelical Lutheran Church in America (formed by the union of the American Lutheran Church, Lutheran Church in America and the Association of Evangelical Lutheran Churches — the former two already members)

Asia

1987 Methodist Church, Upper Burma

1990 Gereja Kristen Protestan Angkola (GKPA)* (Christian Protestant Angkola Church, Indonesia)

Central America

1984 Moravian Church in Nicaragua

Latin America

1984 United Presbyterian Church in Brazil*

NEW ASSOCIATE COUNCILS SINCE VANCOUVER

Africa

1984 Sudan Council of Churches

1985 Christian Council of Tanzania
Christian Council of Zambia

1987 Christian Council of The Gambia
Liberian Council of Churches

Caribbean

1985 St Vincent Christian Council
1987 Ecumenical Council of Cuba
Jamaica Council of Churches

Latin America

1987 National Council of Christian Churches in Brazil (CONIC)

Pacific

1989 Melanesian Council of Churches

Withdrawals
   The Igreja Evangélica Pentecostal "O Brasil Para Cristo" (Evangelical
Pentecostal Church — "Brazil for Christ") has withdrawn its membership
from the WCC for the time being due to internal reasons.

RELATIONSHIPS WITH OTHER CHURCHES
AND ECUMENICAL BODIES

Non-member churches
   Since Vancouver the WCC has further developed its relationships with
non-member churches through contacts, ecumenical events at national
and regional levels and through some programmes in Faith and Order, the
Commission on World Mission and Evangelism (CWME), the world
convocation on "Justice, Peace and the Integrity of Creation" (JPIC), and
others. The most significant of these relationships has been with the
Roman Catholic Church (RCC).

Roman Catholic Church

As a structural expression of collaboration between the WCC and the RCC, the Joint Working Group (JWG) has provided a platform for common reflection and action on ecumenical issues. Between 1984 and 1990 the JWG has held five plenary meetings; in addition the executive of the JWG has met several times. In 1985 the WCC initiated a survey of co-operation with the RCC. The following year a report on the extraordinary synod of Roman Catholic bishops and an aide-mémoire on Roman Catholic relationships were presented to the executive committee of the WCC. A consultation on national councils of churches as instruments of unity (Geneva, 1986) affirmed the values of collaboration in this area, and revealed some problems. In 1988 a WCC staff paper on "Relations and Collaboration Between the WCC and the RCC" was sent to member churches and the central committee.

A full review of common activities within the JWG since Vancouver is made in the sixth report of the Group (presented to the central committee meeting in Geneva, 1990). It indicates the substantial results in areas of collaboration between WCC programme units and Roman Catholic partners at various levels, as well as between WCC member churches and local Roman Catholic churches around the world. It reflects also the progress made in some priority areas for co-operation within the JWG: "Unity of the Church — the Goal and the Way", "Common Witness" and "Ecumenical Formation", with important studies related to these themes. The document acknowledges difficulties which have been experienced in our collaboration, particularly in the field of social thought and action, and indicates possible areas for future common work.

During recent years, collaboration between several sub-units of the WCC and their Roman Catholic partners has increased. Valuable Roman Catholic contributions have been made to a range of WCC conferences and consultations, such as the San Antonio conference on world mission and evangelism and the Faith and Order Plenary Commission meeting in Budapest. The desire has been expressed for greater reciprocity regarding invitations for participation in ecumenical gatherings (for more detailed information, see sixth report of the JWG and the sections of programme units' reports).

Regional and national ecumenical bodies

Work with councils of churches was highlighted by the holding of the second world national councils of churches (NCC) consultation in Geneva, 20-24 October 1986. In the 15 years since the first (1971) consultation the family of NCCs has grown considerably; at the 1986 world consultation 120 leaders represented 70 NCCs. Their frequent cry during the consultation was for more regular opportunities to meet and work together within the NCC community. The report of this meeting was published by the WCC in 1988: *Instruments of Unity: National Councils of Churches Within the One Ecumenical Movement.*

Consultation with representatives of the NCCs has continued, especially at the time of central committee meetings. Plans have emerged from discussions in Hanover and Moscow with a group of some 35-40 NCC leaders; one important aspect of these is the decision to have a third world consultation of NCCs 18 months after the Canberra assembly.

A seminar at Bossey before that consultation will bring together around 20 new members of NCC staff, introducing them to the ecumenical movement and, in particular, to the programmes of the WCC.

Representatives of NCCs at Canberra will meet on the question of relationships with the WCC, the regional ecumenical organizations (REOs) and local ecumenical bodies. Consultation has continued with leaders of European NCCs on several occasions.

Finally, the development in regional resource sharing, heralded during the period before Vancouver, has become broader and better defined. The "Guidelines for Sharing" from the 1987 El Escorial consultation, have been widely and enthusiastically accepted. These highlight the importance of the regions and call for responses from the REOs.

The WCC programme on "Justice, Peace and the Integrity of Creation" (JPIC) has been supported especially by the REOs in Asia, Latin America, the Pacific and Europe. This kind of collaboration is vital to the ecumenical movement and the churches' concern for confronting the survival issues of today.

Christian World Communions

The relationship between the WCC and the Christian World Communions (CWCs) has remained on the agenda of ecumenical reflection and discussion. How can these different expressions of Christian community and ecumenical involvement be held together as serving the one ecumenical movement? How can they be brought into a constructive and confident relationship so that, despite their specific tasks and goals, they complement each other? These questions require attention and positive response in every new phase of the ecumenical movement.

In earlier phases of the history of the WCC, critical questions were raised about possible negative implications of CWC membership for church union negotiations. After 1970 many CWCs became actively involved in bilateral conversations with each other and especially with the Roman Catholic Church. This new and active ecumenical role of CWCs raised the question whether this would lead to an ecumenism parallel to, and disconnected from, the ecumenical efforts of the WCC. This led to an intensive period of conversations between the WCC and CWCs before the Vancouver assembly; some misunderstandings were removed and common perspectives clarified.

As a result of this development, Vancouver noted that "a deeper partnership has developed between the WCC and the Christian World Communions within the one ecumenical movement as they have faced the common calling to Christ". Accordingly, Policy Reference Committee I recommended "that the assembly *recognize* the ecumenical importance of the CWCs and the conference of secretaries of CWCs as partners in the quest for the full visible unity of the church and encourage the development of closer collaboration between the WCC and the CWCs". More specifically, this recommendation refers to common reflection on the goal of the unity we seek, the continuation of the forum on bilateral conversations, and discussion between united churches and the CWCs.

This new relationship of trust and co-operation has clearly marked the period between Vancouver and Canberra. In several instances the WCC has co-operated with some CWCs in the area of interchurch aid, emergency and refugee service. Common statements (for example, on South Africa) have been issued and joint studies have been undertaken (on new religious movements). The WCC has been invited to send representatives to major CWC meetings and assemblies (such as the World Methodist Council in 1986, the Lambeth conference of the Anglican communion in 1988, the general council of the World Alliance of Reformed Churches, the general assembly of the Christian Church (Disciples of Christ) in 1989, and the assembly of the Lutheran World Federation (LWF) in 1990; CWC representatives have visited the WCC and were invited to participate in the 1990 WCC world convocation on JPIC, as well as in the Canberra assembly. A first consultation with the Lutheran World Federation in 1981 was followed up by a second consultation at the Ecumenical Institute in Bossey in February 1989.

The annual conference of secretaries of CWCs has become an important occasion for sharing of information and discussion of common concerns, including developments and special events in the life and work of the WCC. The lively interest shown indicates that the CWCs' specific ecumenical tasks are undertaken in relation to the broader ecumenical activities of the WCC. This relationship is of particular significance for bilateral conversations between the CWCs.

The number of bilateral dialogues has increased since Vancouver. They represent on the international, regional and national levels a major expression of present ecumenical endeavour. The Commission on Faith and Order has followed developments in these dialogues by sending observers to some, and by making use of the fact that several members of the commission are involved in them; as a result, insights from these dialogues have been taken up in the work of Faith and Order. And the convergences expressed in the multilateral Lima document on *Baptism, Eucharist and Ministry* (BEM) are now taken into account in nearly all bilateral dialogues.

To strengthen this inter-relation Faith and Order, authorized by the CWCs, has organized the fourth and fifth meetings of the Forum on Bilateral Conversations in 1985 and 1990. These meetings dealt both with the coherence between the different dialogues and with their complementary relationship with the multilateral dialogues of the WCC. The 1985 forum focused on common orientations between the BEM document and bilateral results; the main subject of the 1990 meeting was "Common Perspectives in the Ecumenical Dialogues on the Understanding of the Church". The meetings of the forum have thus become most helpful in building a constructive relationship between the WCC and the CWCs in their common endeavours to lead the churches towards visible unity.

Other ecumenical partners

During the period from Vancouver to Canberra partnership with the Frontier Internship in Mission, the World Student Christian Federation, the YMCA and the World YWCA, and ad hoc consultations on mutual concerns, have continued. Such collaboration (which may be illustrated by the participation of the YWCA in the WCC Eminent Church Persons' Group) has been mutually beneficial. The YMCA contributed generously to the relief work operated by the Commission on Inter-Church Aid, Refugee and World Service (CICARWS) during this period, and the YWCA joined the WCC to initiate a non-governmental organization working group on refugee women.

A significant breakthrough in this period has been the decision to work together on a global ecumenical youth gathering to take place in 1992, which will also have the participation of Roman Catholic youth organizations such as Pax Romana, the International Movement of Catholic Students and the International Young Catholic Students. This process of rebuilding the ecumenical youth movement is expected to culminate in the gathering of 1992 and to generate energy which will move the co-operating organizations to work together in their local situations.

The experience of the general secretaries of the organizations looking to the global ecumenical youth gathering shows that regular meetings of the group are necessary for more intensive sharing of information and joint approaches to common concerns. There are other Geneva-based ecumenical bodies, such as the World Conference on Religion and Peace, whose involvement will enrich our partnership. Explorations about collaboration on the Ecumenical Decade of the Churches in Solidarity with Women have begun.

Through its sub-units, the WCC has maintained a wide variety of contacts with the United Nations and its agencies and with many non-governmental organizations. This aspect of the Council's work has been reported on by the respective sub-units.

Evangelical organizations

At the Vancouver assembly about 300 participants signed an "Open Letter of Evangelicals" which, while critical of some WCC positions, encouraged communication of those who define themselves as "evangelicals" with the WCC. It is fully recognized that many "evangelicals" are members of WCC member churches. Given the evangelicals' primary concern for evangelism, most of the WCC contacts have been channelled through the CWME — though the WCC as a whole, and its policies and statements, are closely watched by evangelical organizations.

Relationships have been maintained with the World Evangelical Fellowship (WEF; a WCC observer attended its world assembly in 1986) and with the Lausanne Committee for World Evangelization (LCWE; three WCC staff persons were observers at its July 1989 "Lausanne II at Manila" congress).

In 1987 CWME convened a consultation at Stuttgart, FRG, to which were invited a number of evangelical leaders. That consultation issued a statement, which has been widely circulated and discussed, on the nature of evangelism, local Christian communities and evangelism, evangelism and the unity of the church, evangelism and the renewal of the church, the role of para-church organizations in evangelism, and evangelism in the context of other faiths. A proposal that the WEF, the LCWE and the WCC officially constitute a joint committee for further work on matters of common concern was approved by the WCC executive committee, but rejected by WEF and LCWE.

However in February 1989, at the invitation of the church of Württemberg (FRG), WEF, LCWE and the WCC did send representatives to a joint consultation where areas of convergence and divergence were discussed openly and frankly. There was unanimous agreement that this type of consultation should be repeated in the future.

In many WCC meetings there has been a deliberate effort to invite "evangelicals" representing evangelical organizations of many kinds, and often these invitations have been readily accepted. The WEF and LCWE, as well as other evangelical organizations, sent observers to the WCC conference on world mission and evangelism at San Antonio, Texas, USA, in 1989. Here again, as at Vancouver, some 200 participants signed a letter drafted by evangelicals, this time directed to the LCWE, expressing appreciation for much that was done at San Antonio, and suggesting that in the future it might be well for LCWE and the WCC to hold their world conferences at the same time and place to facilitate interaction and understanding between the two. This proposal was presented to "Lausanne II at Manila", and it is anticipated that further conversations on this possibility may take place.

At Vancouver the *Nairobi to Vancouver* report stated that two basic reciprocal challenges needed to be faced. These still remain today. The evangelicals ask the WCC whether it takes seriously enough its evangelistic responsibility to the many who have never heard the gospel of Jesus Christ, and whether the WCC's passion for justice for the poor is matched by a similar passion for the proclamation of the gospel to "the unreached". On the other hand, the WCC asks evangelicals how they foster the unity of the church in the service of the kingdom, and how our evangelistic and missionary obedience embrace the total demands of the kingdom and the manifestation of the unity of the church.

The WCC should exert every effort to foster communication with Christians of these persuasions, and do everything possible to create "space" for mutual discussion and understanding.

WCC 40TH ANNIVERSARY CELEBRATIONS

In 1988 the WCC celebrated the 40th anniversary of its founding. This important milestone was celebrated by special events at the 1988 central committee meeting in Hanover, as well as ceremonies in Amsterdam (where the inaugural assembly was held) and in Geneva, and by the publication of a special issue of *The Ecumenical Review*.

WCC GOVERNING BODIES

Central committee

The 150-member central committee, elected by each assembly from the assembly delegates appointed by the churches, has met six times since Vancouver: in Buenos Aires, Argentina (1985); Hanover, FRG (1988); Moscow, USSR (1989); and in Geneva (1984, 1987 and 1990).

In response to the need underlined by the sixth assembly "to increase the Council's flexibility in allocating available funds for programmes and its ability to undertake new programmes of a short-term or experimental nature within the availability of undesignated funds", the central committee in Geneva (1987) approved the following procedure: that interest earned on the general reserve, the emergency reserve and the exchange fluctuation reserve be made available for new, short-term experimental programmes of not more than two years which cannot otherwise be funded, with one half of the interest money being allocated within the regular budget process and the other half to be decided by the central committee outside this process.

In Moscow the central committee voted to establish a new rule entitled "Responsibilities of Membership in the World Council". This stated, in summary form, that:

> Membership in the World Council of Churches signifies faithfulness to the basis of the Council, fellowship in the Council, participation in the life and work of the Council, and commitment to the ecumenical movement as integral to the mission of the church. Member churches of the WCC are expected to appoint delegates to the WCC assembly; to inform the WCC of their primary concerns, priorities, activities and constructive criticisms; to foster and encourage ecumenical relations and action at all levels of church life and to pursue ecumenical fellowship; to interpret both the broader ecumenical movement and the WCC, its nature, purpose and programmes throughout their membership; to encourage participation in WCC programmes, activities and meetings by proposing persons who could make a particular contribution, by establishing links between their own programme offices and the appropriate WCC programme offices, and by submitting materials for and promoting WCC communications resources; to respond to decisions of the central committee; and to make an annual contribution to the general budget and programmes of the WCC.

The report of the committee on the General Secretariat in Hanover "affirmed suggestions for the study of the organization of the WCC. The committee urged staff to explore further the questions raised in the general secretary's report related to style of work and future planning.

Ideas and guidelines should be brought to a future meeting of the executive committee and then to the central committee for consideration." In its February 1989 meeting, the executive committee appointed an ad hoc committee which prepared a paper on programmatic reorganization for consideration by the executive in Zagorsk and the central committee in Moscow. After discussion the central committee appointed a group to bring proposals for programmatic reorganization to its March 1990 meeting. The Committee on Programmatic Reorganization (CPR) met twice between central committee meetings. In Geneva a proposal of the CPR was presented in plenary and, on the basis of the discussion there and in the unit committees, modified. This later version was not discussed, however, but by means of a privileged motion both reports of the CPR were received and referred to the next central committee for study and action.

In Moscow the central committee also requested the general secretary to develop a process of consultation on the common understanding and vision of the WCC and on the relationship of the WCC to its member churches, to non-member churches and to other Christian groups. A proposal outlining a process of reflection and discussion with the churches, to be developed after the assembly, was accepted by the central committee in Geneva.

Executive committee

This committee oversees the work of the Council between meetings of the central committee, and often prepares a number of policy matters on which the central committee can act. It has also provided occasions for discussion in depth on major concerns such as vital and coherent theology, the WCC-Roman Catholic relationship, Namibia, dialogue with the black churches in the USA, programmatic reorganization, and others.

The executive committee has met twice annually: seven times in Geneva; and in Buenos Aires, Argentina; Kinshasa, Zaire; Atlanta, Georgia, USA; Istanbul, Turkey; Loccum, FRG; Zagorsk, USSR; and Granvollen, Norway.

An ongoing discussion was resolved in the action of the central committee (Geneva, 1990) that, at its first meeting after the assembly, the committee will make a schedule for rotation of all non-ex officio members of the executive committee.

Officers and presidium

The officers have maintained constant contact with one another between and during executive and central committee meetings. The moderator has represented the WCC in visits to various countries, including Norway, Indonesia, India and Romania.

Since Vancouver the presidents have been very active in representing the Council and in assuming specific responsibilities; examples are their participation on the Eminent Church Persons' team, in the JPIC moderatorship, in the team visit to Central America, and at the United Nations. They have continued to issue their annual Pentecost message, which has been widely distributed in the churches. They have also fully participated in the meetings of the central and executive committees.

PUBLIC ISSUES

After the Vancouver assembly there was again discussion on the role of the WCC in international affairs and on the special role of public statements. In 1976 the central committee had identified the following criteria for public statements, namely that they should address:
— areas and issues in which the WCC has a direct involvement and long-standing commitment;
— emerging issues of international concern to which the attention of the churches should be called for action;
— critical and developing political situations which demand of the WCC to make known its judgment and lend its spiritual and moral voice;
— expectations from the churches and various secular bodies that the WCC should speak on particular issues;
and that they should:
— set the policy and mandate for the WCC secretariat.
In the official report of the sixth assembly, the chapter on "World Affairs in Ecumenical Perspective" begins as follows:

> The making and breaking of human life anywhere and for whatever reason is the legitimate and necessary concern of Christ's church: on that score the churches as they work together through their World Council have never had any doubts. Moreover, an assembly that had meditated at length on the Vancouver theme was bound to try to bring the insights of the gospel to bear, quite specifically, on the life-denying forces rampant in the year of our Lord 1983. But where to start? Where to stop? And how to select?

The Commission of the Churches on International Affairs (CCIA) prepared a document on "The Role of the World Council of Churches in International Affairs". This was commended to the member churches by the central committee in August 1985. As its foreword says:

The document explains the rationale and theological basis of the WCC's involvement in international affairs, the procedures and forms of action and implications of such involvement for the fellowship and unity of the churches. It draws on the affirmations, findings and thinking of various parts of the WCC. It therefore underlines the linkages existing between work in international affairs and work connected with mission and unity.

The document makes clear that public statements must be seen within the context of the WCC's involvement in international affairs through various means and forms of action. It emphasizes that public statements are only one form of action, and to judge the WCC's role in international affairs on this basis alone is misleading.

Under the general term "public statements" the WCC has published a wide variety of texts, including assessments of situations, appeals to member churches, representations and appeals to governments and inter-governmental bodies, pastoral letters and resolutions. A careful procedure is followed for preparation and presentation of public statements.

The authority of public statements is defined in the rules of the WCC. They are not binding on the member churches; their "authority will consist only in the weight which they carry by their own truth and wisdom".

During the period of this report the central and executive committees have adopted statements on a wide range of issues and situations: human rights, peace and disarmament, the international food disorder, the international debt crisis, Southern Africa, Korea, the Philippines, Sri Lanka, Poland, the USSR, Central America, the Caribbean, the Middle East and the Pacific. In addition, the officers or the general secretary have issued a number of statements on specific developments in conformity with policies established by WCC governing bodies.

Other forms of action, which are also part of the Council's witness in the realm of public affairs, have included delegations and pastoral visits to conflict situations, representations (sometimes on a confidential basis) to governments and intergovernmental bodies, and facilitation of communication between parties in a conflict, etc.

ASSEMBLY PREPARATION

In one sense all work of the WCC following one assembly is a preparation for the next. Nevertheless there is a point between assemblies when the focus of attention shifts from what the last assembly said to what the next assembly will do. In these years from Vancouver to Canberra, the turning point was the central committee meeting in 1987. At this time, the Assembly Planning Committee (APC) was appointed and the assembly theme adopted.

Assembly preparation, however, had already begun. Following invitations from churches in several countries and staff exploration of the different possibilities, the invitation from the Australian churches to meet in Canberra was accepted by the executive committee in September 1986. In January 1987 the central committee appointed 21 of its members to serve on the APC with the Rev. Dr Avery Post, then president of the United Church of Christ, USA, as moderator.

By the time of the Canberra assembly the APC will have met six times. The assembly worship committee, appointed in 1988 with Grand Proto-presbyter Georges Tsetsis of the Ecumenical Patriarchate as moderator, will have had four meetings. Both committees have met once in Canberra. They have engaged in intensive and creative work for the preparation of the seventh assembly, and much gratitude is due them.

At the central committee meeting of January 1987 support was expressed for an assembly theme centred on the Holy Spirit. After careful consideration, the APC made specific recommendations to the central committee, and the theme, "Come, Holy Spirit — Renew the Whole Creation", was chosen together with four sub-themes. It was agreed that each sub-theme would be the focus for one of the four sections of the assembly, where consideration would include both the theological content and the programmatic issues arising from the sub-theme.

Two special consultations on the theme were held in 1989, one to develop the sub-themes and issues, and one on the theme and sub-themes from the Orthodox perspective.

The central committee in 1988 decided on the allocation of seats for delegates to the member churches, who were then invited to name their delegates.

Meanwhile, a national committee was formed in Australia for assembly preparations with Mr John Denton, general secretary, Anglican Church of Australia, as moderator and Ms Jean Skuse, former vice-moderator of the central committee, as national co-ordinator. The Canberra churches' assembly committee has been chaired by the Rt Rev. Owen Dowling, Bishop of Canberra and Goulbourn.

The programme of the assembly has been developed to provide adequate time for consideration of the theme, sub-themes and programmatic issues, for committee work and for the business of the assembly including policy guidelines for the future work of the Council. The Bible studies, section papers and the present report are seen as major contributions to this end. The Bible studies have been translated for publication in the languages of many member churches.

The planning of the assembly has also recognized the need to give importance to the participation of Australian Aborigines and to their concerns, to receive the large number of visitors expected, and to foster the participation of children. Regional preparatory meetings are taking place around the world; new publications and visual aids have been produced.

In Geneva more than one hundred staff members have been involved in over twenty task forces to support the work of the APC and the assembly worship committee in preparing the assembly.

STAFF STRUCTURES AND RESPONSIBILITIES

Staff Executive Group

The Staff Executive Group (SEG) is composed of the staff of the General Secretariat, the heads of all sub-units and departments, the moderators of the regional task forces and other representative staff members. Its function is to advise the general secretary on the implementation of policy established by the central and executive committees.

SEG has met regularly as a forum for corporate reflection on policy matters. Its work has been facilitated by a wide variety of task forces on regional relationships, travel, finance policy, communication, publications, relations with Orthodox churches, etc. There has been a regular review of the work of each sub-unit and department during the period.

Personnel

Personnel-related matters, particularly the question of staff balances, have occupied a significant place on the agenda of the governing bodies during this period. The desirability and necessity for the WCC to have a staff characterized first by their Christian commitment, and their competence for their particular responsibilities within the Council, was reaffirmed. Furthermore the purpose of the WCC can best be fulfilled if the Council, in selecting its staff, takes advantage of the vast, rich diversity of its member churches. This diversity includes different religious traditions, cultures, and political and social environments. While it is not possible for the WCC to represent all the diversity of its member churches within its staff, it is necessary that it have sufficient diversity for all churches to have some point of identification through which they may be encouraged to pursue their ecumenical commitment. The staff of the Council is important to this goal.

In 1987 the central committee approved "directions" in which the WCC should move in its search for a better-balanced executive staff. It agreed on a series of guidelines, such as:

1) a minimum and maximum of staff persons to come from each region, as follows:

	Minimum	Maximum
Africa	10	14
Asia - Australia - New Zealand	10	14
Eastern Europe	6	10
Latin America - Caribbean	5	10
Middle East	3	6
North America	12	20
Pacific	3	6
Western Europe	15	20

2) that regional, sub-regional, confessional and gender balances should be taken into consideration when recruiting new staff.

In 1987 the central committee approved two documents: one on "Staffing Procedures" and another on "Procedures for Renewal and Non-Renewal of Contracts". These clarify procedures for the advertising of vacancies, screening of applications, shortlisting of applicants, interviews, and so on, as well as the role of commissions and committees in the process. Through the years progress was achieved in staff balancing and representation. The composition of the staff at different periods is as follows:

— in 1969, from 44 churches and 37 countries;
— in 1974, from 49 churches and 45 countries;
— and in 1990, from 89 churches and 63 countries;

There is a conviction that fewer administrative centres can better ensure the staff balances needed in the whole Council, especially in relation to the number of women and Orthodox.

The total number of staff was 315 by March 1990, representing a 7.5% increase for the period between Vancouver and Canberra. (It should be noted that of the 315, 74 persons are employed part-time.) By comparison, in 1970 there were 373 staff, and 329 in 1974. The following table summarizes the composition of staff:

STATISTICS BY GRADE, MARCH 1990

Grade	Women	Men	Average age
01	4	—	38.49
02	4	3	33.99
03	27	4	42.26
04	74	5	41.80
05	70	9	45.32
06	13	6	47.25
07	21	45	47.82
08	4	14	47.73
09	—	9	54.23
10	2	1	58.97
Total	*219*	*96*	
Total (men and women)	*315*		*44.89*

Rules and regulations: In October 1988 a revised edition of the Staff Rules and Regulations was introduced; it included a series of improvements in the general conditions of service of the staff. The rules and regulations form an integral part of the contract between the Council and its staff. The salary scale was also reviewed during this period and some of its basic assumptions re-affirmed, including the conviction that:
1) the system must reflect the philosophy for which the WCC stands and the objectives towards which it works;
2) it must be a scheme that is equitable and fair to all, and which is seen to be so;
3) it must attract and retain staff of the calibre necessary, at all levels, to conduct the work of the WCC efficiently both now and in the future;
4) it must motivate employees to improve their performance and to accept greater responsibility.

Maximum years of service: The rule of maximum years of service approved in 1974 was designed to increase the turnover of the staff, to ensure that the staff return to their churches to share their international ecumenical experience, and to improve regional representation among staff. In 1984 the central committee called for a re-examination of the maximum years of service rule. An interim report was presented to the meeting in Buenos Aires in 1985. In 1987 the executive and central committees carefully assessed the result of the implementation of the rule and decided to abolish it, "with the understanding that the contract system and the performance appraisal system remain unchanged and that the executive committee's actions are implemented" (these "actions" refer to the above-mentioned document on staff procedures and the procedures for renewal and non-renewal of contracts).

This period showed an improvement in staff procedures, though certain areas remain to be worked out; these have to do with staff recruitment and development, and the re-integration of staff into their churches following service with the WCC.

THE ECUMENICAL CENTRE: THE NEW WING

The growth of the ecumenical family "living" in the Ecumenical Centre — which includes not only the WCC but also related organizations — obliged the executive committee to approve the extension of the Centre through the construction of a new wing, offering some eighty new offices and several meeting rooms for small groups. Many of the offices are not presently needed for the WCC, and have been rented to other church-related and human rights organizations which desire to be located in Geneva. This new wing enlarges the "patrimony" of the WCC and provides support facilities for the ongoing work of the ecumenical movement.*

One facility in the new wing deserves special mention. On the ground floor, in a bright and comfortable suite of rooms, the Ecumenical Women's Group (EWG) re-opened its "Open House" in May 1987. Besides welcoming visitors and staff members on weekday afternoons, the Open House is used for meetings of the EWG and other in-house groups (including the Ecumenical Centre Staff Association, ECSA), receptions, language classes and family potluck suppers. It is also available to certain outside groups, such as a young mothers' group once a week and an African women's group once a month. Recently some refugees, being housed temporarily in Grand-Saconnex parish and receiving noon meals at the Ecumenical Centre cafeteria, found a haven in the Open House where a bit of family life could continue.

ECUMENICAL INSTITUTE, BOSSEY

In the winter of 1986-87 the Ecumenical Institute celebrated its 40th anniversary, in a spirit of gratitude for the years that it had served the

---

* For additional details and the financial aspects of the new wing see pp. 79-80.

WCC and the wider ecumenical cause. During these four decades, moments of crisis had threatened its existence. Fortunately, as mentioned already in *Nairobi to Vancouver*, this situation was stabilized by restructuring, making better use of the facilities, and the securing of a new basis of support to replace the large WCC grant which had previously subsidized the Institute.

A better regional balance among faculty was achieved during this period, with staff coming from Europe, Asia and the Caribbean. The post of associate director was changed to a fourth teaching staff position, and at that point the oversight of the Institute's total operation was shared by the members of the teaching staff. After an initial trial period, this structure of collective leadership has generally worked well. Regional balances have been maintained — in spite of staff turnover — by inviting tutors or visiting scholars to come for shorter periods from regions not represented. Moreover, the Institute has had each year the assistance of a *Vikar* from one of the West German churches to accompany the many German guest groups, and had for one year the help of a "faculty assistant", seconded by a volunteer in mission programme of the Presbyterian Church in the USA.

In an agreement with the holy see, a Roman Catholic theologian was appointed as seconded staff in September 1989.

In Moscow, the central committee approved a recommendation that the Ecumenical Institute and the Programme on Theological Education (PTE) begin a process of joining their efforts, to serve the theological renewal and ecumenical formation of the churches more effectively. The director of PTE was appointed also as director of the Ecumenical Institute until the end of his term at PTE, in June 1990.

Programme

The Institute offers programmes which contribute to the general task of education for ecumenism, including the graduate school, short courses and seminars, and programmes for visiting groups.

1. The Graduate School of Ecumenical Studies — and the continued discussion about its form and methodology — continues to be the most substantial part of the Institute's programme. Semesters are divided into two parts, the first devoted principally to academic input on the theme and to the preparation of a paper by each student, and the second focused on perspectives for the renewal of church and society in different regional contexts, and on how participants can follow up the theme ecumenically on their return home.

The themes of the graduate school orient the overall programme of ecumenical learning; they are formulated in relation to ongoing discussions in the larger context of the WCC as a whole. Recent themes have been:

1983-84: The unity of the church and the unity of humankind
1984-85: Faith and Christian discipleship today
1985-86: Gospel and culture I
1986-87: Gospel and culture II
1987-88: Unity and mission
1988-89: Justice, peace and the integrity of creation
1989-90: The Holy Spirit and the prophetic witness of the church
1990-91: Come, Holy Spirit — renew the whole creation

Ecumenical learning during the graduate school is a rich and complex experience. The fact that participants come from many countries and churches, live together for almost five months, study together, pray together, and discuss together a crucial ecumenical theme, is in itself extremely important. Certainly this being together of many persons from different confessions, theologies, cultures and approaches is not without its difficulties and tensions; but it also provides creative opportunities for enlarged vision and deepened commitment. Graduate school participants are not considered primarily as students coming to learn, but rather as resource persons who can best interpret their own context, in which they must "live" ecumenism.

As was the case before Vancouver, the two graduate schools prior to Canberra have studied the assembly theme in all its aspects. This preparation of local churches' representatives is a contribution to the growing awareness that a WCC assembly is not simply the affair of specialists and staff. Rather it is the responsibility of all member churches to invest their best in this process of mutual communication. And indeed, churches are regularly using their Bossey-trained members for ecumenical tasks.

2. The second pillar of the Bossey programme is the shorter courses and seminars offered every year. Many of these are planned and organized in co-operation with sub-units of the WCC, or with other ecumenical bodies. They offer a concentrated process for reflection on a specific ecumenical theme and are for many who cannot participate in the longer graduate school programme a first encounter with ecumenical thought and sharing. The so-called "summer programmes" for 1989, for example, were:

— the ministry of the ministry;
— Orthodox theology and spirituality;
— workshop on inclusive liturgy and music;
— ecumenical youth conference;
— the ministry of the laity;
— partnership in ecumenical leadership formation.

The seminar on Orthodox theology and spirituality, which takes place each year preceding Orthodox Easter, was created to introduce the Orthodox tradition to members of the non-Orthodox churches. As an example of co-operative work the seminar on "Models of Renewed Community" (May 1987) may be mentioned. This was planned and conducted by staff from Bossey, Faith and Order, the Sub-unit on Women, the Programme on Theological Education and the Office of Women in Church and Society of the Lutheran World Federation; it sought not only to study but also to build community among an exceptionally diverse group of participants. The papers, reflections and creative productions are recorded in *The Search for New Community: a Bossey Seminar*, a book published by the WCC Publications department on behalf of the consultation.

3. The third pillar of the programme has become increasingly the visiting groups who stay for shorter periods, for whom specific programmes about the WCC are arranged according to their need and preference. The Bossey staff takes responsibility for preparing the programmes, inviting guest speakers and giving lectures. Although these experiences cannot give the same thematic coherence as a graduate school or a seminar, they do have a very valuable effect in promoting local ecumenism. For many it is the only way to become acquainted with the work of the WCC outside its official sessions and conferences.

4. There are new developments in programme possibilities. The *Nairobi to Vancouver* report stated that the "Bossey extension" plan could not (as yet) be implemented; but it was understood that joint ventures with other centres of ecumenical education, or theological and lay training, should be explored. Through the increase in staff and a grant from the interest of a special WCC fund for innovative projects, a beginning has been made with what is now called "Bossey in Partnership".

a) As a part of this programme the teaching staff went to Cuba in May 1988 to work with pastors and theological students of the evangelical churches. Bossey, with the help of local ecumenical bodies, conducted workshops in Matanzas and Santiago de Cuba on the theme of "Unity and Mission".

b) The teaching staff had ecumenical team visits to the Romanian Orthodox Church, the Ecumenical Patriarch (Istanbul), the Greek Orthodox Church and the Russian Orthodox Church in order to strengthen the relationship between Bossey and the Orthodox churches.

c) A consultation on "Partnership in Ecumenical Leadership Formation", organized together with the Sub-unit on Renewal and Congregational Life and the Programme on Theological Education, was held at Bossey in September 1989 to foster collaboration with other regional ecumenical centres, lay academies and theological seminaries. The participants committed themselves to a partnership covenant to work, in collaboration with Bossey, towards local and global ecumenism.

Bossey and the Programme on Theological Education

More far-reaching perspectives are on the horizon with the coming together of the Bossey programme and PTE. After preparation by the Bossey board and PTE commission, a recommendation on such implementation was accepted by the central committee in Moscow in 1989. This will give Bossey a better contact with the regions from which candidates for the graduate school and shorter courses are recruited, and gives PTE (with its emphasis on intercultural theology) new possibilities for experimentation in ecumenical learning. With a common, larger staff it is hoped that this process will strengthen both Bossey and PTE in the task of ecumenical theological education and leadership formation.

Everyone who has had the privilege to live and work in Bossey will have had the same basic experience of both its uniqueness and fragility. The uniqueness is its situation, its own beauty and that of its location, the "space" around it, the contacts with "Geneva". It is the "space" which invites the participants to open themselves to one another, to discover the richness of the gifts which God bestows on us in the encounter with those who are so different from us. But Bossey is also a fragile, vulnerable place. All the conflicts which arise from the encounter of cultures arise here as well. But conflicts are a necessary part of learning in community and growth as a community.

Bossey has the power to survive and to change with new challenges of the times and with new opportunities in the ecumenical movement. It was Visser 't Hooft's vision that the Ecumenical Institute will be "an energizing centre and laboratory for the whole movement". That vision still remains.

COMMUNICATION DEPARTMENT

Introduction

"Communicating Credibly" was one of the eight issues in Vancouver. The only other occasion when communication as a specific issue figured on an assembly agenda was at Uppsala in 1968. The Vancouver issue report reflected a certain disenchantment with the values and structures of the media which had by then been revolutionized by technology. This report was distributed widely, together with a booklet entitled *Credible Christian Communication*.

The mandate

The Department's mandate dates back to 1973 when it was administratively relocated within the General Secretariat and for the first time allowed to have its own advisory committee.

The mandate describes the *aims* of the Department in general terms, and then goes on to list its *functions*. The overall aim is "to extend and strengthen the ecumenical movement", and that is to be achieved "by assisting the WCC and the member churches" in three areas.

The first of these is "to share in the development of mutual understanding and renewal in the church and in the world".

The second aim is more specific. The Department must "communicate and interpret the life and work of the Council and its members". Two points need to be underlined here. First, that it is asked to *interpret* and that it is seen not just as a purveyor of news but also as spokesperson for the Council. Second, the life and work of both the Council and its member churches must receive the attention of the department. What is prescribed is more than public relations (PR) for the Council; it involves also the communication and interpretation of the Council as a fellowship of churches.

The third aim has to do with communications media in general. The expression "to promote the liberating and creative role" of the media reflects the media optimism of the 1970s, which was even more evident in the Uppsala 1968 statement on "The Church and the Media of Mass Communication".

Ecumenical formation, communication and interpretation, mission to the media — these, broadly speaking, are held up as the aim of the Department.

In the following section of the mandate ten functions are identified. The first five deal with the Department's role as an agent of the

ecumenical movement and the churches, and concentrate on the institutional needs of the Council. Through the years these have been the
functions on which the Department has concentrated.

This means that the remaining five functions have received relatively
less attention. Serving the units and sub-units in devising new communication possibilities for the sharing of information and insights, sharing in
the exploration by units and sub-units of communication issues,
stimulating the participation of member churches and related bodies in
the study and use of the media, in the dissemination of ecumenical
information and in the development of ecumenical communication
strategies — in all these the Department has not been able to contribute
a great deal. One of its functions is to co-operate with the World
Association for Christian Communication (WACC) and other agencies
in the field of communication. The LWF/WACC/WCC co-ordinating
committee has fulfilled this function. The last function envisaged for the
Department is "to conduct or participate in research", and here too, due
to lack of time and resources, not much has been achieved.

The mandate reflects the communication situation of the early 1970s
and the traditional print-media bias of the churches. Its thrust is on
ecumenical communication, though it is nowhere explicitly defined. It
does not understand such ecumenical communication as the monopoly of
the WCC, or as originating only in Geneva; both in terms of production
and distribution it is as much the responsibility of the churches as of the
Council. The mandate does not sell the department into institutional
captivity; it does not see its work in terms of "PR". The mandate provides
room for co-operation, innovation, research and even for a measure of
decentralization. The importance of all these has been repeatedly re-
affirmed by the Communication committee. To do justice to the present
mandate, it needs to be taken more seriously than it is at present, both in
terms of staff and budget, and in terms of winning the commitment and
understanding of the WCC constituency. In any case, the present mandate
will have to be either re-affirmed or revised — keeping in mind the
limitations mentioned above — within the context of any future re-
organization of the WCC.

Director's office

Co-ordination and administration of the Department's very diverse
activities are the major responsibilities of this office. During the period
under review the Department's leadership changed three times.

To a limited extent, the office has been involved in research on the issue of church and communication, and in various communication projects in liaison with ecumenical partners, in particular the WACC and the LWF, through regular meetings of the LWF/WACC/WCC co-ordinating committee.

This has included studies on theology and communication, made possible as part of the communication enabling resource, which started in 1980 as the "project team". Staff and consultant time has been set aside from the ongoing production work of the Department in order to focus on specific communication needs and problems of member churches and the Council.

Projects have included sending a team to Ethiopia at the request of the Ethiopian Orthodox Church (EOC) to evaluate their communication needs, which resulted in a creative and useful report which was transmitted to the EOC and to all organizations involved in the EOC round table; assistance to the Greek Orthodox Church in factual reporting on the conflict between church and state; assistance for a series of consultations for communicators and church leaders in francophone Africa; assistance to the Russian Orthodox Church for ecumenical communication of the millennium; workshops for the promotion of dialogue between creative writers and theologians in Kerala, India; the production of a film on the Council; and a workshop on culture and communication in Rwanda.

A presentation on "Communicating the WCC — a Task to Share" was made to the 1987 meeting of the central committee. The presentation focused on the role of central committee members in communicating an ecumenical vision and the programmes and activities of the WCC. Among issues highlighted were the importance and difficulty of relating the global ecumenical concerns of churches and Christians in each local situation, and how churches could make better use of the Department's "products". The presentation and discussion were a learning exercise both for the Department and for the members of the central committee, as the appropriateness of these products to various social, cultural and political contexts was considered.

Special attention has been given in past years to the development of an intern programme, which has enabled young people interested in ecumenical communication to familiarize themselves with the WCC communications operation and with the ecumenical movement. Interns have come from New Caledonia, Japan, India, Antigua, the Congo, Scotland, the Netherlands, Poland, and Germany. In light of the difficulty of finding ecumenically and professionally experienced communication staff from all continents, it is hoped that the intern programme can be continued after the assembly and expanded into a training programme.

The co-ordinating role of the director's office has been occupied exclusively with responding to the challenges posed by the call for improved communication with our constituency on the one hand, and continuing financial pressures and constraints on the other.

News and information

Beginning with the WCC Communication committee meeting in January 1986, proposals to improve WCC news-and-information efforts have been seriously discussed by committee members and staff, as well as by colleagues in other organizations and around the world.

The fundamental conviction behind the proposals for change which have emerged from this process is that separating the journalistic and public-relations aspects of news-and-information work will make it possible to do each more effectively on behalf of the WCC — considered both as a Geneva-based institution and as a global fellowship of more than 300 member churches.

Under proposals before the central committee at its March 1990 meeting, what has been the News and Information section would be re-born as three entities: (1) an Office of Information and Interpretation (lodged in the General Secretariat); (2) the Ecumenical News Service (ENS; to be formed in co-operation with other ecumenical and confessional entities such as the Lutheran World Federation and the World Alliance of Reformed Churches); (3) the Ecumenical News Network (a co-operative of regional and national ecumenical and confessional news agencies, of which ENS would be one member). Both the present *Ecumenical Press Service* (EPS) and the *Service oecuménique de presse et d'information* (SOEPI) would be superseded by the ENS during 1992.

During the Vancouver-Canberra period efforts were made towards better integration and co-ordination of EPS and SOEPI, and for better service to our German-speaking constituency.

The arrival of a senior press officer in 1988 relocated tasks such as co-ordinating media operations at major WCC meetings and in-house information flow, making them again the chief responsibility of one person in the Department.

Production of the monthly audio magazine *Intervox* continued in English and French during this period, for use primarily by stations in Africa, Asia, the Pacific, the Caribbean and Europe. It was supplemented by special news feeds, and by the new sound bank series, which promotes topical items. A start was made on a computerized index of the WCC audio archives, which go back to the very beginnings of the Council.

Apart from the regular generation of several products, much of the work of the section involved responding to inquiries from journalists from a wide variety of media, and the organization of press conferences. The section also spent significant time and effort to ensure that journalists — both those who do attend and those who cannot — receive assistance and information before, during and after major WCC meetings and other WCC-related events both in Geneva and around the world.

Publications

Progress has been made in developing a coherent and comprehensive publishing strategy. The publications board (consisting of the general secretary, the unit moderators, the publications manager and the editor) meets regularly throughout the year to plan and approve WCC publication projects.

Since Vancouver almost 200 new books have been published under the WCC Publications label, reflecting issues and concerns of the Council and the wider ecumenical movement. Special attention has also been given to books on ecumenical history. Sales have increased in this period, and so have co-publishing ventures with outside publishers in various language areas. Although for financial reasons most of the books are published in English, approximately 30% are also published, through such arrangements, in one or more other languages.

In 1988 the *Risk Book* series celebrated its tenth anniversary. The four books published yearly in this series provide perspectives on emerging themes and concerns in the ecumenical movement, and are meant for a general church readership. The series reaches a steadily increasing number of readers.

Other books to be highlighted include the new ecumenical prayer cycle *With All God's People*, published in July 1989, and the major project to produce a *Dictionary of the Ecumenical Movement* — a one-volume, 1000-page alphabetical reference work on the modern ecumenical movement. This was initiated in 1986 and will be published early in 1991.

Difficulties remain in the marketing, distribution and promotion of books — tasks that call for a greater investment of time by the member churches as well as the Council — and in the imbalance of the distribution of WCC publications. Seventy percent go to persons in the North, and prices are too high for many countries in the South, with currency restrictions often presenting insurmountable problems. A pilot project in

India suggested that when books and periodicals are distributed at a price which is comparable to that of similar books published in a country in the South, the response is excellent. However, carrying out such distribution on a wide scale would require funds for subsidy, and an investment in staff time, which are presently not available.

A *shared subscription fund* was founded to enable people in the South to subscribe to WCC publications at a reduced rate, or to receive them free; but the amount available through the fund has been minimal.

The editorial responsibility for *The Ecumenical Review* came back to the publications office in 1985. An editorial strategy in which each quarterly issue focuses on a single theme has considerably increased interest in the journal. The policy is to offer sub-units and Council-wide programmes the opportunity (and co-responsibility) for a theme-based issue. Special issues of the *Review* have focused on "Fifty Years of Ecumenical Social Thought", "Commemorating Amsterdam 1948", marking the 40th anniversary of the WCC, and "Come, Holy Spirit". Issues in 1990 are devoted to academic resources important for the preparation of the assembly.

One World, the monthly magazine of the WCC, has strengthened its role as a popular, general-interest interpretation of the Council's life and of the wider ecumenical movement. It has made a serious attempt to cover the concerns of the Council's sub-units, as well as issues and events of ecumenical importance outside Geneva. Since 1985 a special annual issue, giving an overview of the Council's activities over the previous year, has been published successfully in various languages. A "super-story" covering the years since Vancouver will be published in September 1990. Extra-long, well-illustrated and well-received special issues have covered the Vancouver assembly and the WCC's 40th anniversary. The latter was published in book form under the title *"And so set up signs..."*, and is still very much in demand.

What has been said about distribution, marketing and promotion of WCC books applies also to the WCC's periodicals: it is a task to be shared between the member churches and the Council.

Visual arts

Since the restructuring of this section in 1983 the emphasis has been on providing visual services to the WCC, member churches, church agencies, ecumenical bodies, press and other "multipliers".

Since Vancouver the photo service has been growing steadily, and demand has increased from a few thousand prints to roughly 12-15,000 annually. The improved indexing of the photo and slide files has been a great asset, as have the new mailing list, better production quality and faster service and the introduction of computers in the daily work.

Graphic and design services have continued to be in heavy demand by all programme units, especially with the increased diversity of products from WCC sub-units in the last few years and the holding of at least one major conference each year.

The section has felt the increasing demand for more visual communication in all forms. Responses to a questionnaire sent in 1987 to member churches confirmed that there is a general trend of far more dependence on visual aids for communication.

The demand is felt especially in the field of audiovisual and video material. Some promotional and interpretative films, videos, slide-sets and exhibitions have been produced, sometimes in co-operation with outside artists and visual arts offices of member churches. However the 1982 central committee recommendation asking for a visual arts co-ordinator, a photographic services co-ordinator, and a film and video co-ordinator for this section has, for financial reasons, yet to be implemented fully.

Language service

To provide translation and interpretation services for the day-to-day work of the WCC and for meetings and conferences, there are eight translators (two per working language, with the exception of Russian) and two administrative assistants, supplemented by the over one hundred freelance translators and interpreters whose services are frequently used by the WCC. A second Spanish translator joined the staff in 1985. Whenever possible, the service also provides translation and interpretation services to other ecumenical and confessional organizations. Since Vancouver the service has streamlined its administration and continues to work with a collective style of leadership and sharing of responsibilities. Despite serious efforts to increase productivity the costs of providing a professional service remain high, so much so as to limit its use.

Besides providing its professional services this section has continued to participate actively in the work of the Language Policy Task Force, a WCC staff group which advises on language policy and practice. The task force is conscious that the present policy of five working languages does not do justice to the range of languages, especially African and Asian, represented in the Council's membership, in spite of the fact that these working languages function also as link languages in different parts of the world. This policy is often challenged, the argument being that all languages should be treated on the same basis. Since Vancouver, regular discussions have taken place within the Council about the fairness and appropriateness of the present policy, but with no tangible results. The task force believes that — at least up to now — no realistic alternative has been found.

To try to correct the imbalance the task force proposed to the 1989 central committee that, where appropriate, provision should be made at meetings and conferences to include the local language in addition to the working languages.

Before the Canberra assembly, a new edition of the reference text "Ecumenical Terminology" in English, French, German and Spanish will be published.

Some tasks ahead

Among the tasks ahead are the following:
1. Further development and implementation of the proposal for a new ecumenical partnership in news and information.
2. As a consequence of the changes in news-and-information work in the Council, a focus on other communication services oriented towards producing and disseminating material which communicates and inter-prets the concerns of the WCC and the wider ecumenical movement. This could be done through publications, audiovisuals, language services, and showing a special interest in the needs of the member churches and in the justice issues related to communications media in today's world.
3. Development of consultative services to the churches on the social and theological implications of communications and the media, and on church and church-related communication projects.
4. Further development of the use of video for providing both informa-tion and interpretation.
5. A continuing search for a realistic policy which would correct the imbalance in the languages used at WCC meetings.

The WCC itself is "an organ of communication", as former general secretary Philip Potter once stated, "finding ways in which the whole people of God participate in the ecumenical movement through listening to one another, sharing each other's insights and experiences and entering into ever widening and deeper relationships for the sake of living and witnessing to the gospel".

The Communication Department has assisted the WCC to play this communication role. But a great deal remains to be done. The Department is an instrument of the communication process at the WCC, not that process itself. That instrumental role, in turn, is dependent on the day-to-day co-operation with units and sub-units in the Council, central committee members and the media, as well as member churches and national and regional councils of churches.

WORLD COUNCIL OF CHURCHES' LIBRARY

The library was formed during the period when the WCC itself was "in process of formation", in 1946. Its mandate has been from the beginning to serve the staff of the WCC and, since 1964 in the new WCC headquarters, to serve related ecumenical organizations there as well. It also serves the worldwide church constituency, aiming to render the best possible bibliographical, documentary and information service about the history of the ecumenical movement and the programmes and activities of the WCC. Each year a comprehensive strategy is followed to acquire ecumenical literature produced throughout the world in all languages.

Service

In 1986 the library was computerized and its administration changed radically. The computer system now covers all the needs of an international library. It is multilingual, powerful, simple and easy to work with. It allows for equal processing of all kinds of documents preserved in the library, including archival documents, and is compatible with other equipment commonly used throughout the world. This makes it possible for ecumenical institutions to have direct online access to our data bank, and to leave us their book orders by electronic mail. It is expected that the inter-library loan service will continue to expand.

Hundreds of people visit the library every year. Many borrow books or periodicals, prepare teaching material, and work on ecumenical dissertations. A public computer terminal is at their disposal in the reading room.

The library staff continues to provide a wide range of services, including compiling indexes and bibliographies and liaison with, and consultancy to, other theological libraries. The team has been joined by a full-time archivist who is responsible for the preservation of our archives and who facilitates access to the archives for readers. The library works in close co-operation with the library of the Ecumenical Institute, Bossey.

Acquisitions

Since 1983 the library holding of books and pamphlets has grown from 80,000 volumes to almost 90,000 volumes. The library continues to receive over 530 current periodicals, most of them exchanged with WCC journals and periodicals. The library also collects 200 current serial publications of national and regional councils of churches, ecumenical press services and publications of ecumenical institutes.

In 1989, IDC Zug published 7,021 microfiches representing the complete International Missionary Council and the Commission on World Mission and Evangelism archives housed by the library; these are now computerized.

In 1989 the World Council's documentation service was integrated into the library. This service is able to consult online many data banks throughout the world, thus providing WCC staff and other library users with useful information.

OFFICE FOR INCOME COORDINATION AND DEVELOPMENT (OICD)

Background

As the WCC member churches in Vancouver re-affirmed their commitment to the ecumenical vision of faith, renewal and unity they once again posed the question: "Do the member churches raise, receive, contribute and spend their financial resources in relation to the WCC in ways that manifest the unity of which we speak?"

The Office for Income Coordination and Development (OICD) was created in late 1978 in response to the Nairobi assembly's concern for inter-relating the ways in which the WCC and the churches raised and administered funds, and for enabling non-competitive funding among world, regional, national and local church bodies. At that time separate sub-units of the WCC presented individual budgets, most frequently to historic funding partners in the member churches, and there was no unified budget. The wholeness of the Council, its intention of being a fellowship of churches acting together towards unity, was reflected neither in the funding patterns of the churches nor in WCC structures. OICD was designed to help Council programmes build and reflect a wholeness and integrity in relation to each other, to the member churches and to other donors. The stability reached in WCC funding by 1983 was, in part, a reflection of these planning and co-ordination functions. OICD's major concern was, and continues to be, developing income for the tasks decided upon by the central committee.

In 1983, when the Vancouver assembly assessed the financial situation of the Council, the serious problems of international monetary disorder from the early 1970s had eased. In the context of inflationary economies the member churches had increased their giving, thus assisting the WCC to reach a fragile stability after the deep indebtedness and financial chaos at the time of the Nairobi assembly (1975). Even so, reserves were depleted. And although income exceeded expenses in the year of the Vancouver assembly, the moderator of the Finance committee then cautioned that the Council would not be able to sustain its existing structure much beyond 1985.

Since that warning, the general economic situation of the WCC and its member churches has changed significantly. The international debt situation has pushed many of the member churches to the edge of economic despair. The combination of strained domestic finances, and the decline in currency exchange value of the US dollar (which lost more than half its value against the Swiss franc in an eighteen-month period from mid-1985) and related currencies, yielded an effective loss of nearly 20% of the Council's income from traditional donors by the end of 1986.

The results of successful income development in the face of these factors, and the many financial and administrative steps taken since the last assembly, are reported in detail in the chapter on finance (page 53 below). The fundamental policies and assembly directives which have formed the mandate for OICD are reviewed here briefly within the context of the General Secretariat, of which it is a part.

OICD is relationship-oriented; on the one hand, it brings together various programme endeavours into a WCC-wide perspective, and on the other it identifies the priorities for — and obstacles to — the participation of the member churches. The Vancouver assembly actions and concerns which were the basis of OICD planning, reflection and action during this period focused on fuller participation and responsibility, the need for increased funding, and greater coherence in financial and programmatic planning.

Participation and responsibility

In Vancouver the Finance committee was deeply concerned by the fact that not all member churches support the WCC's work financially. It encouraged all members to provide undesignated income to the Council (this had also been recommended in Nairobi), and asked further that a statement of financial responsibilities of WCC membership be included in the rules, together with specific guidelines by which this principle could be made workable.

Encouragement was also given to alternative forms of support (such as paying travel costs, hosting meetings, etc.), and to developing methods for reporting the receipt and use of alternative support for the programme budget (such as material aid and in-kind contributions).

There has been a longer-term request to develop for the WCC rules a statement of principle that each member church should provide a "minimum tangible sign" of its membership in, and commitment to, the Council. To provide background for this discussion OICD has undertaken a two-part study:
1) on ways to receive and use alternative support (such as material aid and in-kind contributions) towards the programme budget; and
2) on the funding models and patterns through which member churches can, and do, contribute to the WCC.

Alternate, or other, contributions

In February 1985, based on a staff survey of information from 1980 to 1984, five "alternative contribution" models were developed based respectively on the factors of personnel, hospitality, external travel, information and material aid. These became the basis for questionnaires sent to all member churches and to WCC programme staff. The models of non-financial contribution remain valid, as all identified items can be attributed to one or another of them (whether categorized in this way by the survey respondent or not). No new models have been suggested either in the context of this study or in the process of dialogue on resource-sharing (see page 47 below).

A report on funding patterns was also prepared; this included "alternative financial routes" by which member churches may contribute to the WCC. Since 1985 the full membership has been surveyed annually about their contributions to the WCC other than financial transfers. Reports of such contributions are solicited, and have been included in the financial report, annually since 1986. Informed estimates of the cash value of "other contributions" towards the WCC budget average not more than Sfr.200,000 in any given year.

Responsibilities of membership

Following the study of non-financial giving to the WCC by member churches, and of various ways in which cash transfers can be credited, a text on financial contributions to the Council was approved as part of a broader statement on the responsibilities of WCC membership. This full statement was approved by the central committee at its meeting in Moscow in 1989 as new Rule II of the World Council of Churches.

The Canberra assembly may wish to review the implications of Rule II for the nearly one-third of present Council members who, despite annual correspondence on this matter, neither make an annual contribution nor report on other types of contributions which they may make. The intent of the sixth assembly Finance committee in drawing attention to these issues was to assure more stable and broadly participatory funding for the WCC. This area needs further careful work.

Decision-making, women and finance

The Vancouver assembly challenged the WCC to incorporate women's concerns and perspectives into all WCC programmes as part of its ongoing search for unity. Following the 1985 meeting in Nairobi which brought to a close the UN Decade for Women, more and more funds have been made available by donors interested in encouraging women to become agents of a just, peaceful and ecologically sustainable society. OICD, in co-operation with various sub-units, has sought substantial funds in support of a wide range of WCC activities which meet this criteria. The WCC's 1987 El Escorial consultation on resource-sharing identified additional changes needed to give women greater access to financial resources, and to financial decision-making processes, within the ecumenical sharing network.

With the launching in 1988 of the Ecumenical Decade of the Churches in Solidarity with Women, the WCC executive committee authorized a survey of the financial impact upon women of activities related to the Council's sharing network, as well as women's access to financial decision-making within the network. This is now underway.

A preliminary survey suggests yet other areas for future work. There seems to be consensus that women's participation in decisions to allocate resources is as desirable as it is rare. Though expressing it in different ways, respondents in every region indicate that women's concerns and perspectives are "invisible", or artificially segregated from those of the broader community.

The assembly may wish to study and comment on how women can be encouraged to fuller partnership in the activities of the WCC and its member churches, how particular programmes enable or impede the empowerment of women, and how women's concerns and perspectives may become more visible in the next period.

The funding of the WCC is dependent upon the full participation, and commitment to the ecumenical fellowship, of its member churches. Certainly the Council's search for unity has become more complex due to the increasing pluralism in both the world and the churches.

The need for increased funding

The Vancouver assembly challenged the churches to increase giving both as a sign of their commitment to the ecumenical vision and as a "necessary financial base for the continuity and creativity of the WCC". The assembly asked major donor churches to set a goal of increasing undesignated funds given in 1984 by 30-50% over the level of 1982; other contributors were asked to increase giving by at least 25%, and those who had made no contributions were asked to begin doing so.

The results of the assembly's challenge are detailed in the chapter on finance; we give here a brief description of the current situation of donors and special funding requests, and of OICD's approach.

Donors

Virtually all member churches and major donors in North America and Western Europe report that their own financial situation is not keeping pace with inflation. Despite higher per capita giving, reduced church membership figures, and the tendency to keep more funds at lower judicatory levels, suggest that this trend will continue. In tighter economic situations, and with a greater number of non-governmental organizations (NGOs) competing for the same funds, reporting requirements are also becoming more stringent.

OICD is also highlighting the concern that, due to the above factors, the traditionally well-supported activities relating to the churches' mission, to interchurch aid and to theological education — which account for a large portion of the WCC's total programme — cannot be maintained by their historic donor group. Substantial new donors have not yet been identified in these areas.

OICD carries special responsibility within the WCC for the issues raised by government funding, and this involves it in a broad yet specialized set of relationships. On a whole range of programmes and projects within the wider ecumenical sharing network, OICD helps to sharpen both church-related and NGO advocacy positions vis-à-vis the World Bank and other government-linked funding instruments.

Member churches should recognize that any specialized funding which might be channelled to the WCC from government agencies will, in most cases, simply not be available for activities which are "theological" and traditionally "church". As we look to the future the balance of WCC activities must be kept in mind, and donors identified who can help to support its work in such essential areas.

Special funding

Since the sixth assembly, some Sfr.13,265,000 has been authorized for special funding appeals in addition to the annual programme budget, projects, and trust funds. This figure does not include the planned Faith and Order world conference, which is now planned for 1993, and reflects not the total expenses but only funds sought with special authorization.

Among these items were consultancies on government funding and on persons with disabilities, International Youth Year events (1985), the meeting for leaders of national councils of churches (1986), the "Learning in a World of Many Faiths" education project; the world consultation on resource-sharing, El Escorial (1987); the Commission on World Mission and Evangelism world conference (1989); the "Justice, Peace and the Integrity of Creation" world convocation (1990); the seventh assembly (1991); the global ecumenical youth gathering (1992, with Sfr.1.4 million being sought); and the mid-Decade meetings on the churches in solidarity with women (1992-93, with Sfr.450,000 being sought). As the vision of Canberra takes shape, the assembly may want to consider how "special funding" activities relate to the priorities expressed in the WCC budget.

Working methods

The Vancouver assembly's emphasis was on increasing undesignated funds. OICD encourages this systematically — and at least annually — with all member churches. As requested by the assembly, OICD has also been able to "explore and implement more flexible funding patterns, including re-allocation, following consultation with the donor, of part or all excess designated funds on a given programme when that programme has been oversubscribed in any budget year". In light of the situation outlined above, OICD also persists in seeking funds which can be used flexibly enough to address internal imbalances created by tightly-designated monies.

Often programme staff find it difficult to interpret their own work while interpreting, and seeking funding for, the Council's work as a whole. OICD's task is to clarify the links between the issues and programmes addressed by different parts of the Council, so that one aspect of the work does not prosper at the expense of another.

Along with its efforts to identify potential new donors and to match highly specialized needs with funding sources, OICD tries, whenever possible, to give a function- and issue-oriented interpretation of the Council's work. This has yielded a greater flexibility among donors, and a greater willingness to support work on important issues wherever it happens to be lodged in the WCC structure — an extremely important point as we consider programmatic re-organization. The "Council-wide" programmes launched in Vancouver have assisted this process in many ways. In addition, the encouragement of block grants to programme clusters has given particular programmes some security against currency devaluation. Internally, WCC staff have taken more seriously their common responsibility for each other. But much is left to be done in building understanding across both the financial and the programmatic structures of the Council.

WCC income and budgetary dilemmas are discussed in the chapter on finance. One analytical tool developed since the Vancouver assembly is presented here as an example of our concern to link broader participation, greater coherence of Council programmes, and increased funding.

The giving index

After studying patterns of financial support and mechanisms of fund transfer, OICD sought new tools to look beyond raw income figures and to understand the giving of member churches in terms of their own economic situation. This study led to the development of a "giving index" which permits the analysis of financial contributions from churches of widely varying size and circumstance, reveals the substance of South-to-North support within the membership, and enables us to challenge the churches realistically, in light of the resources available to them.

The OICD data base and "contributions index" has identified patterns of sharing and enabled us to answer sensitively and clearly that deceptively simple question: "How much does our church 'owe'?" This has demonstrably encouraged giving; more churches are making annual undesignated contributions, and the index has provided the basis for ongoing dialogue with certain large churches about the size and designation of their contributions. It has also been an invaluable guide in determining askings for the seventh assembly.

The study permits descriptive — not normative — discussion. In light of the new WCC Rule II mentioned above, it should be a valuable help towards the more intentional discussion which we anticipate with the churches about their WCC membership contributions.

Greater coherence in financial and programmatic planning

The area where there has been the least progress is that of the many assembly recommendations for greater coherence, simplicity, and transparency in financial and programmatic planning. Details of the efforts which have been made to provide "clearer and simpler administrative and organizational structures and budgeting procedures that lead to greater co-ordination of the total programme of the WCC" are scattered throughout this report, and budgeting details are found in the chapter on finance. By the time of the seventh assembly, progress may have been achieved through the long-term process towards re-stating the vision of the WCC and re-organizing its programme.

In calling for "integrated long-range programme and financial planning which reflects the wholeness of WCC programme and assures its financial stability", the sixth assembly addressed one of the Council's greatest difficulties in income development. Although broad programmatic themes emerge quickly after an assembly, the absence of a central process for planning programmes — and their financial support — means that communication with potential donors suffers from a certain "ad hoc-ism". This hampers our ability to gain both programmatic and financial support for activities. The delegates at Vancouver noted that ongoing (i.e. long-range, or more than three-year) programmes should be funded within the ongoing financial structures and programmatic relationships of the WCC and its member churches and their related agencies, and that such programmes should not be dependent on undesignated funds. This has not yet been possible; for a variety of reasons the Sub-units on Faith and Order, Dialogue, Church and Society, Renewal and Congregational Life, and Youth remain dependent on undesignated monies. Nor has Vancouver's call for truly co-ordinated income development for continuing programmes been acted upon.

Despite a sizeable reduction in currency values against the Swiss franc from mid-1985 to mid-1988, increases in giving have so far allowed the WCC to maintain a stable income level and to complete special funding activities. But giving rates are not increasing at present as they have done in former years and, given our exposure to fluctuating exchange rates, more energy is needed to maintain present funding levels, particularly for budget support. In light of the donors' changing situations and priorities, WCC income stability and growth requires — even more than in the pre-Vancouver period — increased Council-wide planning and co-ordination of programme development, interpretation, financial analysis, and both programmatic and funding mechanisms.

In summary, our goal is to develop, on the basis of realistic assessments, co-ordinated and transparent policies and mechanisms which will link the relational, programmatic and financial resources of the Council to fullest effect in support of the unity sought by our member churches.

UNITED STATES OFFICE

Background and functions

The US Office has existed since the founding of the WCC. From its earliest days its role has been to represent and interpret the work of the WCC in the US, to facilitate the relationship of the Council with US member churches, and to serve as a channel for interpreting the ecclesial and secular realities in the United States to the WCC. The US Office also facilitates co-operation with other organizations, especially the National Council of the Churches of Christ in the USA.

The US Conference of the WCC (an advisory group which includes representatives of all the WCC member churches) has been re-invigorated, and is now a forum where the churches can share issues and concerns with each other and with the WCC.

Relationship to the member churches

In the seven years since Vancouver the relationship between the WCC and its US member churches has been greatly strengthened. A WCC presence has been assured at the major meetings of most member churches. Four member churches (United Methodist, Evangelical Lutheran Church in America, American Baptist, and Presbyterian) have set up special committees to study and evaluate their membership in the WCC. The US Office resourced these committees, providing extensive data and linking the committees with appropriate Geneva staff. Three of the churches affirmed their membership in the WCC with a deepened commitment to global ecumenism; the new Evangelical Lutheran Church in America joined the WCC with an enthusiastic and nearly unanimous vote.

It should be noted that a major constellation of churches or their agencies are now located in mid-America: the Evangelical Lutheran Church in America (Chicago); Christian Church (Disciples of Christ) (Indianapolis); Brethren (Elgin, Illinois); Presbyterian Church USA (Louisville, Kentucky); United Church of Christ (Cleveland, Ohio); Friends United Meeting (Richmond, Indiana); International Council of Community Churches (Homewood, Illinois); United Methodist Council on Ministries (Dayton, Ohio); World Headquarters of the National Baptist Church (Nashville, Tennessee).

Historic black churches

A special effort has been made since Vancouver to increase the sensitivity of the WCC to the gifts and needs of the historic black churches in the US, and to deepen the involvement of those churches in the WCC. A meeting between the leaders of the black churches and the executive committee of the WCC was held in Atlanta, Georgia, in September 1987. As a result the black church liaison committee was formed and two WCC presidents, Dame Nita Barrow and the Very Rev. Dr Lois Wilson, were asked to maintain a relationship to this committee. In 1988 the black church liaison committee planned and carried out a solidarity journey to Southern Africa. In January 1989 the leadership of all seven historic black churches came together in Washington, DC, to launch a black church action to bring the strength of these churches to bear on US policies towards South Africa. The black church liaison committee has also concentrated its efforts on increasing the participation of persons from the black churches in the life and work of the WCC.

WCC presence in the United States

Planning for visits of WCC staff to the US churches has been a major activity of the US Office. In 1989 alone 79 staff visits were arranged and connections made with appropriate denominational and ecumenical persons. The US Office has also been involved in the co-ordination of the various WCC meetings in the US during this period. These meetings provide an opportunity for US Christians and US churches to deepen their global understanding, and for the WCC to interpret its work and witness in the US context.

Global education and ecumenical development

At the central committee meeting in Argentina the US participants asked the US Office to hold regular forums to interpret the work of the

WCC. The first of these, called "Embrace the World", was held in Cleveland, Ohio, in October 1986, and attracted 700 persons from 42 states.

The Programme to Combat Racism (PCR) commission meeting included a forum on racial justice in January 1987, and was the most diverse gathering of ethnic persons to be held in the US. The forum issued a challenge to the US churches and ecumenical bodies to "be silent no more" on the issue of racial justice. In August 1988, Faith and Order held a consultation with representatives of black churches in the US which made a significant impact upon the Faith and Order study document on "The Unity of the Church and the Renewal of Human Community".

In May 1989 the WCC conference on world mission and evangelism met in San Antonio, Texas. This was the first CWME world conference to be held in the US and brought some 700 international participants to the United States. Opportunities for learning were created through the "participating congregations" programme and through a parallel conference called "Encuentro". The participating congregations programme enabled 75 local congregations from Yarmouth, Maine, to San Diego, California, and from Fayetteville, Arkansas, to Puerto Rico, to get the flavour of a global event by receiving team visits. "Encuentro" exposed 500 North Americans, including 119 seminarians, to major plenary speakers in the world conference. In workshops and seminars they discussed the conference theme and sub-themes, and studied emerging issues in mission and evangelism.

Communication

The US Office has developed a network of 10,000 "friends of the WCC". These persons receive a quarterly newsletter called *The Courier* that keeps them informed of WCC programmes and priorities.

The distribution of WCC resources, books and publications in the US has become the responsibility of the US Office in the post-Vancouver period. Co-ordination of communication needs between the WCC and the US churches, and media liaison and involvement in press operations at WCC conferences and events in the US (such as the San Antonio conference on world mission and evangelism, the visit of the Eminent Church Persons Group, and the PCR commission) have continued to be an important responsibility of this office.

ECUMENICAL SHARING OF RESOURCES (ESR)

When in 1977 the consultation on "Conditions for Sharing" was held
— as the first major step in the study on "Ecumenical Sharing of
Resources" — few of the participants expected that the theme would
become so central to the life of the WCC. Ten years later this centrality
was vividly expressed at the El Escorial meeting on "Koinonia: Sharing
Life in a World Community", which was important not only as the
culmination of its own long process but also as one of the five Council-
wide world meetings on the way to the seventh assembly. The El Escorial
meeting was complementary to the Commission on Inter-Church Aid,
Refugee and World Service (CICARWS) consultation "Diakonia 2000:
Called to be Neighbours" held in Larnaca, Cyprus in 1986, as described
in the chapter on Unit II, p. 145 below.

A study, a system, a discipline
The ESR process has gone through several stages. Its forerunner within
the WCC was called Ecumenical Sharing of Personnel. When the central
committee received the report on this study in 1980 it recommended that
renewed attention be given to this area; this became a programmatic
activity of CICARWS, initiating many innovative exchanges of persons.
Reflection on ESR was challenged and enriched by these concrete
experiences of sharing; it has often been said that the greatest resource of
the church is its people, and that ecumenical sharing must always be
people-centred.

ESR itself began as a study programme requested by central committee
after the Nairobi assembly. The effort to implement ESR then concentrated on developing a new "resource-sharing system" to apply such
principles as mutuality, transparency and joint decision-making, first to
the various sharing instruments of the WCC itself but also to the churches
and agencies within the ecumenical resource system. In 1982 the desk
responsible for ESR was moved from CICARWS to the General Secretariat. This search for a sharing system was not without tensions within
(and outside) the WCC, because it created an impression of centraliza-
tion.

ESR was discussed at the Vancouver assembly in issue group IV on
"Healing and Sharing Life in Community". The assembly made implementing the resource-sharing system a WCC priority, calling for a
"comprehensive understanding of ESR as part of a continuing dialogue on
the mission and service of the church... to facilitate models of ecumenical

sharing and not to create a heavy, centralized structure". This meant that a new, more flexible approach was necessary, and led to a third stage which emphasized an *ecumenical commitment* to the sharing of resources — and hence the need to work out a common basis (or "ecumenical *discipline*") as a guide for new relationships of sharing. While the resource-sharing system continued to be developed, the search for this ecumenical "discipline" became the focus for extensive work between 1984 and 1987. This signalled a new orientation in one of the WCC's primary vocations, from administering a project system to promoting the commitment of all those within this system to an *ecumenical* vision. Much clarification is still needed, but ESR has charted a worthwhile course.

"Koinonia: Sharing Life in a World Community"

In 1985 the central committee accepted the proposal for a world consultation on resource-sharing to be held with this title in October 1987; a planning group of ten persons was appointed by the executive committee to work in co-operation with a staff task force. The executive committee approved the group's conviction that the purpose of the world consultation would be "to agree on an ecumenical discipline for the sharing of resources and to foster a process of commitment to such a discipline". The planning group took responsibility for all the major aspects of the consultation; thus this was one of the rare events within the life of the WCC which took place outside the sponsorship of any specific programme unit or sub-unit. Its being lodged in the General Secretariat was intended to emphasize that the concern for resource-sharing belongs to the Council as a whole.

The theme of the consultation reflected the hope of the planning group that sharing would be understood not just in terms of resources but of "sharing life" with all God's people who together form the world community. This is indeed the vision of the "Guidelines" formulated by the consultation: a covenant for sharing life.

The draft of a working document was widely circulated in March 1987 and discussed extensively in March-April 1987 in enlarged meetings of the regional resource-sharing groups in Africa, Asia, Latin America, the Middle East and the Pacific and, in a different way, in Europe and the Caribbean. Reports from these meetings were an important input to the world consultation.

This consultation was conceived mainly as a working conference centred on the draft document. The programme had been planned in three stages: input through plenary presentations, Bible study and testimonies;

a first round of working groups on sections of the draft working document; and reporting followed by a second round of working groups and adoption of a final document. But as the working groups went about their tasks, two trends began to emerge: a sense that the conference could and should do more than review a carefully prepared document, and the urgent need for participants from the South to discuss the issues in their own regional setting. Eventually room was made for the conference to "take its own course". In the final plenary it was agreed that the findings of the working groups should be compiled to become the "longer" part of the conference report, in contrast to the "Guidelines", which were referred to as the "shorter" part, and which should be later supplemented with biblical passages, stories, commentaries, etc. The final plenary was marked by a genuine concern that the commitment taken should actually be implemented; it was proposed to appoint for this a group of participants, but an intensive debate resulted in the WCC being asked to take responsibility for the follow-up.

A description of the consultation proceedings cannot, of course, do justice to the richness of the experiences of its 229 participants. Worship, based largely on a carefully prepared worship book, was central to the life of the meeting and included symbolic acts reflecting the diversity of the participants. The sense of community was sustained by the genuine participation of all. Women played a particularly active role in the consultation process; although women were only 30% of the participants, they assumed 50% of the tasks of leadership (as group leaders, recorders, drafters, celebrants, etc.) and met frequently as a group between sessions. They drafted a set of comprehensive guidelines, which were incorporated into the final report, calling for sustained commitment to participation of women and youth in decisions on resource-sharing. While efforts had been made to reach the target of 15% youth participation, these were not successful. Although young people took an active part in the meeting, they were frustrated not to be able to make their presence felt more strongly.

After El Escorial

The participants at El Escorial committed themselves to give an account within three years to each other, and so to God, of the ways in which they have turned their words into deeds. In August 1988 the central committee, in receiving the "Guidelines" and "Recommendations on Women and Youth", affirmed the WCC's commitment and instructed the sub-units to implement the recommended discipline. In addition it called the WCC member churches to receive the "Guidelines" and "Recommendations", to respond to the commitment, and to work out the discipline in their own situation. A new mandate of the Office for the Ecumenical Sharing of Resources was approved to last until the seventh assembly.

Since the October 1987 consultation the ESR office has followed and encouraged the implementation of the El Escorial "Guidelines for Sharing".

Emphasis was put on follow-up actions within the WCC and with the member churches, and on long-term perspectives for the assembly. Some of the operational responsibilities for the resource-sharing system, in particular the co-ordination of the regional resource-sharing groups, were returned to CICARWS.

Churches, councils of churches, agencies for mission and development, and other bodies have taken up the guidelines and are actively seeking ways to implement the ecumenical discipline. Their responses vary according to their specific situations. Several have taken an official action, adopting the guidelines at the level of their governing bodies; others have initiated a different approach, for example by identifying certain key guideline issues for action (such as the participation of women and youth, the principle of shared decision-making, or the question of mutual accountability); or they have begun a broad process of reflection.

Some concrete examples of action are:
— the resolution passed by the assembly of the Swiss Protestant Church Federation in September 1988 to include 50% women and 20% youth in all its decision-making bodies, and to recommend that its member churches do the same;
— the decision of Norwegian Church Aid to ask for a critical evaluation of its priorities and operations by a team from the South (to be done in 1990);
— the call issued by the follow-up group in the USA for a church-supported consultation in 1990 to determine ways of implementing the guidelines in communities and congregations;
— the acceptance of the guidelines as the basis and framework for the search for a new pattern of partnership between the Church of South India and its related mission partners.

There is a growing awareness that this ecumenical discipline for sharing calls for profound changes in the attitudes of churches, agencies and Christians towards mission and service, and that this requires extensive educational programmes. Especially in churches in the North the world consultation has provided new and fresh impulses for this. The sharing of information about what is being done in various parts of the world has proved to be a powerful incentive.

The guidelines have inspired reflection in WCC-sponsored consultations on personnel in mission (September 1988) and partnership in mission structures (March 1989), and also section IV of the San Antonio conference on world mission and evangelism.

In July 1989 the official report of the world consultation was published as *Sharing Life*, and a progress report on follow-up was submitted to the Moscow central committee meeting.

The WCC staff group on follow-up is working on a computer-supported resource-sharing information service detailing the financial and other support provided by sub-units for projects and programmes of churches, councils, and other bodies. This should help the internal implementation of the discipline and enhance information-sharing and co-ordination and, where appropriate, joint decision-making between sub-units. Other major aspects are the integration of the discipline into new policies and activities of CICARWS, and the growing convergence in follow-up based on the "Guidelines for Sharing" and other new approaches to diakonia.

Some general reflections on the ESR process

Over the years the ESR process has drawn in a widening circle of participants. Those in the first period of ESR reflection came mainly from the constituencies of the interchurch aid project system — the Western European and North American agencies on the one hand and the churches and national councils in Africa, Asia, Latin America on the other. Later, and especially after the Vancouver assembly, the scope became much wider as mission agencies, regional ecumenical bodies, the networks of the Commission on the Churches' Participation in Development, Urban Rural Mission, the Programme to Combat Racism, Women, Youth, and so on were involved. Slowly the churches in the North have begun to see the relevance of ESR for their own life and witness.

The ESR process has encountered many obstacles. One of the greatest has been the difficulty of translating the concept into concrete structural changes in the present relationships of giving and receiving. Related to this is the tension between the search for practical solutions and the attention given to fundamental questions of theology, socio-economic issues, specific regional situations and other factors. Often the priorities of the participants are divided along these very lines! Another problem lies in the distinction between "material" and "non-material" resources, and the difficulty of including both in a comprehensive approach to sharing: spiritual values do not lend themselves to the same type of "transfer" as a project grant. A third question is that of the bilateral relationships "versus" ecumenical channels of sharing, which are multilateral in nature. The great diversity of the participants in the ESR process, and of the regions themselves, has also contributed to its complexity. It is hardly surprising that there is frustration at the lack of change; the kind of transformation which ESR calls for is so radical that it either happens slowly — and changes are evident if one looks back over a long period of time — or comes in unexpected ways.

Finally, an important issue in the context of the project system is the use of government funds, i.e. the role of financial resources from governments of industrialized countries given for church-related development projects. A first ecumenical consultation on this subject was held in 1983. From September 1985 to December 1986 a survey was carried out and the findings published as *The Development Market*. A follow-up consultation in October 1989 focused on the new trend of direct funding of non-governmental organizations in the South, including churches and church-related groups, by governments in the North. The question of government funding is discussed in more detail in the chapter on finance.

Future perspectives

Many of the issues central to the process on ecumenical sharing of resources will come before the assembly through the plenary presentation on "Sharing our Life: Towards New Community", and the work of related sections. A joint meeting with CICARWS should be called after the assembly to take stock of the implementation of the commitments which were made at the world consultations on diakonia (Larnaca 1986) and resource-sharing (El Escorial 1987).

Finance

I. Introduction

Financial discussions at the Vancouver assembly were brighter by far than the debt-burdened deliberations at the fifth assembly in Nairobi in 1975. For 1981 and 1982 — for the first time since before Nairobi — reports showed that the Council had had more income than expenses. The Council's financial stability had been achieved during this period of increased giving through the use of now-depleted reserves, curbs on spending, and distribution of costs.

Since 1975 the WCC has remained essentially at zero growth financially, and has experienced a mounting sense of urgency to set programme priorities and to consolidate programmes. The Council faces shortfalls in income against expenses in both 1989 and 1990, as it has in every year since 1985. For the Finance committee and the assembly, these numbers call for many hard decisions.

Previously the central committee had placed the financial emphasis on unifying the many budgets, programmes and structures of the WCC itself. Vancouver's emphasis on integration, both within the ecumenical movement and within the WCC, led to a financial agenda designed to promote greater:

— participation and responsibility of member churches in financing the Council;
— increases in (and more flexible) funding;
— transparency in financial and administrative operations to permit fuller participation; and
— coherence and integration in financial and programmatic planning.

II. World financial trends and the WCC

The actions of the Finance committee, and the financial difficulties which have been encountered since Vancouver, must be seen within the broader context of world events.

Although the world economy had entered into full-scale recession by 1979, the Vancouver assembly referred to the enormity of the emerging debt crisis only in passing. It failed to highlight the concerns raised by issue group VI about the new international economic disorder, which was then at hand. The assembly did draw attention to the international food disorder, and continued the Council's stance against economic systems and policies which are "one-sided" in distributing benefits. During ten years of economic recession in the 1980s there was a 15-25% fall in per-capita output in the South. Food production has lagged, especially throughout sub-Saharan Africa. Unemployment in both South and North reached levels not seen in fifty years, and financial markets became unstable. The growth of world trade has been low, and protectionism has grown. By 1986 the terms of trade for primary products — except for oil — were at their worst levels since the 1930s.

Disastrous terms of trade, reduced growth and inappropriate domestic investments led to massive external borrowing by the South. Although interest rates remained low in real terms through the late 1970s, they began to rise again in the early 1980s. Since then the poor countries of the South have been transferring more funds to the richer countries in the North than they receive. This accelerated dramatically in 1988, when the South transferred a record $50.1 billion, up almost $12 billion from 1987. The World Bank received $2.6 billion more in interest and principal payments from developing countries from June 1988 to June 1989 than it disbursed in new loans. At the same time, the United States of America has gone from being the world's largest creditor nation to being the world's largest debtor. (Depending on the debt service ratio, debt service payments can push a sluggish economy into recession.)

The loss of financial resources which are needed to "prime the production pump" in the South has also been aggravated by capital flight. Removing wealth instead of re-investing it worsens the gap between rich and poor within the South, as well as between South and North.

The human price of world economic trends over the past decade is shocking. When the poor cannot purchase food and health services there are measurable increases in infant mortality, dwarfism and malnutrition and its related illnesses, as well as shortened life-span. Under the pressures of debt repayment, governments accept toxic waste dumping and environmental destruction for short-term cash; and limited resources may be redirected from health and education to pay for national security forces to avert the civil unrest which arises from conditions of want.

Efforts at "structural adjustment" — restructuring economies to assure national financial "credit-worthiness" — have led to budget cuts in the areas of health and education, reducing these services to those in the population least able to forego them. "Adjustment" has also undermined many projects in the South which are co-financed by churches and agencies in the North, in hospitals, for example, which are no longer able to purchase enough medicine and medical equipment, or in schools now unable to buy educational materials. Much has been written about the disproportionate burden of debt carried by the poorest minorities and the marginalized in both North and South, and about the feminization of poverty which has occurred in virtually all economies.

Largely stemming from the pressure for economic restructure have been the conditions being placed upon the receipt of governmental, bilateral and multilateral funds; these have had a significant impact upon governments, non-governmental organizations (NGOs) and church-related agencies alike.

It is too soon to know what effect the recent developments in Eastern Europe will have on global monetary and spending patterns. Clearly increased emphasis is being placed on market economies, and certain triumphalist claims are being made for capitalist economic systems. There is widespread concern that diminished funding will be available to the South.

There are WCC member churches in more than 100 countries. The massive economic imbalances, both internal and international, and the growing polarization between rich and poor, are affecting their financial relationship with the Council. For example, the new migrant and refugee populations (which the international economic disorder has done much to create), and the increasing economic injustice experienced particularly by women and minorities, are over-burdening church infrastructures for domestic ministry and diakonia. This has a serious impact upon the churches' participation in, and responsibility for, the financing of WCC activities; and it shapes the expectations which they bring to programmatic discussions. All these factors affect the nature of the fellowship which the churches experience in the WCC.

It has become more important than ever to identify explicitly the financial models which operate — often implicitly — in WCC programmes and relationships. The Council should both manifest and advocate "people-centred" alternatives which do not marginalize or exploit any part of creation. It must challenge the broadly-held assumption that the poor are to "blame" for their own poverty. This means disturbing the comforting patterns of charitable action which often "dull the edge" of the struggle for full participation in economic life and the right to social benefits. Finance is an important tool in this search for a new social sensitivity and responsibility.

III. Programme decisions

The programme guidelines adopted at Vancouver used the dynamic language of movement "towards unity of faith, full commitment to justice, peace and the integrity of all creation, towards vital and coherent theology, towards new self-understanding of the churches in ecumenical engagement with the questions of the nature and calling of the church, and towards becoming a community of confessing and learning Christians". What were the financial implications of the programme decisions made within this policy?

A. PARTICIPATION AND RESPONSIBILITY

Significant costs resulted from the increased participation of young people and women (where WCC goals increased to 20% and 40%, respectively), from hiring staff to advocate and facilitate the participation of differently-abled persons, and from physical modifications to the Ecumenical Centre and the Bossey Institute to make them accessible to the differently-abled.

The ecumenical sharing of resources has been a major issue since Vancouver. The fortieth anniversary of the formation of the Commission on Inter-church Aid, Refugee and World Service (CICARWS) in 1986 was an opportunity to highlight the increasing bilateralism in international sharing and to emphasize the local diaconal work of the churches.

Regional consultations involving both churches and action groups were integrated into many programmes, including "Justice, Peace and the Integrity of Creation" (JPIC). A participatory methodology was proposed for the intended third volume of the ecumenical history, but this proved too expensive to be taken up.

In 1984 the central committee reminded churches that they were responsible for assuring the participation of their delegates in assemblies. The Finance committee and the committee on the General Secretariat addressed together the broad range of responsibilities related to WCC membership; this resulted in the new rule II on responsibilities of membership, including an item on finance (see p. 14).

B. GROWTH

The Vancouver theme, "Jesus Christ — the Life of the World", emphasized that life is a gift, and challenged growth towards the vision of one faith and one humanity. After more than ten years of financial consolidation, the imperative was to enlarge the programme budget, to find new ways to work, and to undertake new and experimental programmes as a sign of the vitality of the ecumenical movement. This challenge remains before the WCC.

C. COHERENCE AND INTEGRATION IN FINANCIAL AND PROGRAMMATIC PLANNING

Vancouver adopted guidelines which should "apply not only to studies and action programmes but also to relationships, fund-raising and the allocation of resources for the work of the Council" (*Minutes*, central committee, 1983).

In response, joint meetings of sub-unit commissions or working groups were held, and unit "executive" groups were established to act on common concerns in programme planning, budget co-ordination and funding. The co-operation between the Programme on Theological Education (PTE) and Bossey was extended into a consolidation of the two programmes.

Already in 1985 a timetable of WCC major world meetings to be held before the next assembly, and beyond, was presented. This early listing of these events — in a year when the Council's own budget was not covered by current income — sought to promote coherent planning by both the WCC and its member churches, and to provide a context for the financial decisions and relationships in the period between assemblies.

IV. Income*

A. THE DIFFERENCE BETWEEN MONEY GIVEN AND MONEY RECEIVED

Most of the WCC's income is given by the member churches, their agencies and other donors. Most income is subject to restrictions on its use imposed by the donor. The actual amount received is influenced by such factors as changes in currency exchange rates and inflation. Some explanations may help at this point.

---

* In the following discussion 1981 is used as the base year for comparison, since this was the year used in financial reporting to the sixth assembly. The most recent figures available at the time of writing this report (April 1990) are the pre-audit figures for 1989.

Inflation: This is the term for rising costs of goods and services. The cumulative Swiss inflation of 29.33% from 1981 to 1989 is considerably higher than the 19.2% experienced between the previous two assemblies, i.e. from 1975 to 1981. However, this does compare favourably with the rise in costs of 47.4% in the context of the world monetary disorder between Uppsala and Nairobi, from 1968 to 1975.

Exchange rate: This is the value of one country's currency when exchanged for that of another. Exchange rates vary in the world money market and are completely beyond the control of the member churches and agencies which support the Council. The Geneva expenses of the WCC are incurred in Swiss francs (Sfr.), and thus the income actually received depends on the rate of exchange between the currency in which the donation is made and the Swiss franc. For instance, in 1981, each US dollar received could be exchanged into Sfr.1.80; but by 1989 it converted into only Sfr.1.55 (and by June of 1990 had declined even further, to Sfr.1.43).

A brief look at what has happened to the exchange rates for the currencies of the Council's major donors is revealing:

Table I — YEAR-END RATES OF EXCHANGE TO SWISS FRANCS (Sfr)

WCC Major Income Currencies

	Sfr. 1981	Sfr. 1989
Canadian dollar, 1 C$ =	1.52	1.33
US dollar, 1 US$ =	1.80	1.55
Australian dollar, 1 A$ =	2.45	1.22
New Zealand dollar, 1 NZ$ =	1.50	0.92
Danish kronor, 1 Dkr. =	0.25	0.23
Finnish mark, 1 FM =	0.41	0.38
French francs, 1 FF =	0.31	0.27
FRG D mark, 1 DM =	0.89	0.91
Netherlands guilder, 1 Dfl. =	0.73	0.81
Norwegian kronor, 1 NOK =	0.31	0.23
Swedish kronor, 1 SEK =	0.33	0.25
UK pound sterling, 1 £ sterling =	3.43	2.50
Total Swiss francs	13.94	10.60

The lower total exchange value of other currencies means that the value of the Swiss franc has stayed relatively high compared to other currencies. The composite decline in value of these currencies, after adjustment for inflation, is 41.2%. That is to say, for the WCC to receive the same buying power in Swiss francs donors would need to give nearly twice as much in 1989 as they did in 1981.

Table II illustrates an additional problem with exchange variation experienced between 1981 and 1989. Not only did the combined exchange value of major donor currencies decline, as shown above, but there was also a sudden drop in the US dollar and related currencies between 1984 (the highest year-end rates) and 1987 (the lowest year-end rates).

Table II - VARIATION IN EXCHANGE

Combined Value of Major Income Currencies vs. Swiss Francs

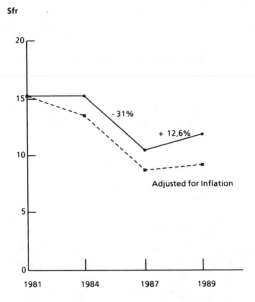

The decline of 30% in the combined exchange value of major currencies given to the Council was due partly to a sharp rise of the US dollar, to a value of Sfr.2.90 before its fall, late in 1987, to Sfr.1.29. The higher dollar exchange enabled the Council to balance its budgets through 1984; but the subsequent precipitous decline of the dollar against the Swiss franc wrought havoc with programme and financial planning. The German D-mark averaged Sfr.0.85 during the period, the 1989 year-end exchange rate listed being its peak exchange value. The slight recovery in composite exchange value apparent at year end 1989 is partly due to a weakening of the Swiss franc.

These figures emphasize the importance of distinguishing between contributions (what the churches actually give) and income (what the Council actually receives). Many donors have greatly increased their giving, but these increases may not be apparent if currency exchange rates produce smaller amounts in Swiss francs. This phenomenon is surely as frustrating to contributors as it is to the Council itself.

Inflation plus exchange: The combined effects of inflation and exchange rate loss account for a major part of the WCC's income difficulties. For example, if an item cost Sfr.13.94 in 1981 it could be purchased with one unit of each of the income currencies listed in table I. In 1989, because of inflation, the same item would cost Sfr.18.03. But, as indicated by the final figure in the 1989 column of table I, lower exchange rates would then yield (for the same contributions in the original currencies) Sfr.10.60 — only 59% of the amount needed.

Depending on the currency of the donor, the exchange variation may give a distorted impression of the Council's actual income and expense situation. To continue the above example, the Sfr. 13.94 item would have cost US$7.74 in 1981 and US$12.69 in 1989, a 64% increase. In DM, however, the item would have cost DM15.50 in 1981 and DM19.76 in 1989 — an increase of only 27.5%.

B. Kinds of income received by the WCC

Undesignated income (UDI): These are the budget-linked funds* given to the WCC without further specification as to their use. Since they come primarily from member churches as their annual membership contribution, they are sometimes referred to as such.

Designated income: These are monies given with a directive by the donor as to how they must be used. Designated funds given in support of the budget are referred to also as either "unrestricted" or "restricted". Unrestricted funds are designated for a particular programme unit or sub-unit, but have no further specification; restricted funds are those for which the donor has indicated a very precise use within the unit or sub-unit concerned (that is, for a particular consultation, publication, etc.).

Trust funds (project money): Income designated for third-party projects and programmes is handled "in trust for" the third party or project-holder.

---

* On this and the next category see the discussion of the "programme budget" on p. 71.

Trust fund income and expenses are reported alongside actual WCC monies but are accounted for separately, in US dollars; they are funds for whose administration the Council is responsible, but they are not Council funds as such. *

In-kind contributions: Some WCC member churches are in countries with currency restrictions. Not permitted to make cash transfers out of their countries, many have hosted meetings and covered on-site costs, provided for travel, locally co-supported activities related to trust funds or projects of other churches as listed by the WCC, and so on. When in 1981 (to take an example from the base year being used for comparison) the central committee met in Dresden, the costs covered by the hosting church amounted to about 1 million marks. Such a contribution cannot be included in the accounts of the WCC; but in this case the Council directly saved Sfr.96,441 of its budgeted amount for the meeting, and the auditors agreed to consider this as "restricted income" for WCC governing bodies. The Vancouver assembly strongly urged the Council to find ways to identify, encourage and report such contributions. The final income and expense report for the sixth assembly was the first attempt (1983) to consolidate references to "other contributions" in the financial report. Efforts in this area (see p. 38) have led to the listing, in the annual financial report, of churches which have provided such contributions.

Material aid contributions: As noted in the section on CICARWS, the World Council also handles the purchasing and transport of non-financial assistance on behalf of member churches and agencies throughout the world. Such aid is largely in the form of agricultural equipment, tools and seeds, clothing, shelter and blankets (primarily in emergency responses or refugee work), transport equipment, medicines and medical equipment; some food aid is provided on request. In 1988 the total value of commodity shipments by church organizations related to the WCC was US$134 million (not including purchases made by local or regional offices). This is the highest turnover recorded during the 19 years in which annual statistics have been compiled.

Although material aid is not included in the financial reports of the WCC, these goods do represent actual contributions or funds for direct purchase; they are mentioned as another aspect of the resource-sharing which occurs among the churches.

---

* See the discussion of "projects" (trust funds) on p. 71.

Table III - GROWTH OF MATERIAL AID CONTRIBUTIONS

TOTAL VALUE OF SHIPMENTS

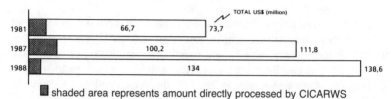

■ shaded area represents amount directly processed by CICARWS

C. Giving: where does the money come from?

With these terms in mind, let us now take a look at Council income. Table IV shows the 13 countries whose churches and other donors provide nearly 96% of all WCC budget-linked support.

Table IV — GEOGRAPHIC DISTRIBUTION OF MAIN SOURCES OF WCC BUDGET INCOME

Comparison of contributions 1981-1989, with % adjustment for inflation (all figures in Swiss francs)

	Undesignated 1981	Budget-linked 1981	Undesignated 1989	Budget-linked 1989
Canada	171,448	1,243,119	208,798	1,802,557
USA	1,706,556	6,829,403	1,630,123	5,860,883
Australia	48,898	344,426	54,014	181,941
New Zealand	22,555	90,752	20,593	59,251
Denmark	70,241	264,614	49,308	296,708
Finland	59,100	60,886	92,000	486,738
France	37,779	90,814	42,352	84,715
FRG	1,984,086	9,244,992	2,260,022	13,429,588
Netherlands	116,018	1,149,520	129,997	1,422,998
Norway	102,455	312,835	116,687	809,506
Sweden	128,998	3,272,196	102,705	5,408,868
Switzerland	136,000	964,592	168,000	975,564
UK	260,582	1,272,570	288,915	1,240,312
Sub-totals	4,844,816	25,140,719	5,163,514	32,059,629
After inflation adjustment			−17,6%	−1,4%
All others donors	205,735	298,047	224,894	578,791
After inflation adjustment			−15,5%	+50,2%
Total WCC Contributions	5,050,551	25,438,766	5,388,408	32,638,420
After inflation adjustment			−17,5%	−0,8%

Among these thirteen countries, donors in the Federal Republic of Germany (FRG) and the United States of America (USA) provided 63% of budget income in 1981, but only 59.1% in 1989. This shift is due largely to four factors:

1) The exchange value of the US-dollar in Swiss francs in 1989 was 14% below its 1981 value (not adjusted).
2) The exchange value of the German D-mark was 14.1% higher in 1989 than in 1981 (not adjusted).
3) A major US grant related to refugee work ended. Apart from this one grant, US donors nearly matched Swiss inflation in support of the budget, despite the lower dollar exchange value.
4) Some churches and other donors elsewhere in the world increased their giving in original currency at higher rates.

D. DESIGNATIONS ON INCOME

One notes in table IV that total Swiss-franc income is up Sfr.7.2 million, a 28.3% increase over 1981. When this is adjusted for inflation, however, the Council experienced a slight overall decline in buying power of -0.8%. (Budget income other than the refugee grant mentioned above increased 4% above inflation for the period.)

Comparing the undesignated funds, however, reveals a far more serious situation: undesignated Swiss-franc income increased only 6.7% over the period, meaning a decrease in buying power of 17.5%.

Despite systematic efforts to increase the Council's undesignated income, it has not kept pace with inflation — and this has been the case since long before the 1975 assembly. Such funds are generated largely as "membership contributions", and it is evident that the number and wealth of new WCC members is limited. This contrasts with other categories of income where, if present members cannot maintain increases which cover both exchange losses and inflation, the Council may hope to attract new donors. Undesignated income remains a precious sign of commitment to the ecumenical fellowship and a valuable support of church-related activities for which government-linked funds are not available.

Table IV illustrates that WCC income is losing the "cost of living battle". There are serious shortfalls in the critical area of the undesignated funds which support many of the Council's fundamental functions and programmes (such as the General Secretariat, Faith and Order, Dialogue, Church and Society, Renewal, and Youth). Clearly other support must be found for these activities, as foreseen in the Vancouver recommenda-tions. In 1975 undesignated income was 30% of total budget-linked funding; in 1981 it was 19.8% of the total, and by 1989 only 16.5%. When trust funds are considered, undesignated monies represent only 4% of the total funds handled. Yet it was precisely with undesignated funds that Vancouver recommended that the Council undertake any new and experimental programmes. Thus although — despite exchange losses and inflation — the Council's overall income is holding steady, funds available for allocation in response to central committee directives have diminished to an even greater extent than in the previous period.

But greater inflation rates, unfavourable exchange rate variations, and weaker donor economies are not the only factors which have changed since Vancouver. Table IV expressed main sources of WCC budget income in terms of Swiss francs; table V shows the increases in giving in terms of the original currencies in which they were given.

Table V — BUDGET-LINKED CONTRIBUTIONS, CHANGES IN ORIGINAL CURRENCY GIVING 1981-1989

Country	% change in giving	Adjusted for inflation
Canadian $	65.7%	28.1%
US dollar	7.4% *	−17.0%
Australian $	5.6%	−18.3%
New Zealand $	6.4%	−17.7%
Danish crown	18.1%	−8.7%
Finnish mark	767.7%	570.9%
French franc	10.5%	−14.5%
FRG D mark	50.4%	16.3%
Dutch guilder	11.9%	−13.5%
Norwegian kronor	243.5%	165.6%
Swedish kronor	116.0%	67.0%
Swiss franc	1.1%	−21.8%
UK pound sterling	33.7%	3.4%
* US dollar giving:		
— Refugee grant	−65.3%	−73.2%
— Other US dollar	27.2%	−1.6%

Donor giving outside these countries, recorded in Swiss francs, increased 94.2%, or more than 50% after adjustment for inflation.

Of the six increases noted above which exceed the Swiss inflation rate, and thus result in real Swiss franc increases, all but that of the UK are, in one way or another, linked to government funding. Giving channels vary; they are primarily via church aid agencies in the donor country, often with matching church funds required. Giving from these sources has increased 50%, largely due to new channels in Scandinavia, where there is state church legislation. Virtually all these funds are restricted, accounting for the enormous increase in restricted funds in the overall budget since 1981, as shown below.

Table VI — DESIGNATION OF BUDGET-LINKED FUNDS

% increases in Swiss francs from 1981-1989

		Adjusted for inflation
Undesignated	+6.7%	−17.5%
Designated and unrestricted	+1.7%	−21.3%
Designated and restricted	+215.7%	+144.1%

Council policy on accepting government funds calls for consultation with the churches in the donor country. The policy limits the amount of funding from a government donor for any given programme, and seeks to ensure that funded programmes represent initiatives of the churches through the central committee, and not initiatives of governments. Since Vancouver, special auditing conditions have been added.

The receipt of government funds through the Council's present partners, and within the policy guidelines adopted in 1982, has not posed a problem — other than the fact that staff levels are inadequate to handle the added reporting requirements, and that such funding is not available for the support of certain critical areas of WCC work (Faith and Order, Commission on World Mission and Evangelism (CWME), Dialogue, Renewal, PTE, Bossey, etc.). However, the funding environment for the Council and its partners has been greatly affected by the increased use of NGOs as channels for government funds. Things to be monitored include the increased bilateralism of Northern donor governments to Southern NGOs (including church partners), increased bilateralism by Northern NGOs using government funds, direct local funding possibilities from government missions, and various conditions tied to use of grants. The WCC advocacy and information role within the ecumenical sharing network should help partners not to compete with one another, or to expose themselves to unreasonable or unfair conditions.

The average annual trust fund income was $50 million. As trust funds fluctuate greatly (rising in response to emergencies), it is difficult to chart meaningful trends. Comparing the US$58,295,432 received in 1981 with the amount for 1989 shows a mere 2.4% increase in project giving, equivalent to -20% adjusted for inflation. Comparing 1981 with 1988 would show a 6% decrease (-14.2% adjusted), and comparing 1982 with 1989 would show a 39% rise (9.4% adjusted)!

The Council's major income currencies suffered a composite decline against the US dollar of 7% from 1981 to 1989. After inflation the decline is 28%, as opposed to a 41.2% decline in exchange of these same currencies against the Swiss franc. No exchange losses affect giving from the USA, and the German D-mark has strengthened against the dollar beyond inflation. This means that smaller increases in original currency giving have been needed to maintain the US-dollar exchange value of project income accounts. Of course for the Council's partners in implementing projects, the decline in the dollar exchange value creates inflationary project askings, in line with local inflation and the loss of exchange value.

Given the exchange situation which has been described, the dollar became "cheaper" over this period. Thus trust funds have appeared to remain at a higher level than the Swiss-franc income for the budget; yet during this period only Canada, Australia, New Zealand, Finland and Norway have actually increased trust fund giving beyond inflation. As noted earlier, most of these increases also involve the use of government funds. It remains to be seen whether the lower increases elsewhere reflect lower assistance to partners worldwide, or increasing bilateralism (i.e. giving funds directly rather than through the WCC).

The following are some general observations on current Council income:

— Traditional member church and agency donors are faithful in their support.
— Churches and agencies give more money to and through the Council.
— Member churches outside the first world, and non-member donors, play a more participatory role in Council funding, mostly through small but undesignated contributions.
— Traditional church donor giving cannot keep pace with inflation and exchange. Per capita giving in most large donor churches of the North is higher, reflecting an older church population, but individual increases are largely offset by declining church membership and "flat" economic conditions. Income received by these churches is below the rate of inflation, so less money is available for allocation; it is no surprise that most of these churches are unable to respond to the Council's need for undesignated giving.
— Overall increases are due to donor churches or agencies which channel government funds, partially due to government recognition of

the efficacy of NGOs, including the churches, in development and emergency assistance.
— More of the funds which are received are designated.
— Reporting requirements have increased substantially, as churches and other NGOs are affected by the conditions attached to government allocations.

Designations in funding may reflect the donors' desire for a closer relationship with their partners who are implementing programmes; in this case they may enhance mutual understanding. But there are also negative factors in the diverse and long-standing trend towards greater designation in giving. These include: (1) The growing general distrust of institutions and bureaucracies since the 1960s, which can also be seen in religious organizations, including many member churches; (2) increases in NGO-channelled government funds which require reporting for their own constituency, and must address the distrust just noted, leading to: (3) competition between more NGOs, including church-related NGOs, for public appeal funds and government assistance budgets, either in the donor country or via government missions in implementing countries; (4) neo-conservatism, either of political or economic origin, which encourages designation in support of — or against — specific actions of the churches and partner bodies.

Broader designations are encouraged as they help provide financial integration across WCC administrative structures. "Functional", issue-oriented designations (for example, for women, health, or education activities) respect the donor's special interests and are available for activities at various points in the Council's structure where those interests are addressed and in light of specific financial needs.

Block grants are another approach to financial integration for more stable programme planning. In the budget, these are grants for the activities of an entire unit, available to particular sub-units as needed. In Units II and III such funds stimulate co-ordinated planning, as well as creating a pool of different currencies, minimizing the exchange risk faced by programmes with a major exposure in one currency.

Trust funds may also be given as broadly-designated "block grants". The Ecumenical Development Fund (of the Commission on the Churches' Participation in Development [CCPD], and Urban Rural Mission (of CWME) have educated donors for block grant support over the years. The pre-Nairobi "category I", or priority project fund, had an annual goal of $3.5 million. Due largely to a higher dollar return on exchange, a new annual goal of $4.5 million has been established for block support of the priority projects of CICARWS. This rise is welcome news to implementing partners around the world. When adjusted for the (relatively low) Swiss inflation, the new target still represents a decline of 17% in purchasing power.

The good news about WCC income is that more churches from other parts of the world are participating in the financial life of the Council. The bad news is that, with few exceptions, the traditional Northern donor churches cannot maintain their own structures — much less increase giving to the WCC beyond inflation — without government assistance. Since 1987 virtually all major donor churches have indicated that their own income does not cover their costs after inflation. The world financial trends described above have become measurable in the economics of the Council's life.

Serious consideration is needed both now and after Canberra as to how:
— the WCC can live within its means;
— current giving can be increased;
— restrictions on giving can be eased;
— the number of donors can be increased, particularly for the historic theological, ecclesiological, educational and mission work done by the churches through the Council.

Other income: In addition to financial and in-kind support by the member churches and other partners, the WCC generates income through investing its reserves and through sales and services (production income).

Interest and investment earnings on all funds since the sixth assembly were as follows:

Table VII - INTEREST AND INVESTMENT EARNINGS, ALL FUNDS

Swiss francs

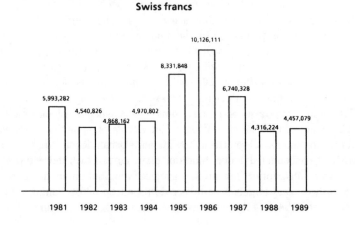

The extraordinary increases for 1985 and 1986 were the result of forward selling of US dollars to cover the budgeted rate. (Since the decline in dollar exchange rates, further sell-forward arrangements have not been possible.) In this manner, the Council postponed absorbing the enormity of the drop in the US-dollar exchange value for two years.

About half of the funds and balances held by the World Council are trust accounts, and most of the interest gained accrues to these accounts. Similarly, unrestricted funds, such as the seventh assembly reserve, accrue interest for their respective purpose. Since 1985 the Council has placed wills and bequests into a General Endowment Fund, which stood at Sfr.848,991 at the end of 1989.

Income from sales and services, which is largely generated by the Ecumenical Institute, Bossey, and the Department of Communication, was as follows since 1981:

Table VIII - INCOME FROM SALES & SERVICES

Swiss francs

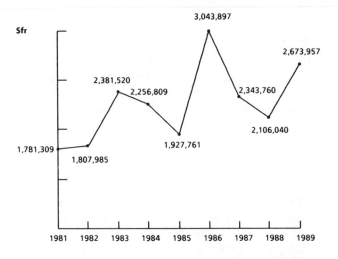

Publications and sales are affected by the variations in exchange rates, as is the rest of Council income. Additionally, due to added delivery costs and lower subscription revenues, increased distribution in developing countries produces a greater net loss over production costs. Adjusted for inflation, the 1989 amount shown is 37% below the 1981 figure.

Special funding: Staff and commissions are encouraged to plan their work in such a way that activities can be included in the annual budget.* However, the executive committee can authorize "special funding" which permits staff to seek funding for additional activities (within, of course, the priorities set by central committee).

In 1981, special funding for the Sheffield consultation on the "Community of Women and Men in the Church" study was completed; and Sfr.5.5 million was authorized in special funding for the sixth assembly. No further such items were authorized until after the 1983 assembly, and authorized items approved were successfully funded.

WCC programme methodology after Vancouver has included a series of world conferences, resulting in authorization for the Office for Income Coordination and Development (OICD) to seek an additional Sfr.13,265,000 in special funding as indicated on p. 41 above.

To respond to the assembly's call for integrated long-range programme and financial planning, a schedule of special funding requests has regularly been shared with the central committee. But "special" events linked to ongoing concerns are paid for largely from the same donor budgets which have been unable to increase overall programme support.

V. Expenditures

A. GLOBAL EXPENSE TRENDS

It is helpful to consider "where the money goes" as the Council and its member churches respond to human needs in areas such as emergencies and refugee assistance, training, advocacy, credit, education and health. All the budgets which follow must be seen in their "world context"; they are not simply abstract numbers but reflect specific situations of need and, in response, partnerships in service and acts of common witness.

In reviewing project activities some shifts are apparent between 1981 and 1989 (any given year will be affected by the occurrence of natural or human disasters). Figures are somewhat approximate and do not fully reflect material aid, personnel placements, and participation of programme staff and resources.

In 1981 large emergency responses in Asia and in Latin America brought the emergency sector to more than a quarter of all project funds;

---

* See the discussion of the "programme budget" on p. 71.

in 1989 they were closer to 19%. Refugee assistance has increased by 20% (-3% adjusted), Urban Rural Mission by 42% (15% adjusted) and the scholarship programme by no less than 300% (293% adjusted!). Inter-church aid declined from 51% of the total to 46%, but this also reflects the changed circumstances in Africa, where refugee expenditures have increased 70% (37.5% adjusted) (see table IX, next page).

B. KINDS OF SPENDING

Funds spent by the Council are of three types:

1. Programme budget: These are the budgeted Swiss-franc expenses which include the essential programme operations of WCC programme units, sub-units and the General Secretariat. Staff salaries and related costs, travel, programme, newsletters and other publications, research, and consultations are all budget expenses. This category represents between 25 and 30% of total Council spending.

2. Programme projects: These are specific short-term activities, in line with sub-unit criteria, which may be authorized in addition to programme budget items for implementation as funds are available. (The central committee has indicated that most of these activities should be planned for and incorporated into the programme budget, so that adequate support can be secured.)

3. Projects (trust funds): These are funds handled in trust in relation to projects and activities of member churches, church-related agencies, and networks. The funds are accounted in US dollars, received separately from the WCC programme budget accounts described above, and trans-ferred to, or spent on behalf of, the respective project or activity. The WCC thus provides a service for member churches, church-related agencies and networks in advocating, circulating information about, and soliciting funds for, activities which they have undertaken. In this process sub-unit staff may consult with the project-holder and assist in the administration of requests and contributions. This category, together with number 2 above, accounts for the remaining money spent by the Council, i.e. 70-75% of spending.

C. THE WCC PROGRAMME

The programme budget is the responsibility of the central committee, which approves it. From Nairobi to Vancouver, a primary task of the Finance committee was to develop a unified budget for the Council, instead of the seven different budgets of its historical parts. With the "Council-wide" emphases following 1983, and the push for greater clarity

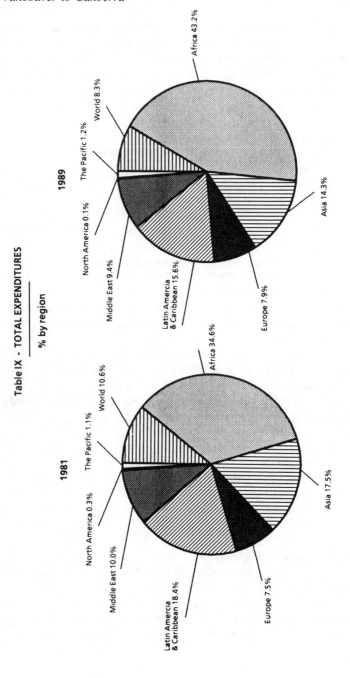

Table IX - TOTAL EXPENDITURES

% by region

1981

Africa 34.6%
Asia 17.5%
Europe 7.5%
Latin Amercia & Caribbean 18.4%
Middle East 10.0%
North America 0.3%
The Pacific 1.1%
World 10.6%

1989

Africa 43.2%
Asia 14.3%
Europe 7.9%
Latin Amercia & Caribbean 15.6%
Middle East 9.4%
North America 0.1%
The Pacific 1.2%
World 8.3%

in finance and administration, this period is characterized by efforts to develop unified budgeting.

Detailed numerical comparison between 1981 and 1989 is cumbersome. Some programmes have come to an end since 1981, and others have moved within the WCC structure. Regular transfers from some sub-units to others (CWME to Dialogue, CICARWS to Scholarships and Youth) have stopped, as sharing of central costs has been rationalized. And new activities have been undertaken, such as the office on Justice, Peace and the Integrity of Creation (JPIC), the programme on "Young Women Doing Theology" (a short-term experiment), and the introduction of word-processing and other computer facilities in the sub-units.

Inflation, which totalled 29.33% over the period, progressed as follows:

Table X - LOSS OF BUYING POWER 1981 - 1989

due to Rates of Swiss Inflation

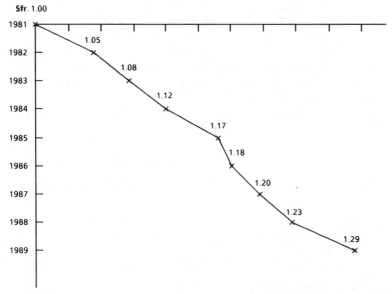

To give a concrete example, this means that goods or services which cost Sfr.5.00 in 1981 now cost Sfr.6.47 (adjusted for inflation).

In the years 1981-89, Sfr.307,468,993 was spent in programme budget-linked expenses. What is the WCC budget spent for? The largest portion of expenses is staff-related costs. Following serious cuts in staff and programme during 1976 and 1977, by 1980 the pre-Nairobi level of Geneva personnel was reached again; and requests for additional staff to implement the Vancouver mandates led to an 8% expansion of personnel by 1989. Staff-related costs were 57% of 1981 budgeted expenses, 64% of those for 1989.

Some attempt was made to consolidate meetings around WCC "world" events, thus saving travel costs. But despite lower US-dollar rates and the general lowering of plane fares, expenses for meetings, consultations and travel have still risen 10% beyond inflation, from 13.8% of total spending in 1981 to 15.3% in 1989. The WCC initiated its own travel and conference office to seek maximum economy in this area; but this incurred, of course, some additional staff expense.

The practical costs of participation — of involving the member churches in the life and work of the Council through travel, meetings, consultations, translation, interpretation, communication — were nearly one third of total expenses in 1989.

Given that overall levels of expenditure have barely kept pace with inflation (2.7% over the entire eight-year period), the growth in personnel-related and meeting costs has had major implications. The additional costs in these areas have meant that the money available for all other activities, including publications, studies, administration, etc., has actually declined from Sfr.9.1 million in 1981 to Sfr.8.6 million in 1989, a reduction (adjusted for inflation) of 27%.

Programme expenses among the units of the Council show considerable stability.

Table XI – WCC PROGRAMMES AS PERCENTAGE OF BUDGET

Figures below total more than 100% due to overlap of distributed costs

	1981	1989
General Secretariat (including resource sharing)	6.2%	7.3%
Library and documentation	1.2%	1.7%
Unit I (without 1981 Community study)	12.0%	13.6%
Unit II (without Resource Sharing or Sodepax; with JPIC)	42.0%	44.3%
Unit III	15.7%	16.6%
Ecumenical Institute, Bossey	5.5%	4.6%
Communication	12.7%	13.0%
Finance and Central Services, administrative costs (including amortization of new building)	9.8%	9.2% *

* The 1981 column totals 105.1%, while that for 1989 totals 110.3%. This reflects the increase in distributed costs.

The distinction between programme budget and projects (trust funds) must be kept in mind (see p. 71). In 1989, budgeted expenses were nearly 30% of total spending, the rest being projects and trust funds. Thus administrative costs are less than 4% of total Council spending.

Looking at programmes in relation to the entire budget is one way of studying their growth; changes in spending levels are also revealing.

Table XII – EXPENSE INCREASE/DECREASE 1989 OVER 1981

Adjusted for inflation

General Secretariat	25.4%
Library and Documentation	17.4%
Unit I (without Community study and Energy for my Neighbour)	6.2%
Unit II (without SODEPAX)	14.8%
Unit III	19.4%
Ecumenical Institute, Bossey	−19.2%
Communication	4.7%
Finance and Administration	0.9%
Total budget spending	2.7%

In understanding the two preceding tables, several factors must be taken into account. These can be grouped under four headings.

1. The budget

The increase for the General Secretariat is due largely to the inclusion of the budget of the US Office (which was not done prior to 1984), and the addition of the Travel and Conference Office (which did not exist in 1981).

The Unit I figures in table XII do not include the Sfr.536,754 spent in 1981 for the study on the "Community of Women and Men in the Church". (That programme was specially funded and staffed, and there is no equivalent in 1989.) Also removed are costs related to the "Energy for My Neighbour" programme, a special activity of Church and Society.

The Unit II figures in table XII do not include the Sfr.275,547 spent in 1981 on SODEPAX, which has since come to a close. The growth of Unit II is due to:
a) increased staff and programme in the Commission on Inter-church Aid, Refugees and World Service (see below), the Commission on International Affairs and the Programme to Combat Racism;

b) increases in the Christian Medical Commission, linked especially to the AIDS programme and to bringing *Contact* and the pharmaceutical programme into the budget; and

c) the creation of an office to staff the process on "Justice, Peace and the Integrity of Creation" (for an average of Sfr.730,000 per year from 1986-91).

These changes mean that Unit II resources have been re-allocated, transfers to Youth and Scholarships stopped, and other programmes in the Unit have kept expenses below inflation throughout the period. If the CICARWS refugee field offices (which were being closed during 1989) are removed from the 1981-89 comparison, CICARWS' programme would still be the largest in the Council (accounting for 13.3% in 1981, 15.1% in 1989), the sub-unit having increased Geneva operations by 56.6% (21.1% adjusted) over this period. And without these field offices, Unit II shows a total increase of 24% (above inflation), the largest increase in activity in the Council.

Unit III has also experienced real growth, 19.4% beyond inflation from 1981 to 1989. This figure, however, hides significant variations within the Unit. A closer look reveals:

Table XIII – UNIT III EXPENSE INCREASE/DECREASE 1989 OVER 1981

Adjusted for inflation

Renewal and Congregational Life	+38.2%
Youth	−11.8% (staff vacancy '89)
Women in Church and Society	+69.4%
Education and Scholarships	+36.4%
Programme on Theological Education	−9.4%

Renewal and Congregational Life has experienced growth in the area of its lay training work; but funding for the programme is limited, and it is largely dependent on undesignated funds. The Youth office decline is largely artificial, as an executive staff position was empty for most of 1989. Full staffing of this programme would have increased the overall growth of Unit III. A third executive staff position was approved for the Youth office in 1989, with a central committee waiver of the standing requirement that 75% of needed funds for a first contract be in hand or pledged prior to recruitment; this position has yet to be filled (this programme is also dependent on the undesignated funds).

The most dramatic shift and budget growth since Vancouver is in the Sub-unit on Women in Church and Society (which was dependent on undesignated income until 1982). Growing from 1.2% of the WCC's 1981 expenses to 2% of those in 1989 — increasing 119%, nearly 70% after adjustment for inflation — this programme reflects the strong interest in, and visibility for, women's concerns in the Council and its member churches, as well as other donors. Vancouver urged that the concerns of women be integrated into all WCC activities; the Decade of the Churches in Solidarity with Women should encourage other programmes to engage women more visibly in their own work, networks and leadership.

During this period the financial stability of the Education Sub-unit improved, with the Scholarships programme more than doubling in size and scope.

A word is in order about the nearly 20% reduction in costs experienced by the Ecumenical Institute, Bossey. This reflects the reduction, in the early 1980s, of one executive position for administration and the vacancy for most of 1989 of the director's position (it has since been merged with the directorship of PTE).

2. Shared central costs and services

Every assembly since 1968 has come to the conclusion that all parts of the Council should share in its central costs and services. Vancouver, indeed, encouraged the central committee to share costs which had not previously been distributed. However, such cost distribution — keyed to specific personnel, programme, budgetary and financial activity — causes a commensurate rise in expenses in the respective programme budgets.

As of 1981 the following costs were distributed: mail, telephone and upkeep services, an office furniture pool, and a cafeteria subsidy; the Library, Personnel Office, and the Office for Income Coordination and Development. Subsequently distributed were the Travel and Conference Office, Documentation Service, and parts of the Communication Department. Beginning in 1989, costs of the US Office were distributed, along with additional parts of Communication and the assembly reserve.

Redistribution has been accompanied by closer scrutiny of central costs, which have been reduced steadily since 1975. Business service costs (mail, telephone, cyclostyle or copying service, and economat or office supplies) have remained below inflation. Although upkeep costs (2.9% of budget) have risen slightly, the 12% increase is partly linked to amortization of the building costs for the new wing. The installation of a telephone system capable of itemized billing has encouraged staff to seek economies in this area; a telefax system has been added to the telex service, and the increased workload has been absorbed without increased personnel. In-house printing facilities have been upgraded, with improved quality and/or lower rates for certain jobs than available from outside companies. Recycled paper is more widely used, and quantity purchasing of standardized supplies has enabled economat to introduce savings. Simultaneous translation equipment has been upgraded to limit outside rental charges, and upkeep and repair services are largely performed by the technical service department.

Finance and administration costs have changed in character as the Council moved from using a computer service company to having its own electronic data processing (EDP) system. This has happened in several stages. At the beginning of this period salaries of data input operators and all other computer-related costs were previously charged to the Department of Finance, it being the sole computer user. Costs were thus distributed as part of the finance "charge". As others began using personal computers, these charges became directly attributable to the sub-units involved. When the Council began to offer a central system for these applications, costs were still handled through Finance, although distributed in relation to use of equipment. In future reporting, transparency will be essential about costs for computer hardware, software and service, both centrally and in specific programmes.

EDP and Finance costs total about 5% of total budget. This plus the remaining administrative costs (Personnel and Central Services, i.e. economat, telephone, telex, telefax, upkeep, reception, etc.), yields the total reported in table XI.

As additional costs were distributed — on the lines which Vancouver had suggested — the debate on sharing of central costs has become more heated. The Canberra assembly may wish to review whether it is feasible and wise to continue this practise, and to explore possible alternatives.

3. Other changes

Council expenses since Vancouver reflect the directives on programme which were established there. However, when salary-related and meeting and travel costs are deducted, the programme funds remaining to implement its mandates have declined since Vancouver by 27% (adjusted for inflation).

The limits on resources have forced the Council to trade off new efforts (such as the programme on JPIC) against ongoing work. Costs have been cut, but the new staff levels increase the Council's exposure to inflation (which recently has climbed in Switzerland).

4. Location factors

Over the years consideration has been given to whether the WCC should move from Geneva. The decision to stay in Geneva is based primarily on non-financial criteria (the availability of visas, multilingual administrative capacities, good international transportation and communications facilities, the absence of government censorship, etc.). Given the combined effect of exchange loss on income and inflation on expense, a word is in order about present facilities.

The last detailed "removal study" considered London and Nairobi. Inflation in both locations has greatly exceeded that in Geneva, and travel costs are higher to Nairobi. These together with other, non-financial factors led to a re-affirmation of Geneva as the WCC's home. The central committee has also reviewed the possibility of having certain programmes, or staff, located elsewhere. Some issues which this proposal raised were the full integration of such staff in the life of the Council, the difficulty of representing the wholeness of the Council in several locations, and equity in remuneration. The proposal was not adopted.

The WCC owns the Ecumenical Centre in Geneva, which was built in 1964 with contributions from churches and Christians all over the world. At intervals since 1977, the executive committee has reviewed the needs of various organizations housed in the Centre, which is operated as a co-operative. In response to the need for more space, in 1980 a temporary annex was erected and (it being understood that moving to a new facility would be more costly) in 1983 a task force began to study options for expansion.

In the following year the executive committee established principles for considering such an expansion, and asked that drawings and a plan for financing be prepared. Construction of a new wing for the Ecumenical Centre began in 1985; it was completed in 1987 for a cost of Sfr.6.2 million. The interest rate for investment was fixed at 5.5% per annum (slightly higher than what could have been obtained on long-term, first-class Swiss bonds). Under such conditions the capital investment will be reimbursed in a fraction of the 50-year reimbursement period of first-rank mortgages in Switzerland. The extension was thus self-financed, calling for no special funding from the churches. The Lutheran World Federation occupies 64 of the offices in the new wing, the WCC translation department 5, and the remaining 23 offices are sublet to other non-profit agencies to help offset mortgage costs.*

D. TRUST FUND EXPENSES

Whereas decision-making on budget expenses is the responsibility of the central committee, project expenses are determined in more than a dozen ways. Most projects are proposed and designed in the countries or regions concerned, and go through national or regional screening committees. Churches and agencies which spend funds in support of such projects through the Council do so, of course, in light of their own guidelines and available monies. Some $523 million has been handled in trust funds from 1981-89.

The volume of annual project (trust fund) expenses compared to budgeted programmes was a concern in Nairobi (1975) because of the Council's financial crisis. Careful analysis of expenses has since permitted a more realistic assessment of the extent to which handling trust funds is a budget expense. WCC costs include staff, production of project listings, and financial services. The Council had intended to provide such services without charge, but given the budget pressures, demands on limited staff, and a more relational style of work needed for participatory decision-making, the real costs are high. There is wide recognition that there is also considerable programmatic relationship between activities within the budget and those done "in trust for others".

The Finance committee has become more interested in trust funds, both in terms of their cost to the Council (either directly through services provided, or indirectly by bearing exchange liability — trust funds being US-dollar accounts), and in the context of the WCC's overall programme and ecumenical relationships. The trust funds have been screened, and their criteria and character reviewed, largely through the commissions or working groups of the sub-units most directly involved (whether because of programmatic or regional ties). The Finance committee recognizes that a more co-ordinated approach to the use of trust funds, and an evaluation of their impact on the work of the Council as a whole, are necessary.

These needs are emphasized by two additional factors which have emerged since Vancouver. The first is the fact that trust funds are given largely by the same donors who support the programme budget, raising the spectre of "competition" for funding inside the ecumenical move-

---

* See also the discussion of the new wing on p. 22.

ment. Secondly, a significant amount of trust funds are staff-managed rather than "project funds received from, held for and disbursed at the specific direction of others", as defined by the auditors in the annual financial report. Policy guidance will be necessary from the next assembly if budgeting is to be transparent and equitable. This is evidenced in the following section.

E. COUNCIL-WIDE EVENTS AND PROGRAMMES

A record number of WCC meetings was held from Nairobi to Vancouver. This reflected a desire to encourage broader participation in the ecumenical movement. Perhaps symbolizing the wish for ecumenical integration, Vancouver spawned a record number of world conferences between two assemblies. The meetings mentioned in the discussion of special funding — Larnaca, El Escorial, San Antonio, JPIC and the Canberra assembly (1991) — added an average cost of Sfr.2 million each year since Vancouver, most of it in addition to the budget. Creating an office to staff the JPIC process and consultation meant (including estimated expenses through Canberra) budget costs of Sfr.3.68 million. (Other Council-wide emphases coming out of the sixth assembly were integrated into existing programme structures.)

VI. Consolidation and transparency: some important shifts

A. PRIORITIES AND BUDGET POSSIBILITIES

The central committee has complained several times since Vancouver that pressure on undesignated income was making it impossible to direct funds according to emerging priorities. In response it took a series of actions, proposed by the Finance committee, to free other funds for direct decision-making by the central committee.

The first of these was the allocation of undesignated interest earned on the general, emergency and exchange fluctuation reserves for "new programmes of a short-term (less than three years) and experimental nature", half within and half outside the budget process. Since 1987, more than Sfr.1 million has been allocated in this manner; the 1989-90 evaluation of this process indicates that it was useful in encouraging creative programming.

Secondly, in 1986 the central committee approved the creation of a general endowment fund from wills and bequests (one-time income) to generate undesignated income. At year end 1989 this endowment stood at Sfr.848,991.

Thirdly, the central committee approved the creation of an endowment fund in honour of Willem Visser 't Hooft, aiming to create a new source of funds in support of leadership development and ecumenical opportunities for young people. This was conceived as being separate from the WCC, in order that it might attract funds not available to the WCC itself. At the time of writing the fund had not been capitalized; there has simply not been enough staff to do the necessary work.

Each of these steps was creative, but the total funds involved are minor in comparison with either the annual budget or special funding authorizations during the same period. As undesignated funds continue to decline as a percentage of total available resources, Canberra will again face the problem of how to fund the priorities which emerge from the assembly.

The central committee also asked that criteria be developed for the allocation of undesignated income (UDI) in light of the basic principles established in Vancouver, namely that:

— new programmes be undertaken on short-term or experimental bases within the framework of central committee priorities and the availability of undesignated funds (as discussed above);
— ongoing work and new long-range programmes be funded by designated funds "within the financial structures and programmatic relationships of the Council, its member churches and their related agencies" — and not be dependent on undesignated funds;
— co-ordinated income development be strengthened to provide financial support for those programmes which the central committee continues, consequently reducing the dependency of such programmes on undesignated funds.

These principles are the basis for the central committee's rejection of applications for UDI to support programmes which had not been dependent on these funds in 1983. A detailed review of past UDI allocations reveals a "rationale" only of "balancing" income and expenses for programmes dependent on such funds. Final recommendations are premature; further work is needed both on the procedures for allocating UDI, and on the criteria themselves. Great similarity exists between the problems in allocating undesignated funds and block grants (unit-wide funds), and some inter-relation (both programmatic and financial) between the two kinds of funds is unavoidable. Key words emerging in the discussion of possible criteria for the use of such funds have been:

— priority (though not in itself a financial issue, and not always correlated positively with the actual receipt of undesignated funds);

— feasibility, i.e. the possibility of reducing a programme's UDI dependence by finding more designated funds; it was agreed that the only "implicit designation" on UDI was support of the General Secretariat;
— need, in financial terms, taking into account: overall programme plans, the possibility of raising designated funds, actual spending levels versus budget or increases/decreases over time, and alternate implementations of plans to reduce costs.

The present financial practice is simply to budget more undesignated income than the Council expects to receive, to count on underspending, and to allocate UDI to programmes in the amount of actual shortfalls at year end. The official allocation of undesignated funds is made by the central committee in approving the budget.

Continued reflection, experimentation, and evaluation are needed along three lines: (a) forums for programme directors to debate the distribution of block grants, including undesignated funds; (b) budgeting consistency so that the determination of "need" is comparable for all programmes, and areas of growth or reduction reflect programme priorities; and (c) incentives to increase programme contributions (shortfalls being covered by UDI or block grants, the present system gives staff little incentive to build financial support for their work).

Several suggestions have been forwarded but no criteria and guidelines have been acted upon by the central committee. This area quickly raises questions of staff and constituency decision-making processes, and the continued disjuncture between programme and financial planning and responsibilities.

Little progress has been made in implementing Vancouver's recommendation to strengthen co-ordinated income development as a way of reducing dependence upon undesignated funds. Sometimes the concept of not only direct, but "unhindered" donor relationships is still advanced, raising the old questions about how historically separate programmes can evidence mutual responsibility for the Council as a whole.

Staff vacancies in OICD, the unit finance offices, and the office of the assistant general secretary for finance and administration, have meant that, since Vancouver, fewer staff have been available to:
— continue work in soliciting and reporting on funds;
— develop new funding beyond the levels of exchange loss and inflation;
— study, describe and circulate information about Council finances in order to increase transparency, and to gain broader participation in analysis of, and decisions about, financial priorities.

In 1984 the central committee asked each programme unit and the General Secretariat to rank (in order of importance) all new projects, proposals for additional staff, and other items with financial consequences.

The central committee continues to address issues it considers essential. In addition to steps aimed at freeing funds for direct support of its priorities, in 1988 the central committee established the Ecumenical Decade of the Churches in Solidarity with Women fund and allocated $75,000 from the operating balance of the Council to launch this work and accord it some priority.

The Finance committee has carefully refused to recommend programme priorities, believing that this responsibility lies elsewhere. But the mechanisms for integrating financial and programme planning are inconsistent, and work is still needed on the central committee's role in Council-wide programme priority-setting in light of both financial and non-financial limitations. Finance committee warnings in 1986 have failed to slow spending — in fact expense increases in 1987 and 1988 were double Swiss-franc inflation, at the very time when currency exchange values were down.

B. BALANCING THE BUDGET

Since Vancouver the Finance committee has given attention to the WCC's consolidated budget, with these results:
— The committee re-affirmed the principle that the use of designated funds should not incur the use of undesignated funds. Fund-use policy further specifies that the most-specifically designated funds should be used first, in an effort to protect the flexibility of block grants and undesignated funds in balancing programme support.
— Sub-units are encouraged to put all activities into their budgets to enable better planning and funding, and to gain transparency. An examination of needs for undesignated and block-grant funds shows that, for historical reasons, some programmes use programme-project trust fund accounts (category 2 on p. 71) for consultations, travel and other "activities" costs. Others have no trust funds, and put all costs and planned activities in the budget. Such variations make it hard to grasp what is possible financially, and what are actually the available options.
— In 1985, faced with the problem of maintaining Council activities despite lower exchange rates, the Finance committee set parameters on the budgeted use of reserves. The policy, which was seen as a

short-term measure until income could be restored to the level of expenditure, established that sub-units with operating balances could budget the use of up to one-third of those balances in any given year. The Council itself operates under the same constraint in supporting budgets for those programmes dependent on undesignated funds. (Budgets were considered "balanced" if they did not exceed the one-third draw down on reserves.) In this manner, from 1984 to 1988 total operating funds (restricted and unrestricted) were reduced by more than half (from Sfr.50 million to Sfr.22.5 million).

— Because programmes dependent on undesignated funds were "squeezed" disproportionately by the assembly reserve transfer which was made from this income, it was agreed that this would be a distributed cost, with all programmes participating.

— Because of the pressures on undesignated funding, and in the absence of adequate designated funds, further redistribution was accepted, as noted in the section on expenses.

C. EXTRA-BUDGETARY SHIFTS

In addition to the central committee's creation of the Ecumenical Decade of the Churches in Solidarity with Women fund, during this period CICARWS created a special action fund. The following also occurred, although no new mandates were involved: PTE established a Swiss-franc trust account, in addition to their US-dollar trust account for partnership support; new efforts to increase the endowment fund of the Ecumenical Institute at Bossey were undertaken; and CCPD renewed the 2% Appeal for the Ecumenical Development Fund (EDF).

The Finance committee has noted the link between budgeted and trust funds, both in financial and programmatic terms; but no action has yet been proposed for establishing a transparent and coherent decision-making process for the creation of specialized, extra-budgetary funds handled by the Council.

The central committee noted with regret in 1989 that the regional resource-sharing groups were no longer a joint undertaking of sub-units (as had been hoped), since only CICARWS projects were being screened. It encouraged sub-units to continue trying to co-ordinate their activities in the regions through such regional groups.

In light of sixth assembly guidelines, and the 1987 El Escorial world meeting on resource-sharing, it is noteworthy that the board of the Ecumenical Church Loan Fund (ECLOF), and the commission of PTE, have been determined to allocate at least half of their resources for the benefit and empowerment of women. (The Ecumenical Development Co-operative Society [EDCS] has done likewise.) Attention has been focused on the special needs of women under racism and refugee and migrant women, and this is being reflected in monetary terms as well. The programmatic and financial impact of such decisions will need to be evaluated by the new central committee.

The assembly may wish to offer guidance for distinguishing between staff- and commission-managed trust funds and (to use the words of the auditors once again) "project funds received from, held for and disbursed at the specific direction of others". This is needed to clarify and improve their relationship to budgeted plans, income and expense.

D. OBSTACLES AND OPPORTUNITIES IN POLICY DEVELOPMENT AND FINANCIAL MECHANISMS

Some would say that the biggest obstacle for the Council is inadequate funding; a review of the overall economic context suggests that this will be difficult if not impossible to change. Others suggest that the biggest difficulty is setting clear and coherent priorities for the work of the Council — that proliferation of programmes inflates budgets but not necessarily income. The dilemma of WCC financing, and fresh hope for the future, lies in facing the elements of truth in both these positions and in finding responsible and creative responses.

At the July 1984 central committee meeting, members of the Finance committee asked that sessions be planned so that they could participate in the other (General Secretariat or unit) committees to which they belonged. They affirmed that: "The Finance committee itself will not take decisions on programmes, but it should see as its responsibility to remind the central and executive committees that there are decisions to be taken elsewhere if the Finance committee is to perform the tasks that are assigned to it... Such decisions will regularly require: determination of priorities, analyzing the realities and selecting options (the WCC cannot do everything!) and, because resources are limited, finding ways to do things differently, so that by spending less, we can accomplish more!" (*Minutes*, central committee, 1984, p.94).

A closer link was also urged between the Finance and General Secretariat committees. But aside from work on responsibilities of membership, and the decision-making process for the allocation of undesignated interest, no further co-ordination evolved.

Several areas for further policy reflection have been identified. Specific proposals which have been made include:

— establishing shared responsibility for financial realism;
— developing a more rational use of computers in financial and programme management;
— establishing monitoring mechanisms to assure that central committee policies are reflected in the financial life of the Council (this implies comparable budget procedures, funds policies, and allocation of funds only to activities consonant with central committee policy — for example, funding meetings only if participation follows WCC guidelines);
— clarifying the limits and rationale of the distribution of central service costs;
— ensuring (through adequate staff) that programmes have the necessary financial information, and vice versa, in order to promote financial and administrative integration. (The tendency to speak of "my" donors, programmes and networks reflects and exacerbates the present structural divisions within the WCC. This makes it difficult to manifest the wholeness of the Council and to define clearly its priorities.)

As noted above, it was pointed out in 1988 that the absence of unallocated financial resources made it difficult for the central committee to implement some of the actions requested by the sixth assembly. To provide financial flexibility after the seventh assembly, instructions were given to restrict 1991 expenses to a level equivalent to the current income for that year, thereby protecting any residual reserves. The Finance committee noted, however, "that the steps necessary to reduce the exposure of the WCC in the pre-assembly period to an acceptable level are not mainly financial". It asked that a small group be established to determine what steps would be necessary to enable the rapid implementation of assembly proposals; but this group has not yet been named, and the 1991 budget will again draw on non-recurring income.

The lack of integration in WCC activity also reflects a fragmentation within the churches and the movements with which the Council lives and works. These internal tensions often have financial, as well as programmatic, symptoms. As specialized church agencies use ever-more-specialized funds, as the Council becomes more truly global and its member churches become, generally speaking, materially poorer, their expectations of the WCC may be stated in increasingly financial terms. Not to understand the economic impact of Council activities in those lives which it touches would be a great disservice.

E. WAYS OF USING MONEY: THE WCC'S RESPONSIBILITIES

This chapter began with a brief review of global financial trends. The proper financial tools should be integral to Canberra's consideration of future WCC programmes and resources. As the Council approaches the third millennium it becomes ever clearer that such tools must be used intentionally, both in direct assistance and as alternative models, as new paradigms for challenging the international economic order. Some examples, questions raised, and implications of this perspective are:

— The criteria for doing business with banks which loan funds to South Africa were widely adopted by member churches prior to Vancouver. They have been modified since 1983 and, in light of the rapidly changing situation in South Africa, will undoubtedly be under review in the post-Canberra period.

— Does the way in which the WCC and its partners handle money alleviate, or contribute to, the economic marginalization of women? This question is being addressed prior to the assembly (see p. 39 above), and further study is necessary. This could be an important contribution to understanding the human impact of our programmes, and a step towards "demystifying macro-economics" (that is, making clear the large-scale human impact of economic policies).

— Addressing the effects of the debt crisis may involve more active exploration of alternative forms of credit for the poor, for women and other marginalized persons. The Ecumenical Church Loan Fund has taken a strong stand on the issue of women's credit; hopefully the experience gained in no-collatoral loans, and credit to poor but organized people, can be used to advocate the broader use of credit as a tool for just, participatory and sustainable development. The world banking order might be challenged by alternative credit experiences to share risks more extensively with the poor, and to increase people's responsibility for their own development.

— More Council programmes and networks may reflect on the need for credit as an option when grant funds are insufficient. In the present global financial situation increased cash flows are unlikely, and credit will need more frequent and more serious consideration.

— Commercial venues of debt for equity deserve to be considered as resource channels.

— The Council helped in this period in the strengthening of the Ecumenical Development Co-operative Society. This sought to provide an alternative for the churches' capital investment, one which did not increase the gap between rich and poor. The central committee continues to encourage WCC member churches to review their investment policy, and to increase their support for EDCS from investment funds.

The Council will need to review its advocacy role with donors, including governments, in light of the impact of the conditions which they are increasingly setting upon funding. (Should the WCC, for example, encourage "positive conditions" in funding in order to empower the poor?) Such conditions, and attendant reporting requirements, will have to be carefully monitored to determine whether government policies are enhancing — or undermining — the WCC's programme priorities. Any new models of resource-sharing, diakonia, and donor-receiver relation-ships, will have to be developed within this changing context. The fundamental principle is clear: that the way in which funds are handled must not conflict with stated central committee programme objectives. But to apply this principle the Council will have to become more sophisticated in coming years.

VII. Final reflections and conclusions

The Finance committee's focus on issues of participation, responsi-bility, growth, transparency and integration has been faithful to the instructions of the sixth assembly. The work which remains to be done might well be characterized in these same terms. New approaches may be necessary to deal with the financial implications of our commitment to participation: there are still some one hundred member churches which take no financial responsibility for the Council. Not all staff feel suffi-ciently accountable for the economic health and life of the WCC.

Delegates to the Canberra assembly, and others who are committed to the ecumenical vision, may sometimes feel that the economic aspects of the Council are less interesting — or less important — than the "issues" around which its work is organized. They are not alone. Even staff do not always sense how necessary it is to grapple with these financial issues and the questions of stewardship which lie behind them; and sometimes the lack of financial information makes programme decisions far from transparent.

Yet visible growth in oneness in Christ may be more closely linked to the possibilities for financial growth than some would want to admit: the transparency of budgets, trust fund activities, management structures and programme planning is perhaps a precondition for coherence and integra-tion in other aspects of the life of the WCC. Both the Nairobi and Vancouver assemblies recognized that the Council's financial situation is

symptomatic of the health and vitality of its programmes and relationships, and that, indeed, these three aspects of the ecumenical fellowship
cannot be fully understood when isolated from one another.

> Giving and receiving belong to the very essence of our fellowship (Van-
> couver assembly Finance committee report).

In Canberra the challenge will be to transform these observations into
new ways of acting.

Unit I
Faith and Witness

INTRODUCTION

Historical roots

Three branches of the ecumenical movement, those concerned with mission, unity, and faith and action in society, have each given birth to a corresponding sub-unit within Unit I: the Commission on World Mission and Evangelism (CWME), Faith and Order, and Church and Society. In 1971 the Dialogue section in CWME became a fourth sub-unit. Because of these historical roots, and its call both to provide continuity with the mainstreams of the historic ecumenical movement and to minister to particular constituencies (some going beyond the membership of the WCC), Unit I has a distinct character and a major responsibility for fulfilling the primary purpose and functions of the WCC.

Mandate and priorities

The programmatic concerns of the Unit on "Faith and Witness" are:
— to seek and follow God's will for the visible unity and renewal of the church, expressed in one faith, in common worship, and in sacramental and conciliar fellowship;
— to help the churches understand and explore together the implications of the gospel in their apostolic faith and action, in missionary and evangelical tasks;
— to enable the churches to relate to religious pluralism, and encourage the churches' dialogue with people of other faiths, various cultures and ideological perspectives;
— to address theological, spiritual and ethical issues posed by science, technology and ecological crises.

Unit I programmes have contributed to the work on basic WCC priorities in the post-Vancouver period in the areas of fostering unity, evangelism, common witness, ecumenical relationships, and work towards a vital and coherent theology. This has been achieved through major Faith and Order studies, including the reception process of *Baptism, Eucharist and Ministry*, the world conference on mission and evangelism (San Antonio, 1989), many consultations and seminars, the work on "theological discoveries through interfaith dialogue", reflection and action on topical issues concerning the "integrity of creation" and environmental ethics, bio-technology, and others. The efforts to involve a variety of constituencies, partners and non-member churches in these programmes, as well as to collaborate with "evangelical" and charismatic/Pentecostal movements, have strengthened WCC relations and joint endeavours with a broad range of co-workers in the ecumenical movement as a whole. The achievements and difficulties of the many Unit I programmes are surveyed in the four sections of this chapter.

Working methods

The distinct histories and different constituencies of the sub-units within Unit I have led to their having varied structures and working styles. Both Faith and Order and CWME have large commissions for programme direction and implementation, and hold world conferences; these special qualities are embodied in the by-laws of Faith and Order and the CWME constitution. The Dialogue and Church and Society Sub-units have comparatively small working groups and specific networks for oversight and interaction, involving specialized constituencies and partners. Despite structural difficulties, the four sub-units of Unit I have accomplished a commendable number of collaborative programmes and other ecumenical tasks.

Working methods and relationships have allowed for interaction between theological studies, other reflection, and action, and for ecumenical sharing of resources, thus fostering a growing sense of interdependence. Unfortunately, due to lack of time and financial resources, the unique experience of the combined Unit I commissions meeting in Potsdam (1986) has not been followed up. Co-operation among the sub-units of the Unit on Faith and Witness, and across other programme units, has been enhanced by consultation among the leadership of the Unit I committee and the various Unit I commissions and working groups. This has found structural expression in a Unit I executive group. The process of the sub-units' interaction, coherence and growing together has contributed to the wholeness of the WCC.

Most of the work of the sub-units has taken the form of issue-oriented study and research, holding consultations and issuing subsequent publications. The emphasis is on "major events" and reflection. Nevertheless, maintaining a wide range of relationships and enabling the ecumenical endeavours of churches, various councils, religious orders, and others, characterizes a creative methodological approach that provides enrichment and complementarity of working styles within the WCC.

Staff

Since Vancouver Unit I has operated with a small programme and a small complement of support staff — whose number has in fact decreased in recent years. This fact, and the arrival of four new sub-unit directors and an extensive turn-over of programme staff, have had important implications for the total life and work of Faith and Witness.

COMMISSION ON FAITH AND ORDER

Mandate

"To call the churches to the goal of visible unity in one faith and in one eucharistic fellowship expressed in worship and in common life in Christ, and to advance towards that unity in order that the world may believe" — this first constitutional function of the World Council of Churches is identical with the first aim of the Commission on Faith and Order of the WCC as stated in its by-laws. Thus Faith and Order's calling is to serve the central responsibility and commitment of the WCC within the wider ecumenical movement. This is implemented by focusing in concentrated theological effort on the task of helping the churches to move towards visible unity. These efforts are seen as part of, and in relation to, many other ecumenical endeavours.

This task of Faith and Order has been confirmed by such programme guidelines of the Vancouver assembly as those affirming the need to grow towards unity, the search for a vital and coherent theology, or work for a community of confessing and learning. The continuing work of Faith and Order clearly corresponds to such priorities set by the Vancouver assembly as unity, the concerns and perspectives of women, fostering ecumenical relationships, and creative theological work or ecumenical learning.

This is illustrated by the programmatic work of Faith and Order between Vancouver and Canberra. Faith and Order's major programmes received the full support of the Vancouver assembly. Thus the ecumenical significance of the Lima document on *Baptism, Eucharist and Ministry* (BEM) was underlined — and indeed experienced — throughout the assembly, and encouragement and guidance were given in view of the process of the reception of, and response to, BEM. In addition Vancouver recommended: "That the Faith and Order Commission continue to give priority attention to its study 'Towards the Common Expression of the Apostolic Faith Today', as outlined at Lima (1982), and that this study should be closely linked with the 'Baptism, Eucharist and Ministry' process of reception... " In its concern for expressing "more clearly the relation between the unity of the church, the eucharistic fellowship of believers, and the transformation of human community", Vancouver welcomed the Faith and Order study on "The Unity of the Church and the Renewal of Human Community" and proposed to "make a theological exploration of the church as 'sign' a central part" of this study.

By concentrating between Vancouver and Canberra on these three major studies, the programme of Faith and Order had a clear profile and could thus be communicated effectively to the churches for their support and participation. The fact that the Faith and Order Standing Commission was already appointed by the central committee in Vancouver made it possible to begin work on the programme in that same year.

Major studies

"Towards the Common Expression of the Apostolic Faith Today"

Agreement on, and common confession of, the apostolic faith is an essential element of that visible unity which is the goal of the ecumenical movement. Such agreement and confession is, at the same time, an important contribution to the task of a common Christian witness in today's world. The apostolic faith study seeks to help the churches move towards such agreement and common confession.

The Plenary Commission meeting in Lima in 1982 had already suggested that this study should distinguish methodologically between common recognition, explication, and confession of the apostolic faith as expressed especially in the Nicene-Constantinopolitan Creed (381) and as related to contemporary challenges. It was decided in 1984 to focus on the second aspect, explication, and in the course of many methodological considerations over these years it became clear that such a contemporary explication could both stimulate and assist the churches jointly to re-appropriate the apostolic faith. This could lead to a mutual recognition of the reality of the apostolic faith in each other's confession and life, and would provide a basis for the common confession of that same faith.

This work on explication began with a consultation in Rome, in 1983, on the biblical and historical presuppositions of common confession *(The Roots of Our Common Faith)*. Three consultations (Kottayam, India, 1984; Chantilly, France, 1985; and Kinshasa, Zaire, 1985) prepared first drafts of biblical, historical and contemporary explications of the three articles of the Nicene Creed (cf. *One God, One Lord, One Spirit*, and the collection of basic texts from church history *The Apostolic Faith Today: a Handbook for Study*). The drafts were discussed and revised at the Faith and Order Plenary Commission meeting at Stavanger, Norway (1985), and at several meetings of the apostolic faith steering group and the Standing Commission. This resulted in the study document *Confessing One Faith*, which was accepted by the Standing Commission in 1987. With its nearly 100 pages this is the longest text so far, and the one with the broadest theological scope, in the history of Faith and Order.

The study document, which interprets the text of the Nicene Creed, its biblical foundation, and its significance for today, has been translated into French and German and has had to be reprinted several times. This lively interest has resulted thus far in over 70 reactions from commissions, consultations, theological seminaries and individuals. The reactions, which serve as material for a revision of the text, have been accompanied by four Faith and Order consultations with the goal of critically re-reading the main parts of the document, and of addressing issues related to their respective themes: Porto Alegre, Brazil, 1987; Rhodes, Greece, 1988; Pyatigorsk, USSR, 1988; and Würzburg, FRG, 1989 (the Porto Alegre and Rhodes reports have been published in the *Minutes* of the Standing Commission meeting, 1988; papers from the consultations will be published in 1990).

The Plenary Commission meeting in Budapest, Hungary, in 1989 discussed the document in the light of the reactions, and presented its proposals for revision. Budapest further clarified the fundamental basic significance of this work of explication for steps towards common recognition and confession of the apostolic faith, and suggested that an additional, short presentation of the goal and contents of the study could help to broaden the discussion within the churches. At present Faith and Order is revising *Confessing One Faith* (most recently at a steering group meeting in Oxford, January 1990), and hopes to transmit a revised text to the churches in 1991.

The wider perspective of confessing the faith today has been served by Faith and Order through its series of texts *Confessing Our Faith Around the World*; volumes II, III (Caribbean and Central America), and IV (South America) were published by the WCC in 1984 and 1985. In relation to the seventh ecumenical council the book *Icons: Windows on Eternity. Theology and Spirituality in Colour* was published.

"The Unity of the Church and the Renewal of Human Community"
The second major study project inaugurated at Lima 1982 is indeed of strategic importance for the WCC and its member churches. The study seeks to inter-relate theologically two main emphases of the ecumenical movement — emphases too often seen, and treated, in isolation from each other: the theological efforts to assist the churches on their way towards the visible unity of the church, and the call and commitment of Christians to common witness and service in a broken world.

It was soon realized that this study must be basically an ecclesiological one, and thus its initial step was to develop a draft on "The Church as Mystery and Prophetic Sign" at a first consultation at Chantilly, France, in 1985 (cf. *Church, Kingdom, World: the Church as Mystery and Prophetic Sign*). It was also decided to inter-relate this ecclesiological focus with two areas of human brokenness in need of renewal. The issue of "the community of women and men in the church" was chosen in continuation of earlier work on this issue done jointly by Faith and Order and the Sub-unit on Women; the second area chosen was the churches' involvement in the concern for justice. These two issues were selected among many other contemporary problems to serve as relevant examples for the theological inter-relation between unity and renewal which was intended by the study.

At the Plenary Commission meeting in Stavanger, the draft on "The Church as Mystery and Prophetic Sign" was discussed and revised, and this work of revision has been continued through 1988 by the unity and renewal steering group, the consultation on ecclesiology in Pyatigorsk, USSR, in 1988, and the Standing Commission. During this period the main work, however, has concentrated on the ecclesiological implications of the concerns for the community of women and men and for justice. Three international consultations dealt with the community of women and men (Prague, Czechoslovakia, 1985: cf. *Beyond Unity-in-Tension: Unity, Renewal and the Community of Women and Men*; Porto Novo, Benin, 1988: papers and report to be published in 1990; and Cambridge, England, 1989); and three with the concern for justice (Singapore, 1986;

Porto Alegre, Brazil, 1987; and Harlem, New York, 1988). The papers and reports of the Singapore and Porto Alegre consultations have been published in *Mid-Stream*, and the Porto Alegre and Harlem reports in the *Minutes* of the Standing Commission meeting, 1988. In 1987 a study guide, *Unity and Renewal*, was published for local groups; it has been translated into several languages and continues to be used in several countries.

After this period of consultations, which provided a wealth of material, the most difficult task had to be accomplished — namely bringing together insights from the consultations, and other reflections on the church as mystery and prophetic sign, into a coherent theological framework and into the form of a study document. The perspective of the kingdom of God was chosen as the biblical, theological and eschatological dimension in which church and humanity, and their inter-relatedness, find their proper place. After preparatory work at the 1988 Standing Commission, and with the help of drafts from members of the unity and renewal steering group, a consultation of this group, together with advisers, in March 1989 at Leuenberg, Switzerland, drafted a document on "The Unity of the Church and the Renewal of Human Community". In its first major section the text presents a reflection on the kingdom of God as the context of promise and challenge for unity and renewal, both in church and humanity. This is further explicated in the second section on the inter-relation between church and humanity in the perspective of the kingdom. Here the themes of community (especially between women and men), and of justice, are already announced; these are then developed in the third and fourth sections. The document concludes with the eschatological horizon of the churches' calling to move already now to a deeper communion within, and among, themselves for the sake of being sign and instrument of God's purpose for all humanity.

The Budapest Plenary Commission meeting in 1989 discussed this draft document and suggested changes and additions. The work of revision continued at a final consultation of the steering group in Mandeville, Jamaica, in January 1990, and it is hoped that the text can be transmitted to the churches in 1990. With this document Faith and Order will have reached a new stage in its work, one which will be of significance for the unresolved questions posed in many churches, and in the ecumenical community, about the proper theological vision of the inter-relation between church and humanity in accordance with God's design.

"Baptism, Eucharist and Ministry"

More than most had expected, the *Baptism, Eucharist and Ministry* (BEM) document, adopted by the Commission at Lima, Peru, in 1982, has marked the working period of Faith and Order — and indeed the ecumenical movement as a whole — between Vancouver and Canberra. The results of Faith and Order work have been taken up by churches and ecumenical groups and organizations at all levels of their life. BEM has become a document of the churches and of their common future. The broad BEM discussion and reception process stands out as an unprecedented event in ecumenical history.

Faith and Order has supported the BEM process by helping with translations (so far into 31 languages) and the sharing of information and advice. Commissioners and staff have spoken and written on innumerable occasions to interpret BEM and to evaluate the BEM process and reactions. The secretariat has been involved in an intensive correspondence, gladly acknowledging hundreds of responses from churches, ecumenical groups and organizations, theological seminaries, commissions, groups in congregations and individuals. There were many requests for information, material and advice for research work on BEM, on the unofficial but widely-used Lima liturgy, and on the responses of the churches. In 1985 the secretariat organized the inter-Orthodox symposium on BEM at Boston (*Orthodox Perspectives on Baptism, Eucharist and Ministry*), and assisted in four BEM consultations organized by the Conference of European Churches. Certainly more than 600 — and probably even 800 — letters have been written between 1983 and 1990. By the end of 1989 some 450,000 copies of BEM had been distributed all over the world, together with over 100,000 study guides in several languages; 185 churches have sent an official response, either individually or, in some cases, as part of the response of a federation or council of churches. Most of them have been published by Faith and Order in the documentation *Churches Respond to BEM*, volumes I-VI, with volume VII due to appear later in 1990.

Faith and Order began in 1986 to evaluate the official responses of the churches to BEM. Three consultations of the BEM steering group (Venice, Italy, 1986; Annecy, France, 1987; and Turku, Finland, 1988) prepared first evaluations, and identified points for elucidation and major issues for further work. A smaller drafting team met four times in 1988 and 1989 to prepare a draft report on "Baptism, Eucharist and Ministry 1982-1989: Report on the Process and Responses". This describes the

BEM process, summarizes the responses of the churches to the three sections of BEM and to the four questions in the preface to BEM, responds to a number of critical comments, and indicates ways in which further work on three issues which are still controversial — scripture and Tradition, sacrament and sacramentality, and the nature and place of the church in God's saving action — could be pursued. The draft was discussed at the 1989 Budapest Plenary Commission meeting; with the help of its comments and suggestions it was revised (the steering group has met most recently in Paris in December 1989), and the report has now been published.

In 1987 the Standing Commission sent a letter of appreciation to the churches for their active involvement in the BEM process. In a formal statement the 1989 Budapest Commission meeting has once again expressed this appreciation, and combined it with the challenge to the churches to implement the consequences of this involvement in BEM for their own life and for their ecumenical relations. The BEM process has already had a broad impact on these areas, and this process of renewal within the churches and reconciliation between the churches continues.

Ongoing concerns

Besides its three major studies Faith and Order has accepted several tasks which are an ongoing and specific service to the churches and the ecumenical movement. There are three of these "ongoing concerns".

United/uniting churches and church union negotiations

Faith and Order serves united and uniting churches by helping to bring their concerns before the wider ecumenical movement, and by organizing regular consultations where they can exchange experiences and reflect together on their distinctive identity and ecumenical significance and contribution. In 1987 the fifth international consultation was organized at Potsdam, GDR (*Living Today Towards Visible Unity*). Participants in the consultation expressed the hope that another could be held about 1992, and that some of the insights of the meeting — for example, those on the relation of unity to mission, on renewal, and on participation — might be of relevance to discussions at the Canberra assembly. Faith and Order has also continued to provide advice and information with regard to union plans and conversations between churches. The biennial *Survey of Church Union Negotiations* for 1983/1985-86 and 1986-88 was published in *The Ecumenical Review*, and one issue of the *Church Union Newsletter* was published.

Week of Prayer and Ecumenical Prayer Cycle
    The Week of Prayer for Christian Unity is one of the oldest ongoing ecumenical endeavours, and still the most widespread form of ecumenical co-operation among the churches. At annual consultations the Faith and Order secretariat and the Pontifical Council for Promoting Christian Unity have continued to prepare the material for the Week of Prayer, to reflect on its forms, and to consider ways of intensifying its observance and impact. Faith and Order has also been involved, in co-operation with the Sub-unit on Renewal and Congregational Life (which carried major responsibility), in the preparation of a completely new edition of the Ecumenical Prayer Cycle and this was published in 1989 as *With All God's People*.

Bilateral and multilateral conversations
    The bilateral conversations between Christian World Communions have become a major expression of the ecumenical movement today. They are also a challenge to the WCC, emphasizing that it must not underestimate the importance of theological dialogue for the sake of Christian unity. Faith and Order's task is to follow developments in bilateral dialogues, to use their results for its own work, and to help ensure a complementary relationship between bilateral and multilateral dialogues within the one ecumenical movement. Commission and staff members have participated in several bilateral dialogues and have been delegated as observers to others. The secretariat organized the fourth forum on bilateral conversations in 1985 at Bossey, Switzerland, on the theme of the inter-relation between BEM and bilateral results (see the *Fourth Forum on Bilateral Conversations: Report*, 1985), and the fifth forum in 1990 in Budapest, Hungary, on ecclesiological perspectives. These meetings have become a unique opportunity for exchange and joint reflection. By clarifying common orientations they have furthered the necessary inter-relation between the bilateral and multilateral expressions of the churches' ecumenical commitment.

The Commission, communication and co-operation
    Given the broad and demanding programme of Faith and Order, the work between Vancouver and Canberra could not have been done without the active participation of all the members of the Standing and Plenary Commissions. The Standing Commission, which met every year, has planned and directed Faith and Order work and, through its three steering groups for the major study projects, was actively involved in their

development. The Plenary Commission, meeting in 1985 at Stavanger, and in 1989 at Budapest (see *Faith and Renewal*, and *Faith and Order 1985-1989: the Commission Meeting at Budapest 1989*), discussed the results of the work and clarified the basic lines for its continuation. At the same time the members of the Commission have provided the core groups for consultations and other activities, and have helped to interpret the Faith and Order programme in their churches.

For the more than 40 international consultations and meetings of steering groups, Plenary and Standing Commissions which have been organized by the Faith and Order secretariat between 1983 and 1990, many participants have also been invited who do not belong to the Commission. These consultations and meetings were used intentionally for contacts with local churches and with theological and ecumenical institutions. Staff members have visited many churches in all regions of the world where they were able both to communicate the work of Faith and Order and to learn much about the local ecumenical situations and efforts. Staff members have given lectures, participated in conferences and spoken to literally hundreds of visiting groups in Geneva and at the Ecumenical Institute, Bossey. All this together with an extensive correspondence has enabled a wide participation of the churches — and without such participation the work of Faith and Order would have been irrelevant and ineffective for the ecumenical movement.

Much time has been given by the Faith and Order secretariat to co-operating with other sub-units, and to involvement in the activities of the WCC as a whole. The new edition of the Ecumenical Prayer Cycle was prepared together with Renewal and Congregational Life. Two joint consultations were held with Church and Society in 1986 and 1988 — the latter on "Creation and the Kingdom of God" — as a part of the "Justice, Peace and the Integration of Creation" (JPIC) process, together with other Faith and Order contributions. A joint reflection on unity and mission was initiated with the Commission on World Mission and Evangelism (CWME). With Roman Catholic colleagues, several Commission members and the director have prepared two documents on the "Hierarchy of Truths" and "The Church — Local and Universal" for the WCC-RCC Joint Working Group. Commission and staff members have also been involved in the WCC discussion on "vital and coherent theology".

Evaluation: future plans

Between Vancouver and Canberra the work of Faith and Order has had an obvious impact on ecumenical developments, especially through the

BEM process. Through its studies on apostolic faith and unity and renewal, Faith and Order has moved towards more comprehensive themes of fundamental importance for the churches themselves and for their ecumenical commitment. The method of focusing on a few fundamental theological issues in a long-term process of study, discussion and reception has proved to be highly effective. Many of the official responses to BEM have explicitly affirmed the mandate of Faith and Order by asking the Commission to continue its indispensable theological service to the churches' quest for visible unity in one faith, sacramental fellowship and common witness and service.

There are, of course, areas in which the work and outreach of Faith and Order should be improved, and the recent Plenary Commission in Budapest has indicated some of these. Faith and Order contacts with churches in the southern hemisphere should be further strengthened, and the involvement of younger and women theologians expanded. A strong plea was made also for more participation of ecumenically-minded theologians from the evangelical and charismatic movements. Because of increasing ecumenical relations outside the structures of the WCC, developments in bilateral dialogues deserve more attention. There is also the request that Faith and Order should seek more actively to relate its theological work to the work of the WCC as a whole.

The 1989 Budapest Plenary Commission meeting gave direction for the continuation of the two major studies on apostolic faith and on unity and renewal, and for further work on several major issues which have been raised in the responses to BEM. Thus priority has been given to efforts to help the churches (a) to move towards a common confession of their faith; (b) to take seriously the theological inter-relation between the search for visible unity and their commitment to be God's agents of renewal in the wider human community; and (c) to broaden the convergence expressed in BEM in relation to issues which are still critical.

This continuing work should, however, be done in the framework of a comprehensive study on ecumenical perspectives of the nature and mission of the church. This theme was chosen on the basis of the experience that both inherited dividing issues of doctrine and church order, and new controversies about the church-world relationship, have their roots in different understandings of the church. The development of basic ecumenical perspectives on ecclesiology, in continuation of earlier work in this area, could thus help to remove barriers to closer fellowship between the churches in faith and in common witness and service. The consultation at Pyatigorsk, USSR, in 1988 has already prepared for this study by reviewing the ecclesiological elements in the three major Faith and Order studies, in the bilateral dialogues and in the reflections of united and uniting churches. As part of the new study, Faith and Order is preparing a draft statement on "The Unity We Seek" for the Canberra assembly and looking towards a consultation on women in the ministries of the church.

Finally, the Commission agreed that the fifth world conference on Faith and Order, originally planned and authorized for 1988 or 1989, be held in 1993. Such a conference is urgently needed as a forum for theological exchange and for evaluation of the progress made so far in the ecumenical movement. It is needed even more urgently as a forum for a worldwide theological discussion towards a new commitment to the search for visible unity, in response to the challenges posed to the ecumenical movement, at the dawn of the 21st century, by a human family crying out for salvation, justice and hope.

COMMISSION ON WORLD MISSION AND EVANGELISM (CWME)

The mandate

The vocation of CWME is "to help the churches understand and explore together the content and meaning of the gospel of Jesus Christ" in the contemporary world, and to support and challenge them in their common calling to worldwide mission and evangelism. Rooted in the missionary vision and heritage of the 1910 Edinburgh conference and nurtured through the heritage of the International Missionary Council, CWME seeks to facilitate common Christian witness to the wholeness of the gospel in word and deed, through celebration of the faith, proclamation, and participation in people's struggles.

The WCC's commitment to the visible unity of the church, the renewal of humankind, and its work for justice, peace and the integrity of creation, is today a major context of CWME's programme, as are the involvement of women and youth and the search for an authentic spirituality.

The ecumenical affirmation on mission and evangelism, adopted by the WCC central committee in 1982, is a basic CWME document. Assisting member churches and others to explore its implications for thought and action in mission today is a continuing responsibility of CWME.

In light of the programme guidelines and impulses for mission given by the Vancouver assembly, CWME's work during the period has been within four broad areas of concern: evangelism, mission in and through participation in the struggles of the poor and oppressed, strengthening relationships in mission, and the renewal of local churches for mission in each place and in all places. In all these areas, CWME seeks to encourage the participation of persons of different theological views and from many confessions, including Roman Catholics, evangelicals, and others involved locally in mission and evangelism in very different circumstances around the world. The central role and primary responsibility of local churches for mission and evangelism are emphasized in contacts with local situations, and through communication with, and the linking of, churches and movements in different parts of the world.

The Vancouver assembly urged the WCC to "help member churches in developing an understanding of the relationship between evangelism and culture in respect of both the contextual proclamation of the gospel in all cultures and the transforming power of the gospel in any culture". CWME has sponsored consultations exploring how the gospel can be communicated with full respect for differing cultures, especially those shaped by religions other than Christianity. What has been done is only a beginning, and much more work is needed in this vital and timely area of concern.

Relevant publications undergirding the major programmatic thrusts indicated above have provided resources for the churches as they explore the relevance of the gospel today and seek a "permanent renewal" in mission. The publication of the *International Review of Mission* (the oldest ecumenical journal in the field of mission), the *Monthly Letter on Evangelism*, occasional Urban Rural Mission (URM) newsletters, books in the Mission series, and other materials, has continued.

Evangelism

During this period there has been a new and widespread interest in evangelism in many communities related to the ecumenical movement in both the North and the South. Several member churches of the WCC, and some Christian World Communions, speak of "evangelism decades" and search for authentic ways of holistic evangelism. CWME has felt that there is an urgency to encourage and assist churches to undertake the evangelistic task *ecumenically*.

In this context, one of the significant developments of CWME's evangelism office since Vancouver has been the formulation and testing of an ecumenical understanding of evangelism, and a methodology for local congregations. This is based on the WCC statement "Mission and Evangelism: an Ecumenical Affirmation", and offers a clear and easily-applied technique for communication of the faith — while offering much room, and incentive, for local contextualization. It consists of three interlocking concepts.

The church in partnership with the world for justice and peace: The God we worship is the God of Isaiah 65, who does not want to see children die, who wants to see old people live full lives, who wants to see those who build houses live in them, and those who plant vineyards eat their fruit.

To be a credible sign of this God, we commit ourselves to this "Isaiah agenda" both locally and worldwide. We declare partnership with one and all who share this agenda; we declare enmity with powers, principalities and policies which violate this agenda.

Christians engage in the Isaiah agenda not because we are strong and others are weak, nor because we have and others have not; not because we are different but because we are similar. We engage because we too are wounded; we act not out of generosity but out of solidarity.

Invitation to worship: Because we are wounded, we declare our own need for worship and intercession as we work on the Isaiah agenda. We invite all to worship the God of Isaiah 65 with us, that they may be made whole and strong. We pledge to bring the world in worship into the living and eternal memory of God.

Invitation to discipleship: Because all are wounded the good news is, "take up your own cross and follow Jesus". This is not a call to suffering and sacrifice, but an invitation to community, to friendship with Jesus and all his followers. It is a rejection of self-pity, indeed an offering of power. It is an invitation to discipleship, a joyful challenge to ordinary people to do extraordinary things with God.

This methodology of evangelism has been tested with churches in the secular West, in a socialist-Marxist setting, in situations where Christians are a small minority, and in situations of poverty and exploitation. In coming years it will be shared much more intensively and concretely.

CWME is also seeking to help address the need for ecumenical and inter-regional institutes on evangelism.

The secular context in evangelism has been a major concern; so also was the context of religious pluralism. The report of section I of the San Antonio world conference on mission and evangelism (May 1989) highlights the urgent need to assist churches in exploring anew the nature of Christian witness and proclamation in these contexts.

The *Monthly Letter on Evangelism* has continued to be an important instrument for drawing attention to significant issues and promoting lively discussion. Responses from the world church indicate its continued relevance.

An important concern since Vancouver has been the building and strengthening of evangelism networks among those actively involved in various parts of the world in witnessing to the gospel.

Since Vancouver the WCC has been concerned with increased contact and dialogue with evangelicals, both within its own constituency and beyond. San Antonio reiterated the importance of this for CWME. Its evangelism office has helped the WCC in general, and CWME in particular, to enhance relationships with evangelicals through both formal consultations and informal visits and conversations.

Mission as participation in the suffering and struggles for justice and liberation

Through the work of Urban Rural Mission CWME affirms that participation in the movements of the poor and the oppressed for fuller life in Christ is constitutive of the mission of the church. URM is "primarily a movement of men and women, rooted in the Christian faith and called, with others, to God's mission of participation in the struggle of the exploited, marginalized and oppressed for justice and liberation... URM has been committed to work with slum-dwellers, the unemployed, industrial and women workers, indigenous peoples, fishworkers, rural poor and landless labourers, migrant workers, and others ("Urban Rural Mission's Self-Understanding", in *URM Reflections*, 1986).

This mission, exemplified pre-eminently in the incarnation of Jesus, is for fullness of life in community with persons, God, and nature. The precondition for such community is justice. It is this vision which motivates and sustains hope in the midst of suffering and struggle.

Reorganization, training and strengthening of networks

Since Vancouver three significant developments have taken place in the work of URM. URM has re-organized and expanded its "structures" in practically all regions so that decision-making increasingly devolves to the local level, ensuring greater participation, accountability and responsibility. Particularly in Africa and Latin America much discussion and planning, training, and inter-regional visitations, have led to growing "networks", both inside and outside the church, of committed groups and communities sharing solidarity in suffering and struggle. Women have, at long last, begun to take their rightful place in programmes and decision-making structures. These two continents, long neglected in URM circles, have provided the impetus for much of URM's theological reflection.

Europe and North America, with their increasingly large sectors of poverty and racism, have recently become more prominent in URM. In North America, the focus is on struggles of native peoples and for land rights, struggles of women of colour and against the resurgence of racism. In Western Europe, URM programmes have emphasized the struggles of immigrants and migrant workers, and the economic dislocation felt most strongly by the urban poor.

In recent years the Middle East has begun to feature more prominently within URM. Training consultations have brought together many victims of war and oppression to aid analysis and action towards the re-creation of community. Inter-regional visitations (particularly with Africa), organizing work with migrant workers in the region, and an "action dialogue" between Christians and Muslims have taken programmatic priority.

Asia has enjoyed much attention from URM; activities there include organizing among industrial workers (especially women workers), slum-dwellers, rural peasants, fisherfolk, and indigenous peoples. The issues related to land have become crucial in both urban and rural areas, particularly for indigenous peoples.

Thus URM is increasingly a movement for "mission in six continents", although much remains to be done in the Pacific and Caribbean. National and regional contact groups continue to encourage and support programmes of community organizing for justice and dignity; their stories inspire and enable a realistic analysis leading to further action. Training in identifying problems and issues, analysis and community organizing, supplemented by programmes of documentation and information, inter-regional visitation, and consultations and seminars for reflection — such action/reflection programmes have dominated day-to-day URM activities in all continents.

The CWME-URM advisory group has kept a "watchful eye" on these activities and has worked hard at supporting and advising the commission and staff; and an unusually high level of undesignated funding has shown how the activities of URM have enjoyed the confidence of its supporting churches and agencies.

Theological reflection

There has been a special and consistent effort to reflect biblically and theologically on the experiences of those struggling for justice. Some examples are:

— In 1985, a consultation in Brazil reflected a CWME priority, "resistance as a form of Christian witness".
— In 1986, after intensive reflection at the regional and global levels, *URM Reflections* was published. Its centrepiece was "A URM Perspective on Mission", which has been published in many languages.
— In 1987, after much travel and research, *A Community of Clowns: Testimonies of People in Urban Rural Mission* was compiled; this is an innovative chronicling of 25 years of WCC involvement in URM.
— In 1988, URM published *We Discovered the Good News*, an effort to share widely an attempt of Brazilian workers to "re-read" the Bible.
— In 1988/89, *(The) Church: URM Perspective*, explored some of the ecclesiological implications of community organizing.
— In 1990, after many years of joint struggle for justice by Christians and peoples of other faith, a seminar in Senegal considered the theological foundations for such common actions.

Various aspects of URM's work have also contributed to CWME's concern to explore the meaning of "resistance as a form of Christian witness". CWME needs to explore further, and to remind the churches about, the missiological dimension of both resistance to war, militarism, injustice and all forms of oppression, and the support for civil disobedience and symbolic acts based on Christian conscience. In this way it seeks to open the corridors of power to the poor, and enable persons to experience creative power in solidarity.

San Antonio in May 1989 reiterated theological insights which have undergirded URM since Vancouver, and raised new missiological issues. Questions such as the meaning and role of the "people", and the nature of the "creative power" that transforms people who merely suffer into those who struggle for transformation, will shape URM's future thought and work.

Relationships in mission

The quest for unity is part of the missionary vocation; CWME seeks to promote relationships in mission and sharing among churches in three ways.

First, CWME seeks to encourage local churches to engage more deeply in fulfilling their common vocation in Christian witness together with other confessions. Thus CWME has found it important to develop models of relationship which promote common witness and dialogue among Protestants of various theological positions, Orthodox and Roman

Catholics, models which avoid proselytism and other acts which contradict the common witness.

Second, CWME as the mission sub-unit of the WCC seeks to link churches in mission in different ways to promote mutual challenge and enrichment as they pursue their common calling for mission in each place and all places. In particular the study of the Orthodox heritage in mission and evangelism, the strengthening of the relationship in mission among the Orthodox churches, and the special efforts of a separate office to enhance their relationship to the broader CWME constituency have all been significant.

Third, CWME emphasizes strengthening local, national, regional and international co-operation and the sharing of human and material resources in mission. Embracing the concerns of the Council-wide programme for encouraging the ecumenical sharing of resources, CWME seeks to challenge mission boards and agencies to explore new models of relationships and partnership. A few examples of each of these approaches follow.

Common witness and relationship with the Roman Catholic Church

A significant development since Vancouver has been the appointment of a Roman Catholic consultant seconded to CWME by the Secretariat (now the Pontifical Council) for Promoting Christian Unity. Sr Joan Delaney, mm, was appointed in 1984 as the first such consultant; she was replaced in 1990 by Sr Monica Cooney, smsm.

This desk should encourage the growing co-operation of WCC member churches with the Roman Catholic Church in their ecumenical mission outreach. This involves informing Roman Catholic missionary orders of missiological trends in CWME, and keeping CWME in touch with Roman Catholic missiological thinking and practice.

Personal visits have been central to this process. The CWME director and two staff have visited Rome. Six representatives from Rome (three Roman Catholic consultants to CWME, the executive secretary of the International Union of Major Superiors of Women Religious, the executive secretary of Sedos, and a representative from the Congregation for the Evangelization of Peoples) visited Geneva for three days. Prior to San Antonio the conference organizer met in Rome with the seven Roman Catholic consultants to the CWME commission and representatives of five dicasteries of the Vatican, Sedos and the Unions of Superiors-General.

The seven Roman Catholic consultants (three women and four men) have been very helpful, particularly in the preparation and follow-up to

San Antonio. Of the present consultants, whose terms ended after the February 1990 CWME commission meeting, three are appointed by the Pontifical Council for Promoting Christian Unity and four are nominated by the Unions of Superiors-General of Men and the International Union of Superiors-General of Women.

The Roman Catholic consultant to CWME has been involved in a wide variety of tasks, receiving numerous visitors and speaking frequently to visiting groups about CWME, the San Antonio conference, or WCC-Roman Catholic relations. In addition she has served on various WCC committees and has assumed many staff duties. Her most intense collaboration outside CWME has been with Bossey, the Dialogue sub-unit, and the Christian Medical Commission. She has also been a member of the Joint Working Group (JWG) between the WCC and the Roman Catholic Church. This has fostered many important contacts.

Within the framework of the JWG, the consultant has helped promote the study of the booklet on common witness.

Orthodox studies and relations

During the period under review, the missiological reflections in the WCC, and particularly in CWME, have clearly been enriched by the Orthodox churches. More Orthodox theologians and leaders have been involved in CWME discussions and programmes since Vancouver; indeed, 19% of the participants at San Antonio were Orthodox. This is the recent and important "moment of harvesting" the results of the work of the desk for Orthodox studies and relationships.

Several publications have contributed to the sharing of Orthodox insights and the building of relationships. *Go Forth in Peace: Orthodox Perspectives on Mission*, the fruit of a long process of discussion, has made several Orthodox insights part of the ecumenical heritage: the "liturgy after the liturgy" as witness to the world, the eucharist as an evangelistic and missionary event, and the local community as the basis of mission. These discussions have stimulated serious reflections within and among the Orthodox churches themselves.

CWME has also stimulated the Orthodox churches to a systematic analysis of the contemporary milieux in which they bear witness. The consultation on "The Future of Orthodox Witness" (Hildesheim, Himmelsthür, FRG, 1984) is one fruit of this process; here Orthodox churches identified together concrete possibilities for, and conditions of, an Orthodox testimony for today both faithful to its heritage and open to responsible renewal.

Such stimulus has also encouraged fresh study and creative appropriation of the Orthodox legacy. For example a consultation on "The Missionary Legacy of Saints Cyril and Methodius" in Sofia, Bulgaria, in 1985 commemorated 1100 years since the death of St Methodius and also outlined, in light of this legacy, an appropriate response to today's challenges.

The involvement of the Orthodox churches to ecumenical mission thought and practice centred around the preparation for the world mission conference in San Antonio. A broadly representative consultation was held in Neapolis, Greece, in 1986 on the theme "Your Will Be Done — Orthodoxy in Mission". This reflected on the martyria (witness) of the Orthodox churches today in their specific environments, taking seriously the testimonies of youth, women and clergy in missionary work in places as scattered as Kenya, Alaska, Lebanon and Ghana. This provided major input for Orthdox participants at San Antonio; the material was published in English in 1989 and, with the assistance of local churches, has also been made available in some other languages.

International relationships in mission

Bringing into being authentic structures and relationships in mission which promote genuine ecumenical sharing of resources, persons and power in mission has been the concern of the WCC since 1961. But during the period since Vancouver there has been a new sense of urgency. As the San Antonio world conference on mission put it: " For more than a quarter of a century the WCC has sought new models to express genuine partnership. There have been many excellent ideas but little has happened. Thus there is a clear and urgent need for a renewed call to commitment and action."

Such a search for new models must be global and must involve national and regional ecumenical bodies. To ensure this, consultations on models of authentic partnership in mission have been held in various regions. As a culmination of that process, an international consultation was held in Chiang Mai, Thailand, in 1989, at which 20 representatives of mission boards and church leaders from North and South sought to identify impediments to mutuality in mission, and blocks for structural changes and deeper ecumenical sharing as well as ways to overcome these problems. Then in San Antonio, participants in section IV furthered the search for a new vision of sharing ecumenically in one universal mission, and considered the obstacles to such a vision and practice.

Psychological resistance to change, ideologies and prejudices which promote injustice and dependence, bilateral relationships which exclude an ecumenical dimension, paternalism in various forms, ideas and strategies which leave no room for cultural diversity, the priority given to financial factors (resulting in the consolidation of the power of the rich to the detriment of the poor) — all these have been identified as significant impediments to a new vision and practice of authentic partnership in mission.

San Antonio also identified several aspects of an alternative vision and practice. They include: the recognition that all God's gifts are common property, mutual acceptance of one another as partners, recognition of cultural diversity as an enrichment, equal access to sources of information, transparency in operations, joint planning and implementation of policies, openness to sharing non-material resources, and mutual accountability and correction.

A consultation co-sponsored by the Commission on Inter-Church Aid, Refugee and World Service on the sharing of personnel in mission critically examined the continued movement of Christians for mission from the North to the South, as well as the factors which hinder the equal participation of churches, particularly those in the South.

These issues of structures, sharing "Christian unity at the local level as faithfulness to the gospel", and "credibility to the good news of the kingdom" will remain on CWME's agenda. They are crucial ecumenical questions which test the credibility of the churches' ecumenical and missionary commitment.

San Antonio has underlined a new issue in mission relationship as well. The period since Vancouver has seen enormous growth in different parts of the world in popular religiosity, renewal movements among the poor, and independent churches (the last particularly in Africa). These movements have demonstrated both the potential of renewal for the church at large, and problems for the unity and wholeness of the church. In several places member churches of the WCC do not engage with these movements due to lack of common understanding. Therefore San Antonio called the attention of the churches to the fact that these movements have missiological and ecumenical significance, and noted that any quest for renewed relationships in mission today should take these movements into consideration.

CWME has initiated a study of these movements. But more basic work is needed to help member churches understand, and relate critically and creatively to, these movements and popular expressions of spirituality.

Such explorations provide yet another approach to the question of the relation between gospel and culture.

Renewal and education for mission

Transformation of congregations in mission

The ecumenical study on "The Missionary Structure of the Congregation", developed after the New Delhi assembly in 1961, took on new relevance through the initiatives of local churches and ecumenical bodies, primarily in Europe. The secular context in Europe challenges the churches to explore anew the nature of their witness today, and has brought a sense of urgency to the study. A pilot consultation on "Missionary Congregations in Secularized Europe" redrafted for today the major impulses of the earlier studies from the 1960s. (The Conference of European Churches has been involved as a full partner in the process.) Several consultations, a document outlining the potential of such a congregation-based study, and an invitation for many churches in Europe to be involved ecumenically in the study process, have all been planned. It is hoped that the concern for the missionary congregation in the context of today could become a central thrust of several WCC member churches in the days ahead.

Ecumenical team visits

Based on the conviction that well-prepared ecumenical team visits remain significant instruments in the process of the education and renewal of churches in mission, various issue-oriented visits have been launched since Vancouver, particularly within the framework of preparation for the San Antonio world mission conference.

Moreover, in September 1989 an ecumenical team of nine persons from different regions visited local congregations in Switzerland. Their visit promoted joint exploration of the search for justice, peace and integrity of creation as an essential part of the mission of local congregations.

Mission in the context of developments in Eastern and Central Europe

In March 1987 the Cuban Ecumenical Council, supported by CWME, held an international consultation in Havana on the topic "The Mission of the Church in Socialist Countries". A significant outcome of that meeting was that a working group was formed at the Ecumenical Centre in Geneva through which the staff, particularly those from socialist countries, could exchange perspectives and assist churches in their countries in their missionary calling.

This led to another consultation in Poland in September 1987 with a similar thrust. Sixty participants from eight then-socialist countries met and affirmed ecumenically the potential for proclaiming the gospel in the midst of a growing spiritual hunger, even among the young. A similar group met in October 1989 in Hungary, primarily to translate the mission impulses from San Antonio for their context. The consultation sensed the rapid changes that were already appearing on the horizon in many parts of Eastern and Central Europe.

But changes swept through the nations in Central and Eastern Europe faster than anyone had imagined. The new situation demanded new eyes to see, new analysis, new energies and new ecumenical commitments. With this in view CWME, along with other WCC sub-units and some Christian World Communions (CWCs), planned a major consultation in Moscow in May 1990, at which church leaders from several Eastern and Central European countries explored together the recent developments and new socio-political realities, and their challenge for the witness of the church.

Mission and Evangelism: an Ecumenical Affirmation has been a significant tool in promoting fresh ecumenical thinking on mission. Seminars for pastors at the national level, regional study guides, and translation of the affirmation into several languages have been attempted.

The concern for "witnessing among children" has been identified as being significant. Not much could be done by CWME, however, apart from the publication of the results of a case-study on this theme in the GDR.

World conference on mission and evangelism, San Antonio, Texas, USA

This world conference, which is mandated to meet once between assemblies of the WCC, was held in May 1989 on the campus of Trinity University.

Concerns for continuity with the theme of the Melbourne mission conference in 1981, and the need to focus upon active obedience in mission, resulted in the theme: "Your Will Be Done: Mission in Christ's Way". A unique feature of the conference emerged very early in the planning process, as expressed in the following words:

> Slowly and with much pain we are learning how surprising is the will of God, and how it challenges us in and from the most unexpected places... often

through the people whose voices and actions are ignored or silenced by the powers of this world. Mission in Christ's way must enable their voices to be heard.

Through careful recruitment, programme design and prior visitations this concern was realized.

The *composition of the conference* made it the most representative and inclusive of mission conferences: 44% of the delegates were women, 19% Orthodox and 14% youth; 70% came from the second and third worlds. There was a delegation of 21 persons from the Vatican, an official delegation from the People's Republic of China, and a few representatives from other faiths. In all there were 649 participants from 106 countries, along with 123 press representatives.

Visitations included 11 team visits by the leadership of various conference sections to different contexts of the life and mission of member churches. In addition, some 207 persons were involved in small team visits to congregations in the USA, Canada and Puerto Rico as they travelled to and from the conference. During the conference more than 150 communities and congregations received 400 participants in teams of two or three as weekend guests.

The conference was preceded by a brief *youth conference* which enabled young persons to articulate their concerns about contemporary issues in Christian mission. Parallel to the opening days of the conference was an opportunity for about 500 persons from North America to encounter participants from around the world. That meeting was appropriately called the "Encuentro".

The basic shape of the conference was designed to give maximum opportunity for the participants to listen to each other, and particularly to the voices of those often ignored or silenced by the "powers of this world". Therefore only five plenary addresses were scheduled during the ten days, four of them in the first 24 hours and the last in the closing session. Much of the work was intentionally done in sections and small groups.

It was at *worship* that the conference became most tangibly a community. From the opening service, at which 2,000 persons were present, to the end the quality of music and liturgy continued to feed and energize the participants. The conference was sustained also by all-night vigils maintained by local Christians in a church near the conference site.

The conference was nurtured within 40 small *Bible study groups* in which participants explored the theme through an inductive study of selected passages from Luke's gospel. This experience, guided by an ecumenical team of three persons, faithfully reflected the wide diversity within the conference.

The *sections:* Most of the work at the conference was done in four sections. Participants met nine times in these four sections to explore the following sectional themes:
— "Turning to the Living God";
— "Participating in Suffering and Struggle";
— "The Earth is the Lord's";
— "Toward Renewed Communities in Mission".
These sectional themes provided the context for exploring the contemporary application of the main theme from a variety of situations around the world. Each section also met in smaller groups around sub-themes. With the help of a ten-page briefing received by each section and reports of workshops or consultations, the delegates were expected to define those aspects of the sectional theme which were most urgent for their lives and mission situation.

The three significant texts of the conference are the "Message" of the conference, the "Acts in Faithfulness" and the reports of the four sections. These together with the other presentations and documents are available in the official report (*The San Antonio Report*), and in the July/October 1989 issue of the *International Review of Mission*.

The "Acts in Faithfulness" were intended to be innovative in both form and function, to be different from traditional conference resolutions and declarations. They were to be "do-able", attain-able and measure-able. (Not all, however, were in the form which had been expected.) Some of these "Acts" from each of the four sections were presented to the plenary, and were affirmed by an overwhelming majority of the official delegates. It is hoped that those who did so will faithfully translate the "Acts" into concrete acts of living witness within the context of their congregations and communities.

Another important action of the conference was amending its constitution to make it possible for the WCC member churches to nominate a larger proportion of the delegates to future such gatherings.

From the stories heard in San Antonio, from the depth of the pain and anguish of the oppressed communities voiced there, and from the midst of corporate search through worship and Bible studies, there arose several theological and missiological insights and issues for the ecumenical movement. Their implications for the life and mission of the church are many. CWME is mandated to assist member churches to explore some, and to give clear programmatic expression to others. The following are some of the significant issues which demand the churches' attention. Not all of them are new; but they were reiterated or highlighted by San Antonio with renewed power:

— the urgency of equipping Christians and local congregations for the proclamation of the gospel for the awakening of personal faith;
— the "two-way" relationship between mission and dialogue;
— the meaning and experience of the creative power of the Spirit in transforming people who suffer into those who struggle;
— the continuing role of "resistance" as a form of Christian mission in Christ's way;
— land as a key mission issue;
— mission in the relation between culture and community;
— the affirmation that "the earth is the Lord's" indicates a new, constitutive dimension of mission;
— the theological and missiological significance of a growing number of popular religious and renewal movements (for example in Africa and Latin America) and their ecclesial implications for the ecumenical movement;
— the urgency for change in patterns of partnership in mission and the relationship between churches, that they may witness to a God-intended way of sharing resources for authentic human community.

Several of these issues will shape the future work of CWME as it seeks to address them in co-operation with other sub-units of the World Council.

Emerging trends/priorities ahead

The world conference in San Antonio re-affirmed the central role of local churches in mission, and therefore the urgent need both for the renewal of local Christian communities and for linking them in meaningful partnership at various levels for effective ecumenical engagement in mission.

During the past few years several member churches, and even a few CWCs, have set for themselves renewed goals in evangelism such as a "decade of evangelism". Others are searching for "authentic" and "holistic" mission, and for evangelism in an ecumenical mode.

The theme of the Canberra assembly, "Come, Holy Spirit — Renew the Whole Creation", engenders a fresh and urgent vision of the renewal of churches in the power of the Spirit to be an effective instrument of God's reconciling love in Christ.

These factors have led CWME to affirm at its last commission meeting (February 1990) that supporting churches in their *equipping local congregations* for mission and evangelism needs to be a *central programmatic thrust and focus* of CWME in the days ahead. Such an ecumenical strengthening of churches for mission at the level of congregations, denominational structures, theological training, and in other ways can be done in co-operation with other WCC sub-units.

Such a programmatic thrust will be strengthened by enhanced dialogue and relationship with evangelicals, a renewed search for authentic models of international relationships in mission, and a continued effort to explore the ecclesial and missiological implications of popular religiosity and renewal movements. The experience of URM over more than 25 years has brought abundant theological and spiritual resources from the midst of the suffering and struggles of people for justice and liberation. Greater effort to use these resources for the renewal of local churches, and in their participation in the struggles of the poor, is an urgent need. So also is the continued search with the Dialogue sub-unit for the meaning and shape of witness of local Christian communities in the context of a religiously plural world. Both a joint consultation with the Dialogue sub-unit in Tambaram, India, in 1988 and the San Antonio world conference have given new impetus for such effort.

In all these ways, CWME will seek to be faithful to its mandate to help member churches "understand and explore together the content and meaning of the gospel in their faith, missionary and evangelistic task" and to "foster common Christian witness."

SUB-UNIT ON CHURCH AND SOCIETY

Mandate

The mandate given to the Sub-unit on Church and Society by the Vancouver assembly was to engage the churches in reflection and action on issues raised by science and technology for faith and witness. Key areas were identified for continuing dialogue and work: (a) technology experienced as destructive power, (b) appropriate systems of technological development, (c) automation, micro-electronics and patterns of employment, and (d) the control of science and technology. Issues of particular concern were identified, and included bio-ethics (and in particular genetic engineering) and long-term choices about renewable and non-renewable energy supplies for all countries. While the Vancouver report mentions only a few of the technological, ethical and social issues raised by science and technology, it anticipated many more arising in the future and stressed the importance of churches becoming effectively involved in the social control of science and technology.

Central to the work of the Sub-unit has been the focus upon integrity of creation, both for its own theological and ethical work and in order to make a significant contribution to the Council-wide "justice, peace and the integrity of creation" (JPIC) process and to the Canberra assembly.

Methodology

Church and Society's distinctive methodology has been described as interactive, that is, that existing moral/theological insights, and the perception of contemporary concrete issues, illuminate and deepen one another. Early meetings of the working group, noting Church and Society's limited resources, stressed that this should not mean avoidance of any practical orientation. One of the meetings affirmed: "The ecumenical movement has always understood that working for justice, peace and the integrity of creation involves the perpetual interaction of theory and praxis in the context of human needs."

The relationships between theology, ethics, scientific and social analysis and action have been represented diagrammatically as shown. It is understood that the scope of the Sub-unit's work should not be identified with any single element, but with each in its inter-relatedness at local, national and international levels:

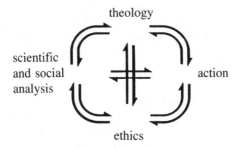

Theology and ethics

Integrity of creation

The ongoing theological work on integrity of creation, or the long-term survival of the earth's ecosystem, has been of fundamental significance to the entire agenda of Church and Society activities, and is becoming foundational for an integrated understanding of justice and peace.

We can neither ignore the magnitude of the ecological crisis, nor be content to treat the symptoms (clean up a toxic waste or oil spill here, plant a few trees there) without dealing with the underlying causes. The root causes of the crisis lie in human arrogance towards creation, in assuming human dominance over nature.

Moderator Held's report to the central committee meeting in 1988 commented upon the "'Western' character of much, if not most, ecumenical theology [that] has so far been based on a pragmatic instrumentalist view of nature which has confined the science/faith debate to those who share these presuppositions and has hampered the development by the churches of an ecological view of the future".

Church and Society has increasingly tried to reflect an understanding of creation in terms appropriate to different regional contexts. This was done in part by holding consultations in places where we could not fail to be affected by different regional and theological traditions, e.g. Indonesia (Puncak Pass, 1989), the Philippines (Manila, 1986), Brazil (Sao Paulo, 1988), Costa Rica (San José, 1988), France (Annecy, 1988), the USSR (Tambov, 1988).

The Sub-unit drew upon the powerful critique of feminist theologians against patriarchal structures, with their dissociation from nature, and listened to environmentalists stressing holistic views on the interconnectedness of life. Theologians from Africa and from indigenous American communities laid strong emphasis upon the sacredness and unity of nature, and upon reverence for life. Latin American and Asian theologians spoke not only of liberation from exploitation and impoverishment but also of liberation from the tyranny of materialism and consumerism.

Increasingly in these discussions, theologians have stressed the immanence of the Divine within the world, rather than transcendence. Mechanistic views of nature, and of a remote deistic God whose only role was to "set the world going" like a watchmaker, have been challenged by more panentheistic views that see God also as immanent in the world, suffering in the suffering of all creatures, and rejoicing in the joy of all creation. Dualistic views which see humanity as separate from nature have been revised by more ecologically-justifiable, inclusive views that see humanity as within, and as part of, nature. This does not diminish the value of personal human life created uniquely in the image of God. Rather, this gives to humanity a responsibility to co-operate with God's purposes in the world.

Particular attention has been given to the task of clarifying what is meant by the "integrity of creation". A consultation in Annecy, France, in 1988 offered this definition: "The value of all creatures in and for themselves, for one another, and for God, and their interconnectedness in a diverse whole that has unique value for God, together constitute the integrity of creation."

Further, major attention has been given to the challenge of bringing together the imperatives of justice and human liberation in the world with the preservation of the ecological foundations for all life. This work is critical to avoid a false and harmful separation between concerns for justice and for the environment. The various theological perspectives developed within the work of the Sub-unit have stressed the inter-relatedness of every part of creation, focusing upon renewing the covenant relationships between God, people and nature.

Environmental ethics

Underlying much environmental concern is the growing realization that creation is an open process within which we take responsibility for our actions. Personal responsibility, arising from commitment to the environment and to the survival of future generations and non-human living creatures, has been seen as the motivation for action.

However, Christian ethicists also have been challenged to move beyond personal and social ethics to a planetary environmental ethic, recognizing that what happens in one place affects the entire global biosphere: that acid rain, toxic waste and soil erosion can impoverish the present and future human community in interlocking ways. Further, within these discussions concepts of development as economic growth have been replaced by those of "sustainability".

In attempting to reflect on questions of environmental social ethics much of the Sub-unit's work has been directed to case studies and to specific issues, such as deforestation. It is hoped that the more detailed study and involvement in these issues has made a substantial contribution to the analysis of theological and ethical presuppositions that underly economic and political decision-making.

Ethical values and science

A meeting held in the Netherlands discussed the means of integrating moral and ethical concerns into scientific education and how to introduce ethics and religion into the science classroom and laboratory. The results were published as *Science Education and Ethical Values*. Similar concerns were raised and debated at length in an ecumenical seminar supported by the Sub-unit and held at the Ecumenical Institute, Bossey (*Science and the Theology of Creation*, 1988).

Bio-technology and genetic engineering

The speed of scientific research and technological development in genetic engineering made it imperative for Church and Society to re-open the ethical debate in this area.

After wide consultation, a report entitled "Bio-technology: its Challenges to the Churches and the World" was produced together with a specific list of recommendations and proposals. After debate and amendments, the following statement was officially approved by the central committee in Moscow in 1989:

> The WCC, recognizing the potential dangers as well as the potential benefits of many forms of bio-technology, encourages its member churches to take appropriate action in their own countries to draw these matters to public attention, and to help governments, scientists, universities, hospitals and corporations to develop suitable safeguards and controls.
>
> In particular it:
> a) calls for the prohibition of genetic testing for sex selection, and warns against the potential use of genetic testing for other forms of involuntary social engineering;
> b) draws attention to ways in which knowledge of an individual's genetic make-up can be, and in some cases is, being abused by becoming the basis for unfair discrimination, for example, in work, health care, insurance and education;
> c) stresses the need for pastoral counselling for individuals faced with difficult reproductive choices as well as personal and family decisions resulting from genetic information concerning themselves or others;
> d) proposes a ban on experiments involving genetic engineering of the human germline at the present time, and encourages the ethical reflection necessary for developing future guidelines in this area; and urges strict control on experiments involving genetically engineered somatic cells, drawing attention to the potential misuse of both techniques as a means of discrimination against those held to be "defective";

e) calls for the banning of commercialized child bearing (i.e. partial and full surrogacy) as well as the commercial sale of ova, embryos or foetal parts and sperm;

f) advises governments to prohibit embryo research, with any experiments, if agreed, only under well-defined conditions;

g) encourages its member churches and other groups to keep themselves informed on how new developments in reproductive technology affect families, and especially women, and develop a pastoral ministry to counsel people facing these issues, including those who choose or are pressured into utilizing such reproductive techniques;

h) believes that animal life-forms should not be patented and calls for further study of the profound moral and social implications of patenting life forms;

i) urges the swift adoption of strict international controls on the release of genetically engineered organisms into the environment;

j) calls on nations throughout the world to cease all use of genetic engineering as part of any biological or chemical warfare research programme, and to reconvene conventions on biological and chemical weapons in order to create new and effective protocols which prohibit their development, production and use;

k) resolves to initiate consultations between international organizations, non-governmental organizations and scientists, with the churches and others, to reflect on the political evolution of bio-technology and its impact on global justice, and to make proposals for maximizing the benefit to those who are most in need.

This step is an important commitment by the WCC in attempting to respond to the theological and ethical issues raised by the various dimensions of bio-technology. By this action the WCC earnestly hopes to stimulate, encourage, and strengthen the engagement of these issues by member churches, related institutions, and centres for study and action, as well as other interested groups throughout the world.

The full report calls for ongoing work, both theological and practical, in response to the challenges raised by bio-technology. Critical theological questions about the nature of human life, and the meaning of the "integrity of creation", need concentrated exploration. Pressing developments, promises, and dangers in certain applications of bio-technology need rapid and clear responses. And, in the long term, a forceful ethic to guide the ways in which this powerful technology will be utilized is imperative. Hopefully, the actions taken by the WCC will be useful contributions to these ends.

Involvement in other critical issues

AIDS

In response to requests from member churches and the World Health Organization (WHO), the general secretary asked the Sub-units on Church and Society, Education and the Christian Medical Commission to consider the escalation of the AIDS epidemic and its implications for the churches. The three Sub-units held a joint consultation in June 1986 on the theme "AIDS and the Church as a Healing Community", calling upon churches to respond to the need for pastoral care, education for prevention and social ministry.

In January 1987, Church and Society organized a hearing on the subject before the central committee. In response to growing demands and requests by member churches a second international consultation was held in Tanzania in December 1988, and the WCC and WHO co-operated in organizing a workshop held in Barbados in October 1989 which produced a manual for church counsellors.

The "liberation of life" and animal rights

The concluding statement at the conference held in Annecy, France, in 1988, read:

> Increasingly during this century, Christians have come to understand the gospel, the good news, in terms of freedom, both freedom from oppression and freedom *for* life with God and others. Too often, however, this freedom has been limited to human beings, excluding most other creatures as well as the earth. This freedom *cannot* be so limited because if we destroy other species and the ecosystem, human beings cannot live. This freedom *should not* be so limited because other creatures, both species and individuals, deserve to live in and for themselves and for God. Therefore, we call on Christians as well as other people of good will to work towards the liberation of life, *all* life.

The report elaborated on human responsibility for all creatures and for the entire environment. This discussion, which has been part of the wider effort to develop an understanding of the integrity of creation, raised a range of questions regarding humanity's relationship to other animals. The theological and practical implications of these matters, which were considered at the Tambov working committee meeting (September 1988), have not been resolved. Rather, Church and Society's role to this point has been that of initiating discussion of these questions.

The negative impacts of technology

Throughout the work of the Sub-unit the role of technology has been examined, including its impact — both negative and positive — on societies. The first two Church and Society consultations following Vancouver were regional meetings to evaluate the effects of new technology, especially micro-electronics, on patterns of work and upon the victims who must live with the consequences of technological development.

The Glasgow consultation papers on "Technology, Employment and Rapid Social Change" were published as *Will the Future Work?* Participants called for new strategies by churches and governments to counter endemic structural unemployment, and urged a rethinking of our theological understanding of work.

The Manila consultation on "New Technology, Work and the Environment" (1986) was held as an Asian regional counterpart of the Glasgow workshop. At the request of the National Council of Churches of the Philippines, which hosted it, the scope of the meeting was broadened so that it dealt ultimately with a wide spectrum of environmental, justice and peace issues. As the Philippines awaited its historic election, Cardinal Sin called for a "people-oriented and environmentally sensitive work ethic". The impact of Asia's electronic industry upon women was studied, as was deforestation and the impact of militarism and the development of nuclear power in Asia and the Pacific. The papers were published under the title *Technology from the Underside* (1986).

Response to technological disasters

In addition to the ongoing planned work of the Sub-unit, critical issues arose which called for appropriate responses. The following examples are illustrative:

1. The Bhopal disaster: A research document was produced on the disaster, a statement prepared and a meeting organized with company representatives, including the chairman of Union Carbide.

2. The Chernobyl disaster: While not all calamities require comment from the WCC, in this case it was appropriate both to express our sympathy and prayers for the victims, and to continue to note how radioactivity crosses international boundaries (thus creating an urgent need for better international monitoring).

Emilio Castro put it this way when he addressed the meeting of the United Nations Environmental Programme (UNEP) on 5 June 1986:

Recent industrial accidents have demonstrated on a large scale what happens when short-term benefits are allowed to endanger the environment and the very survival of whole communities of people... A transformation of technology will be a necessary, but not a sufficient step towards peace and the restoration of the integrity of creation. That will call for a much greater seriousness of purpose on the part of nations, communities and individuals, a commitment to pursue justice between people and nations. It asks that we dedicate human technology and all human endeavours to the common good rather than to the exclusive benefit of some.

Nuclear testing in the Pacific

One of the members of our working committee, Darlene Keju-Johnson, comes from the Marshall Islands in Micronesia, which includes Bikini Atoll. As a child, she was irradiated by fall-out from the 1950s bomb tests, and has had several cancers removed. At the 1983 WCC Vancouver assembly, Keju-Johnson shocked delegates with her account of the dealings between her people and successive US governments. Early in 1987, the Marshallese government (now independent), prompted by Keju-Johnson (who works for the ministry of health), invited a WCC team to assess the overall health needs of the islanders, and it was agreed that Church and Society and the Christian Medical Commission should respond. A delegation visited the Marshalls in the autumn of 1987. Its recommendations included a move away from curative medical services to primary health care, and a request that the US Congress grant the Marshallese the right of access to the medical records of exposed individuals in order to enable their government to plan future health programmes.

The results of the team visit were discussed in a public evening forum at the 1988 Hanover central committee, and were put into the broader context of continued nuclear testing in the Pacific and the Pacific Conference of Churches' efforts to oppose the nuclearization and militarization of the Pacific region.

Toxic waste

In response to the Hanover central committee and to alarm expressed by delegates from many parts of the world, the Church and Society working group meeting in Tambov, together with USSR consultants, drafted a five-point statement concerning the disposal of toxic waste. The statement supported the regulatory work of the UN, deplored international trade in or dumping of toxic wastes, encouraged governments to fund research into minimizing, recycling, or safely storing such substances, and ended by calling for long-term ecologically responsible behaviour and for methods of social auditing that would take into account the social and environmental, as well as economic, costs incurred by industries and corporations.

Nuclear energy generation

The Sub-unit's aim in this area has been to evaluate and make available to the churches and the public accurate and non-biased data on the costs, benefits and hazards of producing and using nuclear energy, with particular concern for third-world experiences and needs.

Church and Society had previously studied the implications of the use of nuclear energy. However, since the Chernobyl and other nuclear accidents, with the escalating costs of nuclear installations, the lack of any significant progress in waste storage, and with advances in alternative energy production and transmission technologies, a review of the question was felt to be urgent and was requested by the central committee.

Thus in October 1989 Church and Society convened a conference in Kinshasa, Zaire, to review the ethics of nuclear energy generation in the light of the most recent technology, information, costs and accidents. The results of this consultation are seen as making a current contribution to the ongoing ecumenical discussion of this question, and, hopefully, influencing the formation of public policy.

The greenhouse effect

Perhaps the most serious environmental threat is the rapid deterioration of the atmosphere. It seems clear, after careful monitoring by meteorologists, that the planet is moving into the early stages of an unprecedented shift in climate which, if not checked, will adversely affect all life on earth. The "greenhouse effect" appears to be caused by the trapping of heat around the earth as a result of the accumulation of a blanket of gases, namely carbon dioxide (50%), nitrous oxide (10%), methane (20%) and CFCs (20%), derived from our intensive industrial and agricultural practices and in particular from the consumption of fossil fuels in vehicles, power plants, etc. These changes are made even more serious by the cumulative impact of acid rain and the deterioration and destruction of the protective ozone layer in the upper atmosphere.

Thus Church and Society, as a response to this urgent issue and in co-operation with the JPIC process, has encouraged discussion of these questions with a view to the churches' contribution. This included background work in preparation for the JPIC world convocation, since the greenhouse effect was selected as one of the three issues that would form the basis for special acts of covenant and commitment by the churches.

Tropical forest destruction

Tropical rain forests are disappearing on average at over 50 acres per minute, or 76,000 acres per day. About 20,000 square miles of tropical forest per year are irreparably destroyed by logging alone. Flooding, road construction and encroachment by settlement add to this figure. The destruction of forest leads to soil erosion, loss of fertility, falling water tables, desertification and eventually to climatic change.

Church and Society has convened a series of three workshops, in Costa Rica, Indonesia and Ecuador, designed to:
— express a critical awareness of the tropical forest crisis;
— encourage church leaders to become aware of, and involved in, the issue;
— produce educational material, both theologically oriented and ecologically sound, on environmental protection and reforestation strategies;
— draw up action plans and strategies to initiate and strengthen local and community-based efforts; and
— initiate networking linkages with church and non-governmental organization groups.

A declaration was issued to the churches in Latin America and Asia calling upon them to defend and maintain the integrity of creation, to educate church members in their ecological responsibility, and to engage in concrete actions to preserve what is left of the forest and to rehabilitate what can be redeemed. A manual of environmental management was produced for use in Latin America.

In these urgent and practical issues Church and Society, while its theology, ethics and hope are founded in our faith in Jesus Christ, finds itself working very closely with environmental and base groups at the local and regional level, and in dialogue with government officials and church leaders. This increases our commitment to the entire community and to the whole of God's creation, so that we are called to participate, work with and co-operate with the whole family of humanity in its struggle against the forces of destruction.

Future directions

The experience of the Sub-unit on Church and Society since Vancouver, and the development of contemporary events in the world, provide helpful guidelines for future directions in the work of the WCC beyond the Canberra assembly.

First, work in the churches to develop deeper and more faithful understandings of the theology of creation must be strengthened in the years ahead. The Sub-unit has begun exploring the theological truth that "all things", indeed, all creation, are being brought together in a unity by God through the work of Christ and the gift of the Spirit (Eph. 1:9-10). In this task, the Sub-unit's work should be seen in light of the whole contribution of Unit I. In numerous ways this work has been undertaken in co-operation with other sub-units such as Dialogue, Mission and Evangelism, and Faith and Order, for these theological questions indeed involve such a coherence.

But obviously this search in the churches is only beginning, and is made ever more urgent by the continuing deterioration of the earth. In ongoing attempts to develop such theological perspectives the experience of indigenous peoples, the insights of other living faiths, the fruits of recent biblical scholarship, the perspectives of women, the insights of modern science, and the theological traditions within the churches (and particularly the Orthodox community), all must be explored and related.

The recasting of theology must always be related to concrete situations. And the task of rethinking the theology of creation must be to help formulate ethical perspectives which can be offered to societies as models and guides in the task of building a sustainable future for the world. As humanity approaches the end of the second millennium, the churches should ask whether and how they can participate in the search for combining ecological wisdom with economic life, as people try to build new structures for the future. This will mean that the work for integrity of creation will have to find a full integration with the imperatives for justice.

For this to take place, co-operation between Church and Society and the ongoing work of the JPIC process, as well as collaboration with efforts of various sub-units in Unit II, should be increased in the future. Thus as the JPIC process becomes integrated in the future into various aspects of the WCC's programmatic work, Church and Society should play a key part. In this process the tradition of offering theological and analytical perspectives on such issues — which is the reason for Church and Society finding its home within Unit I — should be strongly maintained.

These concerns will underscore the churches' role in the search for new economic and social models for societies. The present widespread "ideological confusion" gives fresh urgency to the question, put by the WCC general secretary to the 1990 central committee: "What type of society are we seeking to build?" The general secretary noted that "the specific search for models of society was left on one side" by the ecumenical movement, but that "in the contemporary historical situation, we are challenged to define images of society which can help those who have to take urgent, existential decisions". This requires "studies and practical activities which show how within history we may come close to the coming kingdom". This challenge, undertaken in co-ordination with other WCC resources and efforts, should provide a focus for the energies of Church and Society. This direction was also underscored by the last meeting of the Sub-unit's working committee (Sofia, November 1989).

In this process Church and Society should renew the long tradition of work on the issues of ecumenical social ethics, as they relate to the full range of questions arising in societies about the values, vision and practice which can contribute to the shaping of our common future. This must enable a creative exploration of the possible economic, political, social and ecological structures which can respond to the prayer to be expressed by the seventh assembly: "Giver of Life — Sustain Your Creation!" Many have said that the world is entering a "post-modern" age, when the values which have shaped contemporary societies, in East and West, North and South, will need to be refashioned if the world is to have a future where life can be sustained. This, then, calls for the creative theological and practical contribution of the churches, in societies throughout the world, as they give witness to God's redeeming purposes in Jesus Christ for all creation.

SUB-UNIT ON DIALOGUE WITH PEOPLE OF LIVING FAITHS

The mandate

Today there is greater awareness than ever before that we live in a religiously plural world. Vastly improved methods of communication, greater movements of population, and increased interdependence of nations and societies have contributed to this. Many societies which have for centuries been homogeneous have today become pluralistic, and the churches have begun to look for ways to respond to the call to live and witness in situations of persistent religious plurality.

The Sub-unit on Dialogue with People of Living Faiths was established in 1971 to assist the churches in their endeavour to understand and to relate to religious plurality. The following elements are crucial to what has been an "expanding mandate" over the past 20 years.

The primary task of the Sub-unit is to enable meetings between Christians and persons of other faiths. These meetings are meant to promote understanding and dialogue, so that religious communities which have in the past been mutually suspicious, or in conflict, can become communities in conversation. Even where there has been no conflict, religious groups have lived in mutual isolation and have co-operated little in the search for justice and peace in the world. Therefore "seeking community" has been an important emphasis within the dialogue programme.

The Sub-unit's second main task has to do primarily with the churches. Here the emphasis has been on raising awareness within the churches about the reality of religious plurality, and the need to respond to it in a creative way. Often Christians have built caricatures of people of other faiths (as also others have of Christians), and have done little or no thinking about the theological significance of their neighbours' prayer life and spiritual history. Life in community demands greater willingness to know and understand the "otherness" of the others, and this can only be done through conscious effort.

The third emphasis is a logical consequence of the second. Here attention is paid to theological issues raised in the context of dialogue. What has dialogue to say to our understanding and practice of mission? What about conversion? What can we say — in light of our belief that God is present and active in all creation — about the activity of the Holy Spirit among other believers? Such questions are not easily answered; indeed, there are many different views on these questions among the member churches of the WCC. The Sub-unit provides the "space" within which such theological questions can be explored, and helps to articulate the theological issues which the churches should be facing today.

The Sub-unit's programme mandate has been expanded from time to time to deal with pressing issues such as the church's response to New Religious Movements, to "fundamentalism", to the growing role of religion in conflict situations, and others.

The Sub-unit relates primarily to Hindus, Buddhists, Jews, Muslims, and to persons who follow traditional religions in Africa, Asia, North and South America and elsewhere. It operates under the guidance of a working group appointed by the central committee. Since the last assembly the working group has met four times, in Swanwick, UK (March 1985); Potsdam, GDR (July 1986); Baar, Switzerland (May 1988) and Casablanca, Morocco (June 1989).

The programme on Dialogue works in close collaboration with the Pontifical Council for Interreligious Dialogue of the Roman Catholic Church (formerly known as the Secretariat for Non-Christians). Each year there is a joint staff meeting, alternating between Rome and Geneva, to explore issues in interfaith dialogue and to share information on the work that each party has initiated.

Activities since Vancouver

The theological significance study

One of the major debates at the Vancouver assembly had to do with the theological significance of other living faiths. In its discussion of the report of the section on "Witness in a Divided World", the assembly could not agree on whether God is actively present in the religious lives of our neighbours who are not Christians.

The Sub-unit followed up this debate by launching a four-year study programme in the churches entitled "My Neighbour's Faith — and Mine: Theological Discoveries through Interfaith Dialogue". The study guide for this programme is composed of nine study sections; it has been translated into 18 languages and made widely available. Over 7,500 copies have been distributed in English alone. Reports have been received from a number of groups; these were analyzed at a special study consultation in Casablanca, Morocco. The study will continue beyond the Canberra assembly, but some of its interim findings were followed up at a consultation on the theology of religions at Baar, Switzerland, in January 1990.

The Baar consultation tackled three of the major theological issues in interfaith dialogue: the theological significance of religious plurality, the meaning of Christ in a religiously plural world, and the implications of the belief that the Holy Spirit works outside the boundaries of the institutional church. Some of the theological perspectives stated at this consultation will form the basis for theological explorations after Canberra.

The Sub-unit will continue to be involved in, and animate, discussions on the theology of religions with a view to enabling the churches to respond theologically to the reality of other faiths.

Christian-Jewish dialogue

The International Jewish Committee on Interreligious Consultations and the Sub-unit continue to explore Jewish-Christian relations. In this they are supported by a liaison and planning committee which meets annually. This relationship is monitored and fostered by the Consultation on the Church and the Jewish People (CCJP), a group appointed by the Dialogue working group and consisting of persons engaged, at different levels, in Jewish-Christian relations.

The Sub-unit organized a Jewish-Christian dialogue on "The Meaning and Limits of Religious Pluralism in the World Today" at the Harvard Divinity School, Boston, in November 1984. The consultation affirmed the importance of respecting plurality, and identified the many ways in which fanaticism and bigotry have taken hold of societies which refuse to face this reality.

An important breakthrough in this field was the first Jewish-Christian dialogue event to be held in Africa, in November 1986. African Christians and Jewish participants met in Nairobi for an in-depth dialogue on tradition, creation, scripture and other topics. The success of this meeting has led to a proposal for a meeting between Jewish participants and French-speaking Africans.

One important contribution by the CCJP was the collection and analysis of the theological statements which have been made by member churches, and by the WCC, on Christian-Jewish relations since the formation of the Council in 1948. The most important statements, together with an analysis, have been published as *The Theology of the Churches and the Jewish People*. On the basis of this study the CCJP has also produced a position paper describing where the churches are on the issue of Jewish-Christian relations.

The working group in Casablanca recommended that the WCC should broaden its contacts within the Jewish community. It called for dialogue at several different levels and encouraged the Sub-unit to take up, with Jewish partners, the theological and contemporary issues needing more focused attention in the present context.

Christian-Muslim relations

In recent years there has been increasing interest among WCC member churches in Islam. The religious revival of Islam has created a greater consciousness among Christians of "political Islam". This has arisen from the encounter with "Islamic fundamentalism", the media interest in the Rushdie affair, the migration of Islamic communities into Western Europe, and other factors. In addition, many churches which have for long lived among Muslim neighbours are also seeking ways to preserve, foster and maintain the relationships with them that have been built up over the centuries. In response the Sub-unit has begun a long-term project to develop "guidelines" for Muslim-Christian relations. Islam, however, finds a variety of expressions in different parts of the world and it is not easy to evolve a set of guidelines which take into account the vastly different models of relationship that exist between Christians and Muslims in different societies.

Since Vancouver the Sub-unit has therefore organized five regional meetings between Christians and Muslims: in Porto Novo, Benin, for Francophone Africa; Bali, Indonesia, for Asia and the Pacific; Kolymbari, Crete, for Europe and the Middle East; New Windsor, USA, for North America; and Arusha, Tanzania, for West Africa. In these meetings three main topics affecting Christian-Muslim relations on a day-to-day basis were taken up for debate; these were religion and family, religion and education, and religion and the state.

The Sub-unit is in the process of clarifying the findings from these consultations, exploring the theological and political considerations in Muslim-Christian relations, and working towards guidelines. Since there will be wide consultation with churches and with our Muslim partners on the initial drafts of the guidelines this process will go beyond the Canberra assembly.

An important development since Vancouver is the Sub-unit's effort, in collaboration with the Pontifical Council for Interreligious Dialogue, to create a liaison group between the WCC and the Vatican and world bodies of Islam. A number of successful meetings have been held with Muslim world bodies to explore this possibility.

Much more could be done at this historic moment in Muslim-Christian relations if the WCC, and its member churches, were able to commit more resources in this area.

Christian-Hindu/Buddhist relations

Buddhists and Christians have a long history of association on the Asian continent. Buddhism is also believed to be the fastest growing religious tradition in North America, but since Buddhists do not necessarily organize and count their lay followers it is not known how large the impact has been. This fact, however, has awakened a new interest in Buddhism among Christians in the West, as well as in the lands from which it originates.

Hinduism, too, is today going through a period of self-conscious articulation of its beliefs and practices. There have been several attempts to organize the large groups of Hindus living in various parts of the world into something like a Hindu world fellowship.

In lands which are traditionally Buddhist or Hindu, Christians are often small minorities and are thus engaged in exploring their identity and witnessing within that context. The Sub-unit has attempted to work locally in the field of Buddhist and Hindu relations, particularly in partnership with the study centres in Asia which relate to these religions. A number of dialogue workshops have been held in India on Christian-Hindu relations. One important event in Asia organized by the Sub-unit was the multilateral dialogue held in November 1987 in New Delhi on "Religious Identities in a Multifaith Society". This brought together representatives of the Hindu, Buddhist, Muslim, Christian, Sikh, Jain and Zoroastrian traditions and its findings have been used to good effect in other meetings in India.

An important breakthrough in India occurred when our Hindu partners in dialogue came forward to initiate and organize a number of events. Apart from four such gatherings in different parts of South India, the Hindus, in collaboration with the Sub-unit, organized a three-day seminar in Madras in July 1989 which brought together 105 people to be conscientized about promoting interfaith relations.

Two major meetings brought Buddhists and Christians together for dialogue in North Asia. The first, in December 1984 in Hong Kong, brought together Christians and Buddhists from North Asia (Japan, Korea, Taiwan and Hong Kong). In November 1988 a pan-Asian Buddhist-Christian meeting was held in Seoul, Korea; here Buddhists and Christians from all parts of Asia contributed to reflection on the justice and peace issues of the "Justice, Peace and the Integrity of Creation" (JPIC) process.

Although lack of resources did not permit the Sub-unit to be more extensively involved, it did co-sponsor a Confucian-Christian meeting in North Asia, which was the first of its kind in recent years.

A strong case was made at the working group meeting in Casablanca that the Sub-unit should give attention in the future to Christian-Sikh relations, both in India and in the West. This suggestion will be addressed in the period after Canberra.

Traditional religions

Not every religious tradition can name its founder, or the historical period in which its faith perceptions were "founded" or codified. Over centuries large sections of humanity have received religious perceptions, practices and collective wisdom which have been handed down from one generation to another. These traditional religious perceptions govern the totality of life, directing attitudes to nature, to personal life and to relationships in society. Very often the "founded religions" have acquired converts from these religious communities, often upsetting values that had, until then, preserved and held together whole communities. Today there is a new search to see how Christians can relate to persons who remain in these traditional religions, and to the converts who are seeking to integrate their new faith with the values of their traditional beliefs.

Since the Vancouver assembly the Sub-unit has held two meetings which have sought to address these issues. The first, in September 1986 in Kitwe, Zambia, brought together 20 African Christians from 14 countries to consider the church's approach to traditional religion. The consultation recognized that all African Christians have an ongoing dialogue with their traditional beliefs. It called on the churches to study the significance of this "inner" dialogue more closely, and also to initiate formal dialogue between the church and those who still practise traditional religion. It affirmed that a true encounter between Christianity and traditional beliefs may help incorporate the values, wisdom and understandings of community which have been essential to African culture in the life of the church.

In the second meeting, held at Sorrento, Canada, in November 1987, the Sub-unit brought together for the first time traditional elders from North America, organizing a meeting in which both the agenda and the style were determined by the elders themselves. In fact they did not want a fixed agenda, timetable or written report, but preferred to engage in a conversation on a number of issues, interspersed with periods of silence. A video-tape was prepared on their conversations. The elders strongly felt that more such dialogues — in which mutual listening and learning are emphasized — would enrich the life of all participants.

The working group at Casablanca insisted that the question of traditional religion take a more important place on the Dialogue agenda, and that specially trained staff in this field would be required in the period beyond the assembly.

Collaborative programmes

The integration of the work of Dialogue into the many aspects of the life of the WCC has been given priority in the period following Vancouver. This has been achieved through several collaborative programmes with other sub-units of the WCC.

Dialogue-Programme on Theological Education (PTE): What significance do the practice of dialogue, and the reflections arising from it, have for theological education today? The major thrust for over a decade within the Programme on Theological Education has been the contextualization of theological education, emphasizing ministerial formation within each particular historical situation. On the dialogue side, the emphasis has been on building community across all barriers, including those erected by religious beliefs and practices. In Asia and Africa, and increasingly in other parts of the world, the minister's immediate context is a religiously plural society. How much does this reality shape theological reflection in the seminary? How do we learn about "other faiths" in the seminary context? What is the most appropriate "formation" for ministry in a multifaith society? These questions were addressed by persons who teach theology, mission and religion in Asian seminaries (along with some from outside Asia) at an exploratory meeting held in Malaysia in June 1985.

The value of this encounter, and the good reception enjoyed by its report, prompted another such meeting for African seminaries, held in collaboration with PTE and the Lutheran World Federation (LWF) in September 1989 in Malawi.

Dialogue-JPIC: Since the WCC launched the programme on "Justice, Peace and the Integrity of Creation", many voices have been raised affirming that these questions can and should be explored in collaboration with neighbours of other faiths — who also have much to say on these issues.

Dialogue and the JPIC programme jointly organized in Britain a meeting on the question of the "integrity of creation" attended by persons from five religious traditions. In addition to making a general input five of the participants, from different faiths, contributed to a major JPIC conference on creation held in Granvollen, Norway, in February-March 1988. A pan-Asia Buddhist-Christian consultation also took up the issues of justice and peace, and 10 persons of other faiths participated in the convocation on JPIC at Seoul in March 1990. This experience has shown that in many areas of the WCC's work the regular participation of persons of other faiths would greatly enhance its contribution to the community.

Dialogue-Sub-unit on Women: Dialogue's contribution to the Ecumenical Decade of the Churches in Solidarity with Women has been to organize, in collaboration with the Sub-unit on Women, a meeting in Toronto, Canada, in June 1988 which brought together about 50 women from eight religious traditions. In many ways this was a pioneering venture and an extremely valuable one. The women had the opportunity to take up issues such as scripture and Tradition, authority and leadership, and identity and sexuality, to see how these affected women across religious lines. Many other concerns (for example, the problem of religious stereotyping, the responsibility for handing down religious values, violence) were also debated. Exposure to other ways of worshipping and visits to places of worship enriched the mutual learning. The Canadian Religious Broadcast channel, Vision TV, made eight videotapes of these discussions across religious lines on issues that affect women in church and society today.

Dialogue-Sub-unit on Renewal and Congregational Life (RCL): The Vancouver assembly identified spirituality as one issue needing focused exploration in the post-Vancouver period. This has been followed up closely by the Sub-unit on Renewal and Congregational Life. One important contemporary issue in this field has to do specifically with interfaith relations: a considerable number of Christians often turn to other religious traditions, seeking from them either an overall approach to reality or methods and techniques of spiritual discipline which would help their own spiritual life. It is common for such persons, for example, to turn to meditative techniques of Buddhism, or to worship practices of Hinduism, to help provide the basis for their own spiritual discipline. Others seek ideological values or inspiration from other religions in order spiritually to undergird their social involvement. What does all this mean to Christian belief, and to the church's attitude to other spiritual disciplines?

Dialogue organized a joint consultation with RCL in Kyoto, Japan, in December 1987 which brought together about 30 persons who have followed other spiritual disciplines for many years. They told their stories, shared their joys and fears, and discussed the theological and pastoral implications of their journeys. Their stories and experiences have been collected and published (as *Spirituality in Interfaith Dialogue*) in the hope that this would animate discussion in the churches on one of the more difficult and sensitive areas of interfaith relations.

Dialogue-Commission on World Mission and Evangelism (CWME): What does dialogue mean to the understanding and practice of mission? This has been a persistent question within ecumenical discussions, and has led to controversies at both the Nairobi and Vancouver assemblies. CWME and Dialogue have defined the words "dialogue" and "mission" in ways which are not mutually exclusive. Christian witness takes place in every genuine dialogue; all true mission is dialogical. But the practice of dialogue, and the theology arising from this practice, have also raised deeper theological questions about the Christian understanding of other faiths (the area of theology of religions), and about Christian beliefs and theological formulations which do not take serious account of the reality of other people's beliefs. What are some of these deeper theological questions, and how may they usefully be pursued?

The 50th anniversary of the world mission conference held in Tambaram, Madras, India, in 1938 provided the opportunity. Dialogue and CWME jointly sponsored a "return visit" to Tambaram in commemoration of the event, and followed this up with a consultation on dialogue and mission. This has helped to define some of the primary theological issues in this area which should be examined over the coming years.

Dialogue also facilitated the participation of persons of other faiths at the world mission conference at San Antonio in May 1989 and, at a less formal level, collaborated with the Commission of the Churches on International Affairs in an initial exploration of the role of religion in conflict situations.

Dialogue-Lutheran World Federation: Member churches, especially those in the Western hemisphere, have shown growing interest in and concern about New Religious Movements. As these movements (especially those originating from Asia) have had such an influence on youth in Europe and North America, the LWF, also based at the Ecumenical Centre in Geneva, has also been studying the phenomenon.

The Dialogue Sub-unit and the LWF jointly facilitated a meeting in September 1986 in Amsterdam, the Netherlands, which brought together experts on these movements, sociologists and persons closely related to some of the movements themselves. The churches' attitude and approach to these movements were discussed, and the findings have been published for use in the churches.

Emerging trends and brief evaluation

At both the Nairobi and Vancouver assemblies dialogue became a controversial issue, reflecting the sharp differences which continue to exist among the churches in their theological approach to religious plurality. In recent years the Sub-unit on Dialogue has facilitated discussion of these issues through its study process on "My Neighbour's Faith — and Mine", and the important theology of religions consultation held in Baar, Switzerland. This work should provide a useful basis for the discussions which will follow the Canberra assembly.

Since the Vancouver assembly WCC member churches have taken an increasing interest in interfaith dialogue, and there is a greater awareness of plurality. Churches have begun to take interfaith work seriously in their own ministry, and have made financial commitments to the WCC's work on dialogue — although we are still far from being financially self-sufficient. At the theological level there is a lively debate on the theology of religions, with books and articles on the question of plurality appearing regularly.

On the other hand, there is also increasing conservatism within all religious communities, and the use of religious sentiment for political and social ends is on the rise. The pressures of living together in today's world have also threatened the identity of specific communities, sometimes resulting in a withdrawal from engagement in the pluralistic world. Political considerations strongly influence interfaith relations in a number of nations today.

The working group on Dialogue at its meeting in Casablanca in 1989 studied the present status of each of its interfaith relationships and made suggestions for the future. These include a more active promotion of dialogue in the local context, the need for dialogue at different levels and on more difficult and controversial questions, and the need for emphasis and closer collaboration on issues of justice, peace and human rights.

Since Vancouver the Dialogue staff have travelled widely, conducting seminars, workshops and consultations and encountering along the way many within the church, and in other faith communities, who are committed to, and engaged in, dialogue. A more organized network needs to be compiled of such "dialogue persons" in each geographical area and for each religious community. Not everything has been possible. Limited resources have prevented the Sub-unit from engaging the question of "ideologies", and from having a more active programme in the areas of traditional religions and North Asian religions.

As we look at the world situation beyond Canberra, and the possible developments within and between religious communities, the need to animate, foster and promote dialogue among these communities will undoubtedly remain an important priority for the churches and for the WCC.

Unit II
Justice and Service

Unit II — "Justice and Service" — is called "to assist the churches in combating poverty, injustice and oppression and to facilitate ecumenical co-operation in service to human need and in promoting freedom, justice, peace, human dignity and world community". This is a broad and powerful mandate, challenging the sub-units and programmes of Unit II both to respond to immediate human need and to struggle against the forces which create death and despair.

The Vancouver assembly considered matters related to the mandate of Unit II in several of the issue groups, particularly "Healing and Sharing Life in Community" (group IV) and "Confronting Threats to Peace and Survival" (group V). But the assembly did more than formulate recommendations in these specific areas. The report of the assembly's Programme Guidelines Committee called upon the Council: "To engage member churches in a conciliar process of mutual *commitment (covenant) to justice, peace and the integrity of all creation* should be a priority for World Council programmes" and to explore the "links as well as the tensions between the goals of justice, peace and the well-being of creation... from biblical, socio-economic and political perspectives."

For Unit II the call to churches, and to the World Council of Churches, to make the issues of justice, peace and the integrity of creation a priority in their work has led to new programmatic thrusts, and to a reorientation and new convergence in sub-unit work and activities in response to changing world situations.

In the years since the Vancouver assembly the world has indeed undergone many changes. Violence and repression continue to characterize life in many countries in the world; Southern Africa, the Horn of Africa, Central America, the Middle East and Indochina are only the most well-known cases. In dozens of countries people live in fear — fear of war, fear of persecution, fear of starvation. Despite peace initiatives in

Southern Africa, the Middle East, Central America and Southwest Asia in the mid-1980s, most of the wars continue. But wars are only the most obvious manifestation of the forces of death. In the South the weight of oppressive economic structures and the massive international debt threaten the future of whole generations of children. In the North drug addiction and consumerism give rise to hopelessness and despair, while Northern governments seek to protect themselves from responsibility and even from the awareness of what is happening to human beings elsewhere as a consequence of their political and economic actions. Racism is still thriving in many parts of the world. National and ethnic identity is an increasingly divisive factor in countries of both East and West. And all of these political and economic forces are affecting the air we breathe, the water we drink, the very planet on which we live. In the years since Vancouver there has been a growing realization that the resources of mother earth are finite, and that if we continue to use them with no thought of future generations, human existence itself is threatened. The forces of death are very strong.

But there are also signs of hope. In 1989 prospects for a free and independent Namibia required the concerted action of the churches to monitor and advocate for a democratic process, even while assisting over 40,000 Namibian refugees to return to their homes. In the Soviet Union and Eastern Europe, new leadership and policies of *glasnost* and *perestroika* have given rise to political and economic changes that would have been unthinkable a decade ago. Indigenous people are mobilizing in efforts to reclaim their land and their dignity. The growing importance of "green" (environmentalist) parties and the increased attention given to environmental issues are reshaping national and local political agendas in the North.

Unit II was created to respond to the needs of the world by assisting the churches in their struggle and service. Since Vancouver the churches have moved in new and powerful ways to confront the causes of death and to minister to those in need. While they have always been in the forefront of providing relief and assistance to those in need, the churches now are increasingly taking initiatives to address the root causes which produce suffering. For example, the Programme to Combat Racism (PCR) brought together in 1987 church leaders and liberation movements in Southern Africa to consider ways of working together to confront the evil of apartheid. While talk about root causes, advocacy and solidarity is relatively easy, in fact this witness is often dangerous for the churches and the individuals involved. And at times this witness is divisive, as churches struggle with how the biblical call for justice may be translated into actions by individual Christians and by churches.

Just as the churches live in different settings and contexts and respond to different challenges the Unit II programme thrust is a multifaceted one, but most fundamentally the work of Unit II focuses on the *unity* of the church. The work of its sub-units has shown again and again that the ecumenical movement is strengthened by common endeavours in the areas of justice and service. Churches with serious theological differences over baptism or the ordination of women, for example, are often able to work together in formulating an ecumenical strategy on issues of economic justice, or in serving the immediate needs of refugees, or in confronting racism in their own countries. As the "Justice, Peace and the Integrity of Creation" (JPIC) preparatory group has stated, "surrounding the JPIC process is a call for unity in terms of mission. The image of a broken church in a broken world continues to haunt us." Thus the programmes of Unit II respond to our broken world in its pain and suffering, but also to the broken church in its need for reconciliation and unity.

The Programme Unit on Justice and Service consists of five sub-units which have been established over a forty-year period: the Commission of the Churches on International Affairs (CCIA); the Commission on Inter-Church Aid, Refugee and World Service (CICARWS); the Programme to Combat Racism (PCR); the Commission on the Churches' Participation in Development (CCPD); and the Christian Medical Commission (CMC). These sub-units are supplemented by several unit-wide programmes, set up in response to particular needs, notably the Human Rights Resource Office for Latin America (HRROLA) and, since Vancouver, Justice, Peace and the Integrity of Creation (JPIC).

While the programmes and sub-units of Unit II were created in response to particular situations and issues, one of the Unit's trends since the Vancouver assembly has been the increasing coherence of its approach to the world. Thus work on JPIC has provided a framework for seeing the different aspects of the Unit's mandate as part of a common effort. Co-operation and co-ordination on an operational level between the sub-units has enabled a multi-faceted response to specific issues. For example, support for the churches in Namibia has required the combined efforts of PCR, CCIA and several desks within CICARWS. Certainly the churches in Namibia do not divide their work along WCC sub-unit lines; the ability to respond in a coherent expression of ecumenical support is an important indication of the progress being made to overcome programmatic divisions.

Close co-operation between HRROLA, CICARWS and CCIA has enabled strong co-ordinated advocacy on behalf of those struggling for human rights in Latin America. In preparing its submissions to the United Nations Human Rights Commission, CCIA draws on the concerns and experience of other sub-units in Unit II. Thus in 1989 CCIA presented church concerns on the international debt and on refugee issues to the Human Rights Commission. And increasingly the sub-units are working together to ensure that issues of concern to women (such as economic justice for women, women's health, women under racism, and refugee women) are addressed in a coherent fashion. These cut across sub-unit lines and require collaborative efforts.

The work of Unit II is overseen by the Unit executive group which is composed of the officers of the Unit committee and the moderators and directors of the five sub-unit commissions. During the period since Vancouver the concept of an enlarged Unit II executive group, including all the officers and directors of the sub-units, has emerged. Two meetings of this enlarged group have been held in the period 1983-89. Since Vancouver the Unit executive group has placed special emphasis on encouraging collaboration between the sub-units and in identifying areas needing common reflection and action. In addition to its ongoing work of monitoring and overseeing the programmatic work of the sub-units, the group also provides guidance to the unit-wide programmes which do not have their own commissions or working groups.

Since Vancouver two major WCC consultations of particular concern to Unit II have been held: one on interchurch aid, refugee and world service in November 1986 in Larnaca, Cyprus, and the other on ecumenical sharing of resources, in El Escorial, Spain, in October 1987. These were important not only in reshaping the orientation of two major WCC programmes, but also in providing momentum for common approaches within Unit II. After the Larnaca and El Escorial consultations it has become increasingly difficult to see the world solely in terms of sub-unit emphases. Service cannot be seen in isolation from advocacy; questions related to funding of ecumenical projects cannot be viewed apart from other manifestations of solidarity.

The themes of the two consultations ("Diakonia 2000: Called to be Neighbours" and "Koinonia: Sharing Life in a World Community") were complementary. Service and sharing are two sides of the same coin, two responses of the ecumenical community to the challenges of today — and tomorrow. Both consultations provided input for decades of work by the churches and by the WCC. The need to restructure relationships between churches in the North and South, to support initiatives of churches struggling at the local level, and for an integrated approach to problems of poverty, injustice, violence and environmental degradation came to the fore in both consultations.

Perhaps more than with most WCC consultations, the needs and actions identified were addressed to the churches, while the WCC itself was asked to play primarily a facilitating and empowering role. The messages from both consultations have been echoed by churches in later regional meetings. The two consultations have been described separately in this report (the El Escorial meeting on "Koinonia" has been discussed on pp.48ff. together with the other elements of the programme on ecumenical sharing of resources, which is lodged in the General Secretariat). But they should not be viewed in isolation from each other; their outcomes and challenges are complementary. And, more importantly, they both reflect the yearnings of people for justice, peace and the integrity of creation and for ecumenical structures which can support them in their struggles.

DIAKONIA 2000: CALLED TO BE NEIGHBOURS

In November 1986 about 300 people — church leaders, community organizers, agency representatives, WCC staff — gathered in Larnaca, Cyprus, to discuss the future of interchurch aid, refugee and world service. It had been 20 years since the previous such consultation — 20 years of change and of mounting pressures on the churches' diaconal work. Thus the participants gathered with a sense of urgency and an awareness that time was running out for the churches to address the many global challenges and to prepare for the future.

The theme of the consultation reflected this concern with the future. The emphasis on neighbours reminded participants that all are the people of God, and that all are called to diaconal ministry. The theme of neighbours was developed in the Bible studies and deepened in the unique participatory process of the meeting.

The objectives of the consultation were to develop:

— a clearer view of the world situation as a basis for further analysis and study;
— a theological understanding which, though not committing every church, serves as guidance for further action and relationships;
— an exchange of actual approaches and needs which can serve as a basis and orientation for learning and sharing; and, finally,

— concrete suggestions for the work of the churches at different levels, out of which would come the new directions and agenda for CICARWS in the next 20 years.

Larnaca was intended to be different from most consultations which emphasize the giving of information to participants; it sought rather to use the many and varied experiences of the participants themselves as the principal resource, and its issues, direction and conclusions were to come largely from them. The rich mix of participants ensured that controversial ideas would emerge; yet all were committed to the common search for a new vision of diakonia and to common work to this end.

Following plenaries and intense work in small groups, six "clusters" were identified, each incorporating a number of questions. The clusters, which formed the basis for subsequent work and for the final recommendations, were:

1) affirming the witness of the local churches;
2) equipping the churches for the year 2000;
3) moving towards global diakonia;
4) deepening the prophetic diakonia;
5) focusing on people; and
6) committing ourselves to life together.

Hundreds of recommendations were formulated by the small groups as well as by the regional and issue groups; but certain common themes emerged: the witness of the local churches is the foundation of all diakonia, and the local churches must be strengthened and must become more inclusive; in particular, women and youth must be given more responsibility in directing the churches' diaconal ministry; the necessity of deepening the reflection on the theological bases of diakonia was repeatedly emphasized, as was the necessity of dialogue with other faiths.

By listening to each other, and by recognizing the diversity in Christian service, participants developed a vision of diakonia based on the struggle for survival, liberation, dignity, justice, peace and reconciliation. While expressions of ecumenical solidarity are needed, this struggle must fundamentally belong to those who are oppressed. Christians and churches are called to reconsider their diakonia in the political context; they are challenged to advocacy, to address root causes and, where human lives and dignity are at stake, to provide sanctuary. CICARWS was asked to promote global diakonia through awareness-building and networking, as well as to help give expression to prophetic challenge. The challenge to Christians themselves is a great one; as one participant pointedly said:

"With or without the churches, the people are struggling. The churches must decide which side they are on."

Larnaca emphasized the need to look at people and to shift priorities from financial to human resources. South-South dialogue and exchanges were viewed as fundamental, even as the "North-South" terminology was rejected by many. Problems and inequality in the North were recognized, as was the need to respond to these problems through ecumenical fellowship. The present "project system" was widely criticized, and participants expressed their commitment to work together to create a system for sharing resources based on mutual trust and accountability.

While the recommendations included many specific suggestions for the churches and for the WCC, the "spirit of Larnaca" was much more than a collection of recommendations. Rather, Larnaca embodied the hopes and aspirations of Christians in all parts of the world to reorient their diaconal mission in fundamentally new directions. These challenges have been picked up by CICARWS and by other WCC sub-units in many concrete ways, as the churches themselves struggle to translate the Larnaca message into action.

Diakonia 2000: Called to be Neighbours is the official report of the consultation while *My Neighbour — Myself* presents some of the issues in which the churches are engaged, through interviews, photographs and creative cartoons.

JUSTICE, PEACE AND THE INTEGRITY OF CREATION (JPIC)

The issue group on "Struggling for Justice and Human Dignity" of the Vancouver assembly recommended in its final report "that the churches at all levels — congregations, dioceses/synods, networks of Christian groups and base communities — together with the WCC, enter into a covenant in a conciliar process:
— to confess Christ, the life of the world, and the Lord over the idols of our time, the Good Shepherd who 'brings life and life in all its fullness' for his people and for all creation;
— to resist the demonic powers of death inherent in racism, sexism, class domination, caste oppression and militarism..."
The assembly's Programme Guidelines Committee took up that proposal and declared that "to engage member churches in a conciliar process of mutual commitment (covenant) to justice, peace and the integrity of all creation should be a priority for World Council programmes. The

foundation of this emphasis should be confessing Christ as the life of the world and Christian resistance to the demonic powers of death." The text repeats the examples quoted above and adds to them "violations of human rights, and the misuse of science and technology". The committee underlined as well "that new initiatives are needed to promote education for peace, justice and a caring attitude to nature".

Since Vancouver the WCC central and executive committees have deepened the understanding of JPIC as a *process* calling the churches to a new level of united response to the common threats opposing the wholeness of life. Unlike other WCC programmes or emphases, JPIC is not fundamentally about drafting of documents, or convening of meetings, or supporting of projects — although these may be part of the process. Most fundamentally JPIC is about drawing connections, about weaving together faith responses from the many particular contexts around the world into a diverse but unified whole. JPIC is about enabling and challenging churches and ecumenical groups working on particular issues to see the connections between their work and the larger struggles for survival and peace on the planet. Thus a group working for a nuclear-free Pacific can come to see the relationship between its work for the preservation of the region's oceans and land and the economic and political forces pushing for nuclear expansion. Thus a European group working to educate the public on the consequences of the international debt is challenged to draw connections between economic structures, militarism and the environmental impact of the debt burden.

JPIC is also about participation. Since the Vancouver assembly the call to join in the JPIC process has been widespread. Invitations were sent not only to churches, but also to national councils of churches, regional ecumenical organizations and Christian World Communions to take action on the three inter-related faces of the threat to the future of humankind. JPIC has taken on a concrete reality through several regional meetings; these have affirmed the central thrust of the process, and enriched it through stories of regional challenge and struggle.

Education and communication are at the centre of the JPIC process. The JPIC programme has published two explanatory brochures. It publishes three kits of resource materials per year on its various concerns. These contain papers for theological reflection, Bible studies, and liturgical and other materials for adaptation and use by local churches and groups. It also publishes a quarterly newsletter, *Forum*, in English, French, German and Spanish, to communicate how the process is working in local contexts throughout the world, and to share stories reflecting the struggle for justice, peace and the integrity of creation.

A major concern of the JPIC programme has been the planning and holding of the world convocation on "Justice, Peace and the Integrity of Creation" in Seoul, Republic of Korea, 5-12 March 1990.

About the relationship between the process initiated at Vancouver and the world convocation, the Geneva central committee (1987) said: "The 1990 world convocation for 'Justice, Peace and the Integrity of Creation' is a decisive step towards fulfilling the mandate of the sixth assembly of the WCC in Vancouver. It marks an important stage on the road towards common binding pronouncements and actions on the urgent questions of the survival of humankind."

And the WCC executive committee meeting in Istanbul, Turkey (March 1988), said:

> The purpose of the world convocation will be to make a theological affirmation on justice, peace and the integrity of creation, and to identify the major threats to life in these three areas and show their interconnectedness, and make and propose to the churches acts of mutual commitment in response to them.

The JPIC preparatory group for the world convocation, which included representatives of WCC member churches, the Roman Catholic Church, Christian World Communions and Regional Ecumenical Organizations, met several times, beginning in June 1988, to plan for the convocation. In its planning it did two things in particular.

First, it structured the programme of the convocation — its worship and plenary presentations on the issues of justice, peace and the integrity of creation — around seven moments of the liturgy, both to give cohesion to the programme and to mark the movement from deliberation to common commitment. Each of the seven full days of the meeting had its own liturgical emphasis; these were:

— *praise and adoration* (day 1) recalling the mighty saving acts of God as Creator, Redeemer and Sustainer;

— *repentance, confession and announcing of forgiveness* (day 2) hearing the stories of those testifying to their own experience of suffering from injustice, war and the damage done to the environment; and hearing in them the call for a radical change of direction (repentance) and return to God;

— *proclamation of the word of hope* (day 3) listening, especially through Bible study presentations, to God's message of hope for humanity and the whole creation;

— *affirmation of faith* (day 4) responding in faith to God's word of hope by confessing Jesus Christ as the life of the world, and in declaring resistance to the powers of death;
— *intercession* (day 5) remembering concrete situations calling for prayer and commitment for action;
— *commitment* (day 6) covenanting between churches, and between groups from several regions and national situations, to engage in specific actions on issues and problems of mutual concern;
— *covenanting and sending forth* (day 7) bringing the convocation to a climax with a service that gathers up the affirmations and covenants which have been agreed upon, and expresses the participants' commitment to discuss these, and their practical implications, within the churches and ecumenical organizations or groups.

Second, the preparatory group produced a three-part document for the convocation, the first part analyzing the threats to life in our time and sketching possible responses of the churches, and the second and third parts proposing drafts of the affirmations and acts of covenanting which the convocation would be called upon to make. Using this material, the convocation affirmed:

— that all exercise of power is accountable to God;
— God's option for the poor;
— the equal value of all races and peoples;
— that male and female are created in the image of God;
— that truth is at the foundation of a community of free people;
— the peace of Jesus Christ;
— the creation as beloved of God;
— that the earth is the Lord's;
— the dignity and commitment of the younger generation;
— that human rights are given by God.

It also made commitments for action towards the following goals:

— a just economic order and liberation from the bondage of foreign debt;
— the true security of all nations and peoples, and a culture of non-violence;
— preserving the gift of the earth's atmosphere, and building a culture which can live in harmony with creation's integrity;
— eradicating racism and discrimination on all levels and for all people, and dismantling patterns of behaviour which perpetuate the sin of racism.

The WCC central committee meeting in March 1990 just after the convocation made, among others, the following recommendations to express the need for a continuing commitment to the JPIC process within the WCC:

1. That the central committee re-affirm the long-term commitment of the WCC to the JPIC process up to and beyond the Canberra assembly. Structural arrangements within the ongoing work of the Council and resources for its continuation should be found in order to provide a centre of exchange, information and challenge for churches and movements.
2. That the central committee commend the convocation final document to the churches for study and action, with reports on their reactions and progress in the JPIC process to be brought back to the WCC, if possible to the Canberra assembly.
3. That the WCC facilitate regional JPIC meetings and encourage regional bodies to elaborate their own contextual contributions to the concretization of the covenants.
4. That the central committee recommend that the Sub-unit on Faith and Order as well as other relevant sub-units, with regard to the JPIC process: (a) further explore the concepts of covenanting and conciliarity; (b) continue and strengthen work on the question of the interconnectedness of ethics and ecclesiology. Such work must begin at once in preparation for the seventh assembly and later continue in connection with the upcoming fifth world conference on Faith and Order in 1993.
5. Since JPIC is at the heart of the ecumenical vision for the next millennium, the central committee recommends that (a) the Assembly Planning Committee ensure substantial room at the WCC assembly in Canberra for reflection on JPIC in worship, plenaries, sections and sub-sections; we note with appreciation work already begun in this regard; (b) further cooperation with the Roman Catholic Church on all levels be sought; (c) the Canberra assembly renew a call for commitment to the JPIC process, emphasizing further exploration of the meaning of covenanting, and the conciliar process related to JPIC, inter-regional dialogue, interfaith dialogue, networking among movements, and dialogue with experts relevant to JPIC issues, including scientists, politicians, economists, etc.

HUMAN RIGHTS RESOURCES OFFICE FOR LATIN AMERICA (HRROLA)

"Our delegation was particularly saddened to learn of the increasing attacks on Christian communities and programmes and social projects operated by the churches." Thus the central committee in Buenos Aires, 1985, expressed itself in a substantial letter addressed to the churches in Central America — a region caught up in a violent maelstrom of repression against civilian populations. And an ecumenical delegation visited Paraguay, the continent's oldest dictatorship, in 1988, just before the fall of General Stroessner. At its press conference, the international group expressed firm support to the churches in their defence of the land rights of the Paraguayan peasant and indigenous communities.

HRROLA has been closely involved in these and other forms of the WCC's critical support to churches in the Latin American and Caribbean regions. In face of the spread of repressive regimes and military coups in the 1970s, especially in the Southern Cone region of Latin America, the WCC widened its emergency support to the churches in their defence of those affected by severe violations of human rights by setting up this Unit II programme (in 1975). HRROLA's mandate calls on the WCC to help the churches in Latin America in their work to defend human dignity; to express moral support for these churches on a wide ecumenical basis; to provide systematic information on the human rights situation in the region; and to facilitate and encourage the churches in Latin America to share their rich insights and experience in human rights work across national and regional borders. Its mandate has been renewed several times, including fresh guidelines and emphases underlining an increasing co-operation with the Regional Ecumenical Organizations. Throughout the 1980s the churches reported serious and critical deterioration of human rights in the region, especially in Central America and the Andean area, and responded with pioneering witness and service, calling on the WCC for strong ecumenical solidarity.

Significant changes which have directly affected the work of the churches in human rights have occurred recently in the Latin American and Caribbean regions. Some initiatives, such as those which started the peace process in Central America, still stimulate great hope for those most affected by civil war and violence, i.e. the civilian populations. Other more sinister developments, such as those associated with military attempts to subvert civilian rule, renew fears of continued bloodshed and despair.

Argentina, Brazil, Chile and other countries have returned to civilian rule. The deep-seated economic interests and entrenched institutional power long enjoyed by elites and the military castes in several of the region's countries, are being freshly and effectively challenged in societies where relative freedom of expression and of association has been restored, along with other civil and political rights.

However, the underlying problems which threaten the new democracies impede the full realization of rights and shake the political stability of many Latin American and Caribbean states. On the surface are the continuing dramatic violations of human rights: extrajudicial killings, disappearances, torture, harassment, the persecution of churches, labour unions and popular organizations. The instances of the systematic detention and disappearance of persons in Peru are the highest in the world, according to the UN Working Group on Disappeared Persons. Paramilitary groups have acted with impunity in Colombia, where the rate of political killings has reached alarming proportions in the past two years.

Behind the manifestations of social discontent, of renewed repression and human rights violations, there are three fresh developments which pose serious challenges to the churches and other actors in the human rights area in Latin America and the Caribbean: the assertiveness of the military, the crushing debt crisis and the increasing weight of narco-economics.

The physical presence of representatives of the WCC constituency has been of great importance to churches in crisis situations in El Salvador, Nicaragua, Haiti, Chile, Argentina, Uruguay, Paraguay and Honduras; here the witness, and indeed martyrdom, of men and women has enriched the oikoumene immeasurably in recent years.

Accompanying such pastoral visits have been efforts to gather fresh and accurate information on critical human rights situations in the region, bringing such reports, in collaboration with the CCIA, to the attention of the United Nations Commission on Human Rights and the ecumenical constituency. Guatemala, Peru, Chile, Haiti and Honduras are the most grave instances where torture, disappearance of persons and extrajudicial killings have occurred. Many churches, groups and human rights bodies have built up valuable expertise and organizational strength in the struggle to render effective assistance to victims of human rights abuses, and also to work for a return to democratic rule. Much sharing of expertise in the fields of medical rehabilitation, computerized information management and juridical assistance has been done with human rights groups in the region. HRROLA has focused on enabling such efforts, especially in the inter-regional exchange of analyses, experiences and mutual assistance.

A visit for this purpose took place in early 1987 among Latin American and Asian church leaders who were experienced advocates in the defence and promotion of human rights in their own countries, which included El Salvador, the Philippines, Argentina, Taiwan, Chile and South Korea.

Pastor Carlos Sánchez of San Salvador told one group of Filipinos: "The people of this country look exactly like our people... Your land also looks like our land. And the heat is the same. So it should not surprise you that our problems are also the same as yours." Indeed the sharing showed common features: the structures of domination generally revolved around military power; the issue of socio-economic justice lies at the root of popular resistance; human rights groups work in remarkably similar ways; and some of the churches rediscover new roots of faith and discipleship in the struggle for human rights.

There has been fruitful co-operation with the Latin American Council of Churches (CLAI), the Caribbean Conference of Churches (CCC) and with related human rights networks to promote international standards for the training of persons for human rights work, and to strengthen the churches themselves for human rights advocacy and service. In October 1989 a major meeting of ecumenical human rights bodies, sponsored by the WCC, CLAI and CCC, met in Ecuador to evaluate critically work in the past decade, to identify present trends in the region as they affect the respect for human rights, and to plan together to meet future challenges. HRROLA has sought throughout, in close co-operation with CICARWS, to garner financial support from the worldwide community to meet both the emergency and programmatic needs of the churches in the field of human rights.

In 1988 the central committee appointed a small task force to work with HRROLA to evaluate the impact of HRROLA's experience for the Council's human rights work. This report was presented to the executive committee in March 1990 and will form the basis for HRROLA's future work.

COMMISSION OF THE CHURCHES ON INTERNATIONAL AFFAIRS (CCIA)

Mandate and vision

The mandate and vision of the Commission are defined in its aims and by-laws as follows:

> It shall be the task of the Commission to witness to the lordship of Christ over human beings and history by serving people in the field of international relations and promoting reconciliation and oneness of human beings by creation; to God's gracious and redemptive action in history; and to the assurance of the coming kingdom of God in Jesus Christ. This service is

demanded by the church's participation in the continuing ministry of Christ in the world of priestly intercession, prophetic judgment, the arousing of hope and conscience and pastoral care.

Among the major functions of CCIA, as reformulated in the by-laws approved by the central committee in 1985, are the following:
— advice and assistance in the formulation of the WCC's policies on international affairs;
— monitoring, analysis and interpretation of national and international political developments, especially as they affect the life and witness of the churches;
— promotion of peace, resolution of conflicts and disarmament;
— study and action with regard to human rights;
— representations to intergovernmental bodies (United Nations, etc.) and governments on behalf of the WCC.

Structure

Out of the conviction that concern for social and political affairs is part of the mission of the church, the CCIA was established in 1946 as a joint, semi-autonomous agency of the International Missionary Council (IMC) and the Provisional Committee of the WCC. When the IMC merged with the WCC in 1961, CCIA became one of the commissions of the Council. In the structural re-organization after 1971 it became a sub-unit (with its own by-laws as a commission) within Programme Unit II on Justice and Service. The Commission's special relationship with the General Secretariat must be mentioned: its function of assisting and advising the WCC in the formulation of policies on political issues makes it directly accountable to the general secretary and the governing bodies of the WCC. In practice this means that the formulation of the various forms of action, and often the initiatives for such action, are with CCIA. Careful preparation of public issues is made by CCIA before the meetings of WCC governing bodies with a view to making specific recommendations for action and to providing the necessary background information.

Programmatic emphases

Before describing in detail CCIA's programmatic emphases during this period, some general comments on its functioning may be useful. A review committee appointed by the central committee in 1979 said: "It is important that CCIA work should be considered more as a continuing service to the churches in the field of international conflicts and tensions.

This service should be considered as a permanent thrust of the work of the CCIA, and not as a specific programme."

The day-to-day functions of CCIA, which include monitoring of events and developments, response to crisis situations and advice and assistance on policy formulations, fall within "service" to the Council and thus cannot usually be described in terms of programmes.

In a way the whole world is the area of concern for CCIA. Of course, this may appear presumptuous. But it is a fact that all political developments taking place in any part of the world could be of interest to the fellowship of the churches, and therefore to CCIA. A development which may appear to be minor at a particular time may be the beginning of something major in the future; a dramatic event today might stem from previously unnoticed events. There is a constant demand to be familiar with developments, especially as they affect the life and witness of the churches. Any political development nationally and internationally can affect their fellowship; strains and strengths can be noticed only by carefully monitoring events in the situations where the churches are called upon to witness.

In 1985 the central committee commended to the churches for study a document prepared by CCIA on "The Role of the World Council of Churches in International Affairs". This presents the theological rationale for the WCC's role in international affairs and deals with the basis for action, major areas of concern, various forms of action, special role of public statements, the WCC's role in the UN system and implications for the unity of the churches. It draws on the affirmations, findings and thinking of various parts of the WCC. It underlines the linkages between work in international affairs and that connected with mission and unity. The document concludes:

> As churches and Christians become engaged in human problems and issues they find themselves in a form of unity that transcends confessional backgrounds, ecclesiastical barriers and national boundaries. Unity which has been brought about as a result of engagement in social and political struggle represents a significant trend in the ecumenical movement in recent years.

CCIA faces several problems and challenges in being an actor on the world scene — however modest that role may be — while being primarily an organ of a council of churches. It is challenged to have competence, a degree of specialization and information comparable to those of secular organizations and governments. Naturally, CCIA tends to show more competence on issues and situations in which the churches themselves are actively engaged. The WCC speaks more often, and is listened to more carefully, on such issues and situations.

Major areas of tension and conflict which have received considerable attention from CCIA after Vancouver have included Southern Africa, the Middle East, Central America, the Horn of Africa, Indochina and Eastern Europe. Among national situations which have deserved careful monitoring and responses, the following may be specially mentioned: the Philippines, Korea, the People's Republic of China, Sri Lanka, Namibia, Sudan, Uganda, Lebanon, Cyprus, Grenada, Nicaragua, El Salvador, New Caledonia, Fiji, Poland and the USSR.

A significant initiative was taken by CCIA on peace and the reunification of Korea. This began in a public way with the holding of an international consultation on peace and justice in North-East Asia, in Tozanso, Japan, in October 1984. This set in motion the "Tozanso process", an ecumenical initiative the immediate aim of which was to create a forum for Christians of North and South to meet face-to-face and to contribute towards efforts for peace and the reunification of the divided Korean peninsula. Following a CCIA visit to North Korea in November 1985, representatives of WCC member churches and the National Council of Churches in Korea (NCCK) took part in a CCIA-sponsored encounter with Christians from North Korea in September 1986 in Glion, Switzerland. This was the first such meeting since the division of Korea and happened with the acquiescence of both governments — though technically in violation of South Korea's national security law which makes contact with North Koreans a capital offence.

In February 1988 the NCCK adopted a "Declaration of the Churches of Korea on National Reunification and Peace"; this gave the struggle for reunification a theological underpinning, confessed the sin of hatred underlying the division, affirmed basic principles for national reunification, proposed tasks for both governments of Korea, and committed the churches of Korea to a programme of action towards a jubilee year for peace and reunification in 1995, the 50th anniversary of the liberation of Korea.

The proposals from the NCCK declaration were welcomed by the Korean Christian Federation (KCF) and North Korean delegates at the second CCIA-sponsored consultation on "Peace and Reunification" at Glion in November 1988. The Glion "Declaration on Peace and the Reunification of Korea" supported the decision of churches in both North and South Korea to observe 1995 as the year of jubilee for unification, and to observe each year a common day of prayer for peace.

After the initial visit by the CCIA in 1985, ecumenical delegations from the USA, Japan and Canada have visited North Korea. These visits have helped to break, to some extent, the isolation of the small Christian community in North Korea. Representatives of the KCF have participated in meetings of CCIA, the Christian Peace Conference and the National Council of the Churches of Christ in the USA.

In the KCF the ecumenical community has found a responsible partner for efforts for reunification. There are new opportunities for public worship for Christians in North Korea, and for the building of churches.

The central committee in its meeting in July 1989 adopted a policy statement on "Peace and the Reunification of Korea" which noted:

> There has been good progress in the struggle for peace and the reunification of Korea during the years since the Tozanso consultation. It is a credit to the Korean churches and the solidarity shown by ecumenical partners that so many positive steps have been successfully taken. But there is still a long way to go. The immense tragedy of the division of Korea is still little known. The disproportionate human cost paid by the Korean people for the cold war and geopolitics is little known. The continuing agony of the separation of millions is little known. The potential for escalation of the conflict even to a nuclear conflagration is little known. It is in highlighting these concerns for worldwide recognition that the WCC and the ecumenical community can make a unique contribution.

The initiative with regard to the reunification of Korea is specially highlighted because it points to the type of conflict in which, and the level at which, a body like the WCC can intervene. It is a conflict which governments or intergovernmental bodies have done very little to resolve. To some extent CCIA has been able to promote people-to-people contacts between North and South Korea. The policy statement by the central committee in 1989 is significant also because it is the first of its kind by an international body. The importance of such an initiative for the unity of the churches also deserves mention.

In different ways substantial efforts have been made to facilitate negotiations in the conflicts in Sudan, Ethiopia and Sri Lanka. While the CCIA/WCC may not be able to play the role of mediator in many conflicts, it can act as a channel of communication between the parties involved and thus promote possibilities for negotiations and peaceful resolution of conflicts. A number of initiatives and actions of this nature will necessarily remain unpublicized.

Disarmament and militarism continued to be major areas of concentration for CCIA. The Commission has identified "stimulating and helping public efforts for disarmament" and "support for current bilateral or multilateral arms negotiations" as two of its priorities.

It has analyzed the implications of the new emerging geopolitical situation for disarmament. While there are some hopeful signs, the arms race continues to escalate. The search for common security among nations, as undergirded by the biblical notion of shalom, guides the efforts of CCIA in the area of disarmament. The churches should take the lead in helping develop a new international ethos which offers not only a critique of the current order but also hopeful and rational alternatives to it. Work has already begun in some churches on the notion of a "just peace" as a counterpart to traditional concepts of the "just war".

CCIA has continued its study of militarization. A dramatic growth in militarization — in which politics, societal and international structures are increasingly coming under the influence of military values and control — can be observed throughout the world. Some countries have recently experienced a transition to democratic forms of government, and this development has given new hopes; but they have also proved how difficult it is to reorient the military system towards democracy in societies where militarization has already achieved extensive social and economic penetration. A consultation in October 1989 examined the new prospects and trends in disarmament and demilitarization and their implications for the churches' ministry in peace-making. A special concern has been the militarization of the Pacific.

The Human Rights Advisory Group (HRAG) of CCIA was constituted with a new mandate from the Vancouver assembly to "act as a means for churches and Christians to share experiences with regard to human rights, as well as a place for challenge and stimulation for churches in the struggle for human rights", and "to propose intensive ecumenical work in this field, in particular regarding special human rights topics, such as the problem of torture, religious liberty, etc." The first meeting of HRAG identified three topics as requiring special attention: survival rights (the root causes of attacks against the integrity of human life); religious liberty (new trends and perspectives); militarization and demilitarization (limitations and opportunities in the struggle for human rights).

HRAG has examined various aspects of the current debate on religious liberty in detail. With the adoption of the Declaration on the Elimination of All Forms of Intolerance and Discrimination Based on Religion or Belief, the UN Human Rights Commission has adopted some measures for implementing a universal standard for religious liberty. There is renewed discussion on religious witness and practice in political and social life as an element of religious liberty. Religious revivalism, and the misuse of religious sentiments, are other issues of concern.

In its ongoing work CCIA has supported churches and church-related groups and institutions in their struggle for human rights through taking up human rights cases, the investigation of violations of human rights, and the publication of information and advocacy work within intergovernmental institutions and among non-governmental organizations (NGOs). Human rights work has been considerably strengthened through the creation of mechanisms and structures within member churches as well as national and regional councils of churches which make human rights a priority. The role of CCIA has been to work with and through these bodies for the realization of human rights. This methodology combines the responsibility of each member church for human rights work within its own area, with the responsibility of the ecumenical community to support and strengthen this work internationally through ecumenical solidarity.

CCIA is mandated to maintain contacts with international bodies and to represent the WCC in such bodies. For this purpose CCIA has formal consultative status with the UN and its agencies. It has provided, on a regular basis, both oral and written contributions to several UN bodies. Its most active participation has been in the UN Human Rights Commission and its sub-commission. It has maintained regular contacts, especially through its New York office (for UN liaison), with the UN Secretariat and Department of Political and Security Council Affairs. CCIA has participated in all major UN conferences and special sessions of the General Assembly, and often made substantive contributions to them and their preparatory committees. Its participation in the International Year of Peace (1986) activities and the Second Special Session on Disarmament (1988) may be mentioned. CCIA was honoured by the secretary-general of the UN in being designated as a peace messenger in the International Year of Peace. It has co-operated actively with a number of NGOs seeking to promote the aims and purposes of the UN. Much of the collaboration is carried out in the framework of the Conference of NGOs, which groups together about two hundred NGOs in consultative status with the UN. Through the CCIA accreditation procedure several church bodies have sent representatives to UN meetings. CCIA has also responded to requests from churches and church-related bodies for information on the UN and on specific actions of its agencies. Many churches and Regional Ecumenical Organizations have been particularly interested in the UN Human Rights Commission and the Committee of Twenty-Four (in the field of decolonization).

Changes, developments and special challenges

This period has seen significant changes in international relations. The major developments in international affairs are the result of new policies initiated by the Soviet Union in the last four years; the full implications of these policies are yet to be known, but certainly they have already made a profound impact on international relations. There have been policy changes in the relations of the super-powers, in regional conflicts and in the UN system. The dramatic and breathtaking events of 1989 in Eastern and Central Europe, closely following and accelerating the transformation within the Soviet Union, have altered the course of history. They have obviously brought new dimensions to the issues and the situations with which CCIA deals, demanding new perspectives and approaches.

The agreement on Namibia leading to the implementation of UN Security Council Resolution 435 has been possible mainly because of the new international climate. The independence of Namibia has been on the agenda of the WCC for a long time, and the WCC has steadfastly supported the struggle of the Namibian people. In co-operation with the Programme to Combat Racism (PCR) and the Christian Council of Namibia (CCN), CCIA organized a series of teams of international observers who visited Namibia prior to and during the elections in November 1989, and was represented at the independence celebrations in March 1990.

Another development of particular interest during the period is the expansion of religious liberty in several socialist societies. *Perestroika* and *glasnost* in the Soviet Union have been of direct advantage to the churches there. The changes in Eastern and Central Europe are of even greater significance to the churches.

Though not related to developments in the Soviet Union, special mention may be made here of the growth of relationships between the WCC and the churches in the People's Republic of China during this period. Churches in China were members of the WCC at the time of its founding, but withdrew from the activities of the ecumenical body in the 1950s. They were then isolated due to developments in China, notably the Cultural Revolution. Two official delegations from the WCC have visited the People's Republic of China, in 1985 and 1987, and there have been visits to the WCC from the China Christian Council. CCIA has played an active role in promoting these relations and has participated in both delegations.

Future orientation

CCIA celebrated its 40th anniversary in 1986. In spite of the changes in the world scene and in the ecumenical movement, the basic aim of the Commission has remained the same.

CCIA must continue to work on the basic tasks and major programme emphases described above. Over the years CCIA has been known as a specialized agency of the ecumenical movement dealing with international affairs. At a time when international issues are becoming even more complex, marked by fast and dramatic developments, it is necessary for the WCC to maintain and augment the resources of CCIA as a specialized instrument with a sufficient degree of autonomy to enable it to take initiatives. It will be necessary to strengthen its relationships with and within the UN system and with other NGOs, secular organizations, universities and research institutes.

In the coming period CCIA will have to take into account the profound changes that are taking place in the global scene, the shifts in the nature of national and international conflicts, the new agendas that are emerging as political issues, and the challenges which all these factors pose for the churches.

The changes in relations between the USA and the USSR have already been referred to. There are new prospects for arms control and disarmament. The general reduction in tensions in Europe, the pluralist development of policies in Eastern and Central Europe, the agreements for the withdrawal of Soviet troops, and the impending reunification of Germany have all altered perceptions of security in Europe, and called into question the rationale and future of both the North Atlantic Treaty Organization and the Warsaw Pact. But at the same time there is every evidence of the intensification of civil wars and low-intensity conflicts, with the militarization which they bring. The new international climate is conducive to resolution of regional conflicts — though some of them appear to be intractable. It is evident that CCIA will have to give even greater attention to peaceful resolution of conflicts. There are some conflicts, and some aspects of conflicts, in which the Commission can play a significant role in facilitating communication between the parties involved. CCIA will have to identify such conflicts.

Profound changes are taking place in Europe. The Single European Act of 1992 and the concept of a "Common European House" will usher in major changes, with implications for the rest of the world. This process will be affected considerably by the changes in Eastern and Central Europe. These will offer new challenges to the churches, and CCIA must find means to help the churches to respond to them. New possibilities are opening up for the churches in many countries within Europe and elsewhere, with considerable expansion of religious liberty and general human rights. Church-state relations in many of these countries are undergoing changes.

Another factor to be taken into account is the proliferation of ethno-nationalist conflicts and their increasing significance in international affairs. The importance of understanding ethnic conflict as a force shaping national and international affairs can no longer be denied. Ethnicity is at the centre of politics in country after country; it is a potent source of challenges to the internal cohesion of states and of tensions between them. In many ethnic conflicts religion plays an important role in providing ethnic identity, promoting sentiments for struggle and also in defending nationalism. The use and misuse of religious sentiments in ethnic conflicts thus have a direct bearing upon the life of many of the churches. In addition to their political consequences, there are effects on ecumenical relations. This will demand close attention by CCIA in the form of analysis, interpretation and assistance to the churches in the formulation of their responses.

Ecological issues are bound to influence political agendas in many countries and have emerged as international issues. Several of the churches are engaged in efforts for a better environment, and the political consequences and factors involved deserve scrutiny and action by CCIA.

Within the new international political context, the profile of the United Nations has become more positive. The UN is actively involved in efforts for the resolution of a number of conflicts, and its possibilities for doing so have recently increased considerably. It is important for CCIA to expand and intensify its UN-related activities and to assist the churches in their access to the UN system.

Developments in many countries, and a new definitional struggle between religion and politics, demand a fresh look at church-state relations as part of a wider theological reflection. It is also necessary to build on the theological reflections which have already been done by CCIA on issues such as peace and human rights. A number of churches in many parts of the world today find themselves in situations where apparently there are no immediate political solutions to the conflicts. The situation of these churches cannot be dealt with by prescribing a "solu-tion". And often the churches themselves are divided about what ought to be done. CCIA has to assist the churches in finding new ways of engagement reflecting their pastoral and prophetic responsibilities today.

There are some situations where the churches have become the only organization capable of representing the people in their defence of human rights and their wider aspirations for political transformation. A new kind of responsibility seems to be thrust upon the churches in such situations, and such churches will need special support from the ecumenical movement.

CCIA will complete 45 years by the time of the seventh assembly. It should be prepared to be innovative and daring, with its aim "to witness to the lordship of Christ over human beings and history" in the assurance of "God's gracious and redemptive action in history".

COMMISSION ON INTER-CHURCH AID, REFUGEE AND WORLD SERVICE (CICARWS)

Mandate and structure

Since its formation in 1944 the Commission on Inter-Church Aid, Refugee and World Service has evolved under its mandate to "assist the churches to manifest their solidarity by sharing their human, material and spiritual resources and to facilitate such sharing so as to promote social justice, human development, relief to human need..." But our world is not a static one; the environment, governments, people and needs are all constantly changing. CICARWS is, and always has been, about action — practical action based on reflection and analysis. It is not surprising therefore that it is dynamic, energetic and changing in response to the global environment in which it acts. If "solidarity" is to remain "practical", there must be recognition of those changes and a consequent preparedness to find new and effective responses.

Since the Vancouver assembly CICARWS has undergone major changes, partly as a result of a changing world environment and partly as a direct consequence of implementing the messages received from the WCC consultation on interchurch aid, refugee and world service at Larnaca in 1986. But the mandate and fundamental commitment to assist the churches to manifest their solidarity and to facilitate sharing in promotion of social justice, human development and relief to human need remain at the heart of all of CICARWS activities.

CICARWS is organized around seven area desks (Europe, Latin America and the Caribbean, Africa, Asia, Middle East, North America and the Pacific) and five functional desks (Emergencies, Material Aid, Refugee and Migration, Personnel and Human Resource Development, and the Ecumenical Church Loan Fund). There is, in addition, a communications co-ordinator, a finance secretariat and a directorate. This structure enables both an in-depth regional focus and a global approach to issues that cut across regional lines. The area desks in particular play an important role for the entire WCC, advising it on questions of relationships and regional developments. Since the Larnaca consultation the area and functional desks have worked more closely together through "area groups" which enable the Sub-unit to respond to needs in an integrated way.

Area desks

The emphasis and style of work of the area desks vary according to the region involved. Needs, expectations and resources differ, and these differences are reflected in the priorities of the area desks. But in all cases the area desks work to support the ministry of the churches to those in need, and work with the regional ecumenical bodies in responding and initiating programmes in support of the churches. In addition to their role in monitoring co-operation with, and assistance to, the churches in the region, the area desks play an increasingly important role in building relationships with churches and their related organizations in the area, and in interpreting the needs of the region to partners in other parts of the world. The area desks seek to bring together churches within a particular region to analyze their situations and to devise appropriate responses, and may act as a liaison between local churches and the WCC as a whole. When there is an emergency or a sudden influx of refugees, the area desks always play a central role in determining the response of CICARWS. The following examples give an idea of the range of issues in which the area desks are involved.

In 1984 Western media networks "discovered" the victims of one of the worst disasters in human history, the *African* famine (which had in fact been a reality since before the beginning of the decade). Overnight, the Western world — governments, relief agencies, experts, the public — began pleading for emergency aid for starving people in Africa. At this point both Protestant and Catholic churches, many of whom were already responding to the crisis, decided to combine their efforts. Thus the Churches' Drought Action in Africa (CDAA) was born. In March 1984 it launched an appeal to raise $100 million over five years; this target was reached in a few months, and funds kept pouring in. By March 1986 the total amount raised by all participants in CDAA exceeded $500 million. In a remarkable show of solidarity, donations came not only from "traditional" donor countries, but also from churches in Eastern Europe, Asia, the Pacific and Africa itself. The CDAA was not only an effort to mobilize funds for the African emergency, but also a commitment to provide pastoral care in the region and to raise awareness about the drought and the causes which had led to famine. Assistance for famine relief and rehabilitation was made available to churches and other bodies in Angola, Ethiopia, Ghana, Kenya, Guinea-Bissau, Mozambique, Namibia, Rwanda, Sudan and Zimbabwe as well as the eight Sahel countries — Burkina Faso, Cape Verde, Chad, Gambia, Mali, Mauritania, Niger and Senegal. Moreover, regional and international conferences were held, publications circulated, and a major study involving 52 African experts was carried out. The study's main conclusion was that famine and hunger in Africa are the result of human actions. Economic and political exploitation and oppression are to blame; this being so, the solutions also lie with human beings.

By the mid-1980s more African churches had committed themselves to long-term development programmes as the only viable means of moving beyond a daily struggle for survival. Country programme round tables, and consultations for countries afflicted by drought and violence, focused on ways of moving from emergency to development work. These consultations challenged CICARWS' African partners to show their own local contributions and work for relief, rehabilitation and development programmes.

The Sahel programme, one of only two programmes where CICARWS is operational, works with 140 partners in the eight Sahel countries in an effort to promote long-term development through an integrated development approach. Food aid is discouraged; instead efforts are made to encourage local food production, the purchase of food within the Sahel region, and the establishment of cereal banks. Most of all, efforts are made to develop the human resources of the region. Thus in 1985 the Africa desk organized a month's visit to India for 12 Sahel farmers. They brought back with them from this fascinating experience new ideas, seeds and examples of appropriate technology.

The *Asia* desk has faced many situations of conflict, violence and human need. As the state of affairs in Sri Lanka worsened, the Asia desk, in close collaboration with other CICARWS desks, the Sri Lanka task force and the Christian Conference of Asia (CCA), has made use of a Sri Lanka special fund to respond to the needs of victims of human rights violations both within and outside the country. In February 1985 a consultation was held between Tamil and Sinhalese church leaders in the country. As the violence has continued, further meetings and visits have sought a way out of the civil war which has killed and uprooted hundreds of thousands of people.

The Kampuchea programme has been continued, under CICARWS auspices and under the umbrella of the Indochina round table, as a response to the serious needs in that country. This extensive programme has included input for agriculture, health training and the production of medical cotton goods and pharmaceuticals. Special emphasis has been placed on people-to-people exchange and education in an effort to break the isolation of both Kampuchea and Vietnam; in addition, some initial help has gone to Laos.

Since the Vancouver assembly the Asia desk has taken new initiatives in China and Korea. Bishop K.H. Ting, president of the China Christian Council (CHCC), visited the WCC in November 1983; this was the first visit by a leader of the church in China since 1950. Following an initial staff visit in 1985 the desk worked in support of a long-term development project in a drought-prone area and has been supporting the Amity Foundation (set up by the CCC) in its work in various parts of the country. In Korea the Asia desk worked with the Commission of the Churches on International Affairs (CCIA) to facilitate a process of dialogue and sharing between the churches in North and South Korea, as part of its commitment to reconciliation in this divided country.

Long-term development issues, human rights and the strengthening of local churches, women's questions and leadership training for the future have all been priority concerns of the Asia desk in its work in the other countries of Asia. In seven countries (Bangladesh, India, Indochina, Indonesia, Myanmar [Burma], Korea and the Philippines) this work has been organized within an integrated round-table framework.

Since the WCC's sixth assembly there have been major changes in *Europe*, and indeed the assembly recommended more emphasis on ecumenical relationships in Europe. In response to problems such as cutbacks in European government social welfare programmes, increased poverty, growing racism and changes in East-West conflicts, Europe's churches are searching for new ways of carrying out diakonia and koinonia. The Europe desk has brought churches together to consider their role in local as well as global diakonia. Working in close co-operation with the Conference of European Churches, the Europe desk has responded to requests for assistance in programmes such as drug addiction, peace education, women's issues, the struggle against racism, and assistance to minority and diaspora churches.

Round-table programmes in Portugal, Spain and Italy have been continued and strengthened in the context of changing resources and needs. Casa Locarno (the centre for ecumenical encounter supported jointly by the WCC and HEKS, the Swiss interchurch aid agency) provides a forum for informal meetings between clergy and laity in Western and Eastern Europe.

The movement towards economic, political and social integration has intensified within Western Europe, particularly under the effect of the impending Single European Act of 1992 on the twelve European Community members. But "Europe 1992" will have an impact far beyond its member countries, and the Europe desk is seeking to analyze the effect of these changes on Southern, Central and Eastern European countries as well as on groups which will be particularly affected, including women, migrants and asylum seekers. In the Soviet Union and in Central and Eastern Europe, changes produced by *glasnost* and *perestroika* have created new opportunities for church involvement in diakonia. Efforts to build a "common European house" embracing all regions of Europe are exciting and challenging. A project on local diakonia has been launched to enable Europeans from all regions to study, reflect and act on common themes. The project includes common Bible studies, photographs and study questions which focus on the similarities within Europe. The marginalization and poverty of women have been major foci of the desk since 1987; in 1990 a consultation will be organized in the United Kingdom to enable poor women, and the churches which work with them, to analyze their situation and develop appropriate actions to respond to it.

Since the Vancouver assembly the needs in *Latin America and the Caribbean* have been many. Continuing war and repression in Central America, serious human rights violations throughout the continent, and the human effects of a burgeoning international debt have been the main themes of the desk's efforts to support local churches in their reponse to these challenges. CICARWS has worked closely with the Human Rights Resource Office for Latin America (HRROLA) and with regional ecumenical bodies to denounce US pressure against Nicaragua and support for repressive regimes, and to support the churches in their commitment to peace. The majority of Protestants in Latin America are Pentecostals, and many are involved in grassroots efforts to address social problems. CICARWS has provided several opportunities for dialogue and exchange of experiences among these churches as part of its support of popular religious expression in the region.

With the toppling of the Duvalier regime in early February 1986, the Methodist Church in Haiti and the Caribbean Conference of Churches (CCC) invited the WCC to pay a pastoral visit to the churches there. One week later, a five-person delegation was on the spot; on its return it called for intercession in worship, massive and appropriate economic assistance, co-operation with the CCC, steps to strengthen the democratic process, and the close accompaniment of the churches in Haiti by churches around the world. As the situation in Haiti has deteriorated, the Latin America and Caribbean desk has responded to the needs of churches in that country.

Human rights violations in El Salvador, Guatemala, Paraguay, Peru and Chile required continual monitoring of the situation by the Latin America desk. The growing debt burden, and the conditions imposed on Latin American governments by international financial institutions, have meant an increase in poverty and suffering throughout the region. In many countries CICARWS has supported those struggling for survival. Too often the burden has been disproportionately borne by those least able to do so, particularly by women and children. The Latin America desk has taken initiatives to enable women in the region to meet in order to share experiences and develop common strategies. In 1990 the first ecumenical meeting on Latin American children will be held in Brazil.

Cradle of the world's three great monotheistic religions, the *Middle East* continued to present opportunities for, and staggering obstacles to, ecumenism and peace. Growing religious fundamentalism and its effect on state policies have created a particularly difficult environment for ecumenical work. Presently some ten million Christians, of whom about 85% are Orthodox (Oriental or Byzantine), live as minorities in a region that is unstable and restrictive of the rights of individuals and communities. Solidarity and understanding by churches outside the region are extremely important to them.

The spiralling cycle of violence in Lebanon, leading in 1988 to full-scale war, has demanded new relief efforts, intensified advocacy and programme initiatives by CICARWS.

Working with the Middle East Council of Churches (MECC) Department on Service to Palestinian Refugees, CICARWS provides support for local programmes such as vocational training, family service and home economics centres in Palestinian communities situated in the occupied territories, Israel, Lebanon and Jordan. The programme aims to preserve and re-inforce Palestinian identity, dignity, and initiative through land reclamation, loans and self-help projects. In 1988 this work took on a new dimension as the *Intifada*, or Palestinian uprising, in the occupied territories of Gaza and the West Bank mobilized the energies and the aspirations of the Palestinian people. For more than 35 years CICARWS has attempted to promote peace and reconciliation between the communities in conflict in the area.

In 1985 a round table was created for the Coptic Orthodox Church in Egypt to co-ordinate the church's service projects in leadership training, primary health care, youth, rural development, job creation and social services for disabled people. The Coptic Orthodox Church's six million members make up about half of the Christians in the Middle East.

Throughout this period CICARWS involvement in the Middle East involved much more than financial and material assistance. Building and maintaining ecumenical relationships, monitoring the various situations and needs and interpreting them to churches and people outside the region were tasks assumed by the Middle East desk (in co-operation with other WCC sub-units) through analysis and communication, visits and encounter.

In summary, the Middle East desk has shifted in emphasis from fragmented project work to co-ordinated programme promotion, from fund-raising to advocacy, from technical procedural work to interpretation, communication through publishing, and the building of relations with the local churches.

North America is also a continent in need, and CICARWS has taken initiatives to support dialogue as well as efforts by North American churches to address problems of economic justice, racism, the farm crisis and issues of indigenous groups. A vision of the future is shared by North American commissioners and the CICARWS staff seeking improved relationships, stronger commitment and greater participation by North American churches in realizing the ideals of equitable resource-sharing. However, this vision cannot ultimately be realized without the time and energy of a full-time staff person. CICARWS hopes in the long term to see such a position created to enable greater service to the ecumenical movement; in the meantime, in faithfulness to its vision, the office of the director will continue to guide CICARWS North American involvement.

At the request of the churches in the region, a full-time consultant for the *Pacific* was appointed in 1989 (attention had been given on a part-time basis since 1972), leading to hopes for more active CICARWS engagement with the churches there. The issues in the Pacific have always been of concern to CICARWS and the WCC. The Vancouver assembly drew attention to the "as yet unresolved problem of the self-determination and independence of the Melanesian people of New Caledonia", and urged member churches "to strengthen their support for and solidarity with Christians and churches in the Pacific in their struggles for political and economic independence". The explosive situation in New Caledonia, fuelled by the Kanak people's frustration and tension, has required close monitoring and action by CICARWS in co-operation with CCIA. Continued nuclear testing in the Pacific, church difficulties in Fiji, and the expressed need of the Pacific churches to forge a regional identity were major themes of CICARWS involvement in the Pacific in the post-Vancouver period.

Functional desks

The functional and area desks work as a closely-knit team within CICARWS. Consultation on specific issues is intense and ongoing. For example, when disaster strikes the *Emergencies* desk immediately enters into consultation with the relevant area desk to determine the appropriate CICARWS response. The major functions of the Emergencies desk involve gathering and disseminating information to identify and contact partners in a stricken area. Communication and co-ordination among such partners and a network of agencies and friends providing assistance are ongoing functions of the desk, as is the financial management of ecumenical relief funds and collaboration with other relief agencies. Emergency assistance involves immediate relief (such as food and medical care), rehabilitation (the provision of agricultural and other tools and household goods) and reconstruction (including especially building or construction activities such as housing, roads, irrigation canals, etc.). Longer-term approaches are usually the responsibility of the area desks.

The work of this desk in relief, rehabilitation and reconstruction also involves it in promoting pastoral care for distressed people in situations of death and violence, the restoration of confidence and stability in disrupted communities, and advocacy which aims to prevent those catastrophes which can be avoided by achieving greater social justice.

Since the Vancouver assembly the Emergencies desk, in response to floods, earthquakes, drought, mudslides, war and famine, has channelled millions of dollars to churches and ecumenical partners in some 40 countries. The most serious emergencies are not "natural" disasters at all, but rather caused or exacerbated by human factors.

In recent years the Emergencies desk has focused on disaster preparedness by training churches and ecumenical partners in how to respond if or when disaster strikes. Disaster preparedness workshops have been held in Bangladesh and in Latin America.

The *Material Aid* desk fulfills a technical function in relation to CICARWS' activities by co-ordinating and responding to requests for material resources (goods) in connection with emergency relief and rehabilitation, as well as interchurch aid where it has material aid components. The desk, through its own network, solicits material resources on a worldwide basis and serves as a clearing house and intermediary between donors and recipient partners. The desk provides facilities for procurement and shipping for the WCC as a whole and for national, regional and local groups, if necessary. In addition, the desk participates in and co-ordinates joint food aid action with other non-governmental organizations and intergovernmental agencies, including the European group of NGOs called Euronaid (which co-operates with the European Community), and acts as a liaison in channelling material aid from Eastern European churches to projects in developing countries. Every year some $100 million in material aid is mobilized by the churches; of this, $10 million is channelled through CICARWS.

The *Refugee and Migration* desk works to support the churches in their ministry to uprooted people. One of the oldest programmes of the WCC, the Refugee desk has faced new and more complex problems since the Vancouver assembly. The number of refugees continues to increase; as wars last longer, refugees remain in exile for longer periods of time, requiring a sustained ministry by the churches. Through CICARWS, assistance is channelled to churches in support of their ministry to refugees, with emphasis on finding durable solutions to refugee situations. In some cases this means support for voluntary repatriation, as in Namibia, El Salvador, Uganda and Rwanda. Where refugees are unable to return home, CICARWS works to facilitate their integration into local countries of asylum, with particular emphasis on assisting refugees within the context of the local host community's needs. For a small percentage of the world's refugees, resettlement to third countries is the only option. The Refugee and Migration desk directly facilitated resettlement through its field offices in Vienna, Athens and Rome until 1989 when the offices in Vienna and Rome were closed as a result of an ongoing review of their role and of immediate financial pressures. CICARWS is increasingly involved in advocacy to address the root causes which have provoked the flight from their communities of origin of the world's 15 million refugees and the estimated 30 million persons who are internally displaced.

Another challenge has been the increasing actions by Western governments, frequently acting in concert, to impose policies designed to prevent asylum-seekers from arriving at their borders. For those already there, applications for asylum have been rejected at an alarming rate, and deportations have been more common. These restrictive policies reflect a growing racism and xenophobia in Western countries. Such actions have serious consequences not only for individual asylum-seekers, but for the international refugee system as a whole. Paradoxically it is the very countries which took the lead in drafting the UN Charter of Human Rights and the various international refugee conventions which are now seeking to restrict their application. In response to these challenges the Refugee and Migration desk has taken a more active role in advocacy and in sharing information about these developments through two monthly publications. Working with regional ecumenical bodies, the Refugee Service has facilitated the development of regional refugee working groups in Asia, Latin America, Europe, North America and Africa in order to analyze the refugee situation and to develop co-ordinated ecumenical responses.

In April 1986 CICARWS convened a major consultation on global asylum and refugee protection issues in Zurich. This analyzed trends in refugee movements and governmental responses and mapped out a church strategy for advocacy on behalf of refugees and asylum-seekers. Since then relations within the ecumenical network of refugee-serving organizations have been strengthened and new initiatives taken with Roman Catholic agencies. Since Vancouver the Refugee and Migration desk has worked with churches in some 70 countries in support of local initiatives. At the same time the international role of the desk has been strengthened through increased advocacy vis-à-vis the United Nations High Commissioner for Refugees (UNHCR) and other international organizations. The desk has played an important leadership role in advocating and raising awareness about refugee women's specific needs and resources.

The growing economic crises in many countries of the South have led millions of migrants to leave their communities in search of jobs and economic survival. Some of the migration is internal; thus it is estimated that over 30 million destitute people have emigrated from Brazil's drought-stricken northeast region to the more prosperous, industrialized south. A study on internal migration, focusing on Brazil, was undertaken by the Migration secretary in 1985. Migration between regions is also increasingly evident. In 1985 the desk organized a joint consultation between the MECC and the CCA on the issue of migrant workers from

Asia to the Gulf countries. Just as they are becoming more restrictive towards asylum-seekers, European governments are also reducing quotas for migrant workers. The Migration desk has maintained close contacts with other European ecumenical groups working on issues relating to migration and racism. One of the most important activities of the desk has been the dissemination of information about migrants through its publication *Migration Today*.

Since Vancouver the emphasis of the *Secretariat for Personnel and Human Resource Development* has moved from being primarily a North-South conduit for personnel to becoming a stimulator for multilateral movements of people within the oikoumene. The clear call from the Larnaca consultation to focus on people, and to equip local churches in their diaconal mission, has emphasized the need for CICARWS to develop a broader human resource programme. During recent years the desk has tried in different continents to bring together people in workshops or small consultations to stimulate reflection and initiatives in leadership development, skills development and management, and training for diaconal initiatives at the congregational level. More such consultations and workshops have been planned for the future. The aim is to reach the younger generation in the churches and ecumenical leadership, both clergy and lay, and to encourage them to take new initiatives. Hopefully this would also affect the kind of programmes or projects seeking ecumenical support, bringing them closer to the directions endorsed at Larnaca. The desk has also continued to encourage and assist multilateral movements of people, and to challenge the agencies of the North which send personnel to review their mandates within the scope of this broader human resource development policy. And the Secretariat for Personnel and Human Resource Development continues to be the place within CICARWS which services the personnel needs of programmes and projects supported in other ways, and which enables the exchange of people for learning or for sharing experiences.

Communication is central to all CICARWS programmes and activities. At Larnaca CICARWS was challenged to do more to share the stories of struggle, to share information as a basis for advocacy, and to help churches express solidarity with one another. The Communications desk has established a network for sharing information and resources between the professional communicators of church-related partners, and is moving to expand this network to include more communicators from the South. The desk is seeking to support the establishment of other networks — between individuals and groups — with common purposes or interests.

As communication includes both advocacy and solidarity, the desk has worked to encourage and to participate in these by awareness-raising, skill-development, information-sharing and demonstrating accountability. It has challenged local churches and Christians to action and reflection.

The *Ecumenical Church Loan Fund (ECLOF)* has continued to explore new and effective ways of working in conjunction with CICARWS. ECLOF sees development within the context of the need to realize the full potential of human life, social justice and self-reliance. Thus ECLOF assists projects which promote social justice (such as land-titling movements), community participation and self-reliance (such as co-operatives) and redistribution of wealth (such as gaining credit for marginalized groups).

In practical terms, ECLOF provides low-interest loans in national currencies through a system of national committees to rural or urban grassroots groups to finance specific projects. By providing loans instead of grants, ECLOF encourages self-reliance. Low interest rates make it easier for churches and other groups to acquire capital which would otherwise be unavailable to them. The national ECLOF committees screen and fund projects and are responsible for the reimbursement of loans. Since Vancouver ECLOF has established closer contacts with the Ecumenical Development Cooperative Society (EDCS), which also makes loans but operates with share capital (whereas ECLOF uses donated capital).

ECLOF also works increasingly to respond to calls for support in the development of expertise.

WCC work on the international food disorder

In light of the deteriorating world food situation, which is affecting vast areas of the third world in particular, Vancouver adopted a statement on the international food disorder. This pointed out that at least 400 million people go hungry every day, that malnutrition and starvation have reached crisis levels in many countries, and that the causes of this situation are located both within individual nations, and in international economic and political structures. The statement ended with an urgent 13-point call on member churches to find solutions to the problem through programmatic, education and advocacy channels.

The statement was sent by the WCC general secretary to member churches and councils of churches for study and action. Within the WCC, an inter-unit task force was set up to co-ordinate the various programmes and study activities within different sub-units which touch upon this issue. The task force secretariat (located in CICARWS) issued two resource packets for churches on the global food crisis, established reference and documentation files, and monitored other organizations' involvement in the issue.

In Buenos Aires in 1985 the central committee recognized this issue as an integral part of the struggle for justice, peace and the integrity of creation, and aopted a statement calling on churches and governments to take all necessary measures to redress this tragic situation of hunger and poverty. The central committee further called upon its members to covenant together, promising that they would bring the full dimensions of the international food disorder to the attention of their respective churches and governments. They were to report to the next meeting of the central committee on the specific actions which they had taken.

The Unit II committee followed the activities of the task force, receiving its reports regularly. In 1987, however, a shift of emphasis (towards the global crisis in farming and agriculture) was proposed; the task force has not met since that time.

New approaches
One of the clear messages from the Larnaca consultation was the need to develop widely inclusive regional groups with the capacity to "direct appropriate diakonia" for their own communities. Such regional groups, now in the process of creation and consolidation, will identify priorities for ecumenical action. This process of regionalization is based on the conviction that churches in each region should be empowered to set their own priorities. The objectives of the new regional groups are fourfold: to analyze the situation, identify needs, set priorities among those needs, and develop appropriate strategies for meeting them. Given the variety of regional contexts and issues, the regional groups have naturally taken different forms and made different emphases. Some groups have stressed informing and raising awareness about the reality and the issues of their region. Others have taken the time to identify specific needs. Most of the newly-constituted regional groups met for the first time in March-April 1989, replacing the regional ecumenical resource-sharing groups.

As CICARWS worked towards a new regional focus, new ways of funding were developed. A commission meeting in 1987 agreed that CICARWS should move away from project screening and should phase out the listing service (an alternate mechanism by which donors could identify projects of special concern to them). Priority projects would, however, continue as the most conspicuous and cherished funding instrument, representing the ecumenical partners' determination that decision-making must be transferred to the areas where the needs arise and are identified. Thus the regional groups approve, within given ceilings, projects for guaranteed funding. CICARWS is playing a more active referral role for projects which were previously included in the listing service. CICARWS staff will send requests directly to churches and agencies on the basis of the regional guidelines, and the partner agencies will have to follow up on technical and procedural questions as well as bilateral implementation. With a clear knowledge of agencies' mandates, continuous dialogue and the use of up-to-date communication and computer media, it should be possible to reduce processing time and increase transparency dramatically.

Another new emphasis in CICARWS funding mechanisms is found in the round-table structures. In a round table, CICARWS invites ecumenical partners in a country (or cluster of countries) to sit together "around a table" with a church or council of churches, and to establish a common plan for their programmes. Round-table structures (RTS) are an important step towards transfer or sharing of decision-making. While it is still the donors who decide on the level of support, they make their decisions after working with local partners in approving the programme and a common format of cash flow, accounting and reporting. This process demands compromise and mutual adjustments. RTSs in which donors assume collective responsibility may also ensure the programme against "dropouts" causing problems in full coverage and cash flow. At the same time the very success of the RTS concept, and the consequent possibility of their turning into closed shops, makes it imperative that CICARWS proceed vigorously, but with great care, in relating to them. Presently an enormous amount of staff time and energy is spent on servicing existing round tables, particularly in Africa and Asia.

At the same time as initiatives were being taken in strengthening priority projects, phasing out the listing service and systematizing round-table structures, a new funding mechanism was created to respond to small one-time requests by churches and ecumenical groups. The existing mechanisms all take time; sometimes churches must wait a year before receiving approval for their requests. The special action fund was established to respond quickly and flexibly to requests from local churches for support. Specifically, the fund's objectives are:
— to relate churches to each other for mutual enhancement of their diaconal mission;

— to help churches to express solidarity with each other and the poor and oppressed;
— to challenge churches in their diakonia and sharing.
The support — both philosophical and financial — of church-related agencies has been essential in these developments. At a meeting of agency directors and senior personnel, in April 1989, many of the agencies committed themselves to supporting the process of regionalization and mutual accountability. While it was recognized that bilateral relationships will continue, there was also a recognition of the guiding principles set out at Larnaca, and a growing acceptance of the principle that all ecumenical relationships should be within a common framework which recognizes the policies and priorities set by regional groups.

PROGRAMME TO COMBAT RACISM (PCR)

In 1969 the central committee established the Programme to Combat Racism with the mandate that it be "responsible for working out World Council of Churches (WCC) policies and programmes combating racism, giving expression to solidarity with the racially oppressed, organizing action-oriented research projects, assisting the churches in the education of their own members for racial justice, and operation of the Special Fund to Combat Racism". Until 1988, however, PCR was handicapped in carrying out this mandate fully by a shortage of staff.

PCR has a global programme. The Sub-unit is involved, and challenges the churches to be involved, in the struggles against racism and racial discrimination anywhere in the world. PCR is also involved in the Herculean land rights struggles of indigenous peoples. Women under racism, racism in theology, education and the media are major concerns of PCR. By the mandate of the Vancouver assembly the struggle against apartheid in South Africa remains the major priority of PCR.

Programmatic emphases
   Southern Africa: The sixth assembly said:

> Apartheid raises barriers and denies the fullness of life in Christ. Christians and the churches are called in obedience to Jesus Christ the life of the world, and to maintain the integrity of the church, to oppose apartheid in all its forms, to support those who struggle against this sinful system of injustice, and to denounce any theological justification of apartheid as a heretical perversion of the gospel.

In fulfilment of this call PCR has done the following:
— May 1985: PCR organized a meeting between international and South
  African church leaders in Harare which adopted the Harare Declaration, challenging the churches to express solidarity with the victims of
  apartheid, and calling for "the transfer of power to the majority of the
  people, based on universal suffrage..." The Declaration is now a UN
  document.
— June 1986: PCR organized a world day of prayer and fasting to
  commemorate the 10th anniversary of the Soweto uprising.
— May 1987: PCR called a meeting between international church leaders
  and the Southern African liberation movements, the African National
  Congress (ANC), the Pan Africanist Congress (PAC) and the South
  West Africa People's Organization (SWAPO). The meeting adopted
  the historic Lusaka Statement, which declared the South African
  government illegitimate.
— May 1988: PCR organized a World Day of Prayer for a Free Namibia
  in commemoration of the 10th anniversary of the Kassinga massacre.
  PCR also published a special issue of *PCR Information*, "The Way to
  Namibian Independence, UN Resolution 435".
— May 1988: PCR held hearings on Namibia in Washington, where a
  distinguished international panel heard testimonies from Namibians
  and US legislators.
— September 1988: PCR organized a meeting between international and
  South African and Namibian youth. The assembly had also "called on
  the member churches to intensify witness against apartheid and the
  continuing oppression in South Africa and Namibia and to deepen
  their solidarity with those forces including the liberation movements
  recognized by the United Nations".
— November 1988: PCR organized a meeting on the destabilization by
  South Africa of the Frontline States. Participants heard, as was the
  case in all the meetings cited above, the cries from the heart of those
  in the thick of the struggle. Participants visited refugee camps where
  bread was shared with the refugees who had grown the wheat and
  ground and baked it for the participants.
— January 1989: The Eminent Church Persons Group (ECPG) visited the
  capitals of Switzerland, Belgium, France, the United Kingdom, the
  Federal Republic of Germany, Japan and the United States to call upon
  those governments to impose comprehensive economic sanctions
  against the government of South Africa, in order to force it to negotiate
  with the authentic leaders of the black majority in South Africa.

Developments within South Africa in the period under review have propelled the churches into the forefront of the struggle against apartheid. As that high-level and high-visibility involvement was taking place, there was also serious reflection on the theological and spiritual foundations of political action and even resistance. The Lusaka consultation entrusted PCR with a mandate to explore further the ethical questions raised by violence, and the illegitimacy of the apartheid regime following the questioning thereof by the Kairos document (a significant statement on the political crisis in South Africa, published in 1985 by a group of South African theologians).

Thus it was in faithfulness to that mandate that PCR, together with the South African Council of Churches, sponsored a consultation in Harare in September 1989 to examine in depth the socio-ethical, political and theological implications of the illegitimacy of the apartheid state. The meeting produced a statement of basic affirmations, and a report will be published.

On its own initiative PCR marked the 40th anniversary of the proclamation of the Universal Declaration of Human Rights on 10 December 1988 by launching a campaign against the use of the death penalty in political cases in South Africa. That campaign was supported by the UN Commission on Human Rights, the Lutheran World Federation, the World YWCA, the World Alliance of YMCAs and by Amnesty International (a long-time leader in work against the death penalty).

The indigenous people and the struggle for land rights: Indigenous peoples are the original inhabitants of countries such as the USA, Canada, Brazil, Australia, Aotearoa/New Zealand, to name a few, who have been dispossessed of their lands. For PCR, indigenous people are among the worst victims of racism. The UN defines indigenous peoples as "the existing descendants of the peoples who inhabited the present territory of a country wholly or partially at the time when persons of a different culture or ethnic origin arrived there from other parts of the world, overcame them and, by conquest, settlements or other means, reduced them to a non-dominant or colonial situation". In all cases indigenous people have experienced chicanery and extreme and brutal violence in the process of the sequestration of their land. The descendents of indigenous peoples remember with bitterness and horror what was done, and continues to be done, to them.

Thus in Australia the Aboriginal people painfully recall:

> My mother would sit and cry and tell me this: "They [whites] buried our babies in the ground with only their heads above the ground. All in a row they were. Then they had a test to see who could kick the babies' heads off the

furthest. One man clubbed a baby's head off from horseback. They then spent most of the day raping the women, most of them were then tortured to death..." (Janine Roberts, *Massacres To Mining: The Colonisation of Aboriginal Australia*, 1978, p.19).

And in Brazil there were about 5 million indigenous people when the Portuguese arrived in the 16th century; in 1987 the Catholic bishops conference said that only about 230,000 remained. Conference president Bishop Luciano Mendes de Almeida said: "If the Indians are not defended now they will disappear."

These are only a few of the stories the indigenous people want to tell the world. It pains them that few people are willing to listen. PCR has disciplined itself to learn to listen to the voices of the oppressed, the angry and the exploited, and to challenge the churches to listen and join the struggles for justice of the indigenous people. As the Vancouver assembly so aptly observed: "Land rights claims of indigenous people are often rejected in the name of development and national security."

There is one unifying factor and one highly distinguishing characteristic of indigenous people: no matter where they live or what their political or socio-cultural beliefs may be, they all view land as being the basis of their very survival. It is this world-view, more than anything else, that distinguishes them from minority and other racially oppressed people.

In May 1989 — to highlight the struggle for land rights and to fulfill its mandate "to develop a programme on indigenous peoples and land rights" — PCR organized a global land rights consultation in Darwin, Australia, under the theme "Land is Our Life: Integrity of Creation, Justice and Peace". Australia was chosen as the venue to highlight the plight of the Aboriginal people and to follow up the 1981 WCC team visit. The participants, the majority of whom were indigenous, declared in the final document: "We came together, in deference to Creation and filled with a sense of urgency, to declare that a state of emergency exists in regard to the survival and status of indigenous peoples worldwide."

The meeting's 125 participants, from 14 countries, were united in their objective "to assert our rights as sovereign peoples and to document the atrocities committed against ourselves, our territories and, therefore, our spirituality". The Declaration continued: "The churches of the world have been a part of the problem. As indigenous Aboriginal peoples we believe that we have an inherent and inalienable right to self-determination. We call for global action to cease the cultural and physical genocide and forced removals of indigenous peoples from our lands, of forced removals of indigenous children from our families, of police brutality." To the WCC the Darwin participants said: "We call upon the WCC to recognize that indigenous lands have been taken by the church, without the consent of the indigenous people of that land." They asked for dialogue between the church and the indigenous people to resolve the issue, and demanded that the churches either return the land or pay compensation. They further said: "We request the member churches of the WCC to support the indigenous peoples in their struggle for land rights."

The consultation documents (the Darwin Declaration and Darwin Petition) containing the resolutions were annexed to the report of the UN Working Group on Indigenous Populations sessions of August 1989.

PCR has greatly expanded its work with indigenous communities in Central and South America and tried to raise the visibility of the land rights issue within the church. Activities have also been intensified with the UN Working Group on Indigenous Populations, facilitating the participation of a greater number of delegates. A special issue of *PCR Information* on land rights and indigenous people was produced. The challenge now is to follow up on the implementation of the resolutions of the Darwin documents — one of which is to ensure representation of Aboriginal issues and Aborigine participation at the 1991 Canberra assembly.

Women under racism: PCR has vigorously pursued its "Women Under Racism" (WUR) programme, seeking justice and equality for women who are victims of racism and sexism. Through increased staff visits and participation in consultations on women's oppression, PCR has intensified its support for women under racism and for their liberation. In 1986 PCR organized a global consultation in Geneva on women under racism and casteism, with 20 participants from 13 countries. The women called upon the churches to enable their increased participation in the life of the church and society. They declared: "As Christians we believe that all human beings are created in the image of God, and oppression and violence done to any section of society is an act against God itself... We come together filled with a sense of urgency and determination to end the growing discrimination and repression against us throughout the world." They called upon the member churches of the WCC to join them in their demands for justice, peace and equality.

PCR also co-sponsored the first regional meeting of Dalit women in South India, and convened a seminar to help women gain fund-raising skills in order to increase their activities. PCR, together with the

Women's Sub-unit and CICARWS, convened an African women's consultation on "Justice, Peace and the Integrity of Creation". A data bank for WUR has been established to provide names for church meetings and other events in order to give this constituency increased opportunities for participation and to answer their call for help to "overcome their invisibility in the church and society". The programme has addressed the issues of physical violence and sex tourism, where women under racism are the majority victims, through its programmatic category grants and participation in meetings on this issue. PCR has published *We the Women, We the World*, telling the stories of women under racism.

Race and minority issues in Asia and the Pacific: Staff visits to these regions have resulted in closer co-operation, more support and deeper involvement by PCR in the struggles for justice and equality by the Dalits (India), Tamils (Sri Lanka), Maori (Aotearoa/New Zealand), Aboriginal tribes in Taiwan, Aborigines (Australia), and Buraku, Ainu, Koreans and Okinawans (Japan). The appointment of programme staff with particular responsibility for Asia and the Pacific has meant that those links have been strengthened.

PCR contacts in the Pacific region have historically been few, confined mostly to Hawaii, Aotearoa/New Zealand and Australia. In addition, PCR has worked with the Commission of the Churches on International Affairs in preparing the WCC's response to the changing political situation in Fiji. It is clear that PCR's work in the Pacific will increase, in co-operation with other sub-units of the WCC. The expanding people's movements in that region are demanding the support of justice groups around the world. Following the many years of missionary activity in the Pacific, they seek solidarity from the churches.

The 1989 PCR team visits to North and South India, Japan and Sri Lanka, and the commission meeting in Madras, India, have significantly increased and strengthened its commitment to the struggles for equality and justice in the region.

Racism in theology: Before 1969 the WCC had made many statements affirming the churches' support for racial justice and equality. After 1969 the WCC, through the creation of PCR, went a step further — it took and supported action in the struggle against racism and racial discrimination. But in taking such actions the WCC always explained the theological reasons behind them. In 1983 the Vancouver assembly said: "The spiritual struggle of the church must involve it in the struggles of the poor, the oppressed, the alienated and the exiled." PCR has always been concerned about the need to explain the theological and spiritual undergirding of its involvement in the struggles for justice, equality and peace, and its reasons for challenging the churches to be involved in some of the struggles against racism.

A workshop on spirituality and racism at Corrymeela, Northern Ireland, in 1989 brought groups of activists from the PCR constituency into a common reflection on the spiritual and theological foundations of action for racial justice. It examined the implications of a faith response to the struggle against apartheid or the struggle for self-determination by the people of Namibia, and to those who suffer racial violence in Britain, the USA and France. Participants devised a liturgy of commitment and sought, on the basis of the biblical tradition, an authentic affirmation for those who seek justice.

Since the Vancouver assembly PCR has developed approaches to the concerns raised by racism in theology. A regional consultation was held in Stony Point Center, New York, in January 1986. This affirmed that "the practice of racial injustice is a contradiction of our common participation in humanity and in violation of the faith community's kinship as brothers and sisters in Christ". This was followed by a youth and student forum on racism in theology held in Harare, Zimbabwe, in September 1988. The workshop, which was co-sponsored with the World Student Christian Federation (WSCF), addressed the scandal of faith and doctrine which do not seem capable of eliminating racism and bringing about the unity of humankind.

In September 1989 at Driebergen, the Netherlands, a European consultation on "Black Christians in Europe: a Theological Response to Racial Experiences" brought together black theologians, pastors and church workers to develop strategies for confronting racism in the institutional practices and teaching of the church.

For 1990 PCR is organizing a consultation on racism in Europe which will pay particular attention to discriminatory immigration policies and practices, especially as these will affect migrants in Europe after 1992.

Also in 1990 PCR will organize a consultation in Toronto, Canada, on racism in education, the church and the media.

In all its work PCR has co-operated with international organizations and agencies to achieve the liberation of the oppressed and those who are racially and sexually discriminated against. To fulfill these aims and goals PCR has worked, and will continue to work, with other organizations and agencies. For example, PCR has taken part in the UN debates on human rights; in 1988 the WCC/PCR panel delegation on the Namibian hearings in Washington met with UN secretary-general Perez de Cuellar in New York; the panel also addressed the Council for Namibia. In 1989 the Eminent Church Persons Group met with the UN secretary-general and later addressed the UN special committee against apartheid. The ECPG also met with the Commonwealth Secretariat in London.

In addition PCR worked with ecumenical partners such as the World YWCA and the World Student Christian Federation, as well as with other NGOs such as the World Gold Commission, and with anti-apartheid movements in Africa, Asia, North America and Europe.

At the 1968 Uppsala assembly the late James Baldwin said that he was "one of God's creatures whom the Christian faith has most betrayed". He said further: "I wonder if there is left in Christian civilization the moral energy, the spiritual daring to atone, to repent, to be born again." PCR's constituency in Asia, particularly among the Aboriginal people of Australia, the Tamils of Sri Lanka and the Dalits of India, have told us of the church's betrayal of the calling of the gospel to identify, in word and deed, with the poor, the lonely and the weak. In Brazil the indigenous people face extinction by the middle of the next century. These constituencies have articulated their concerns to the global church community through PCR, and it remains their voice of hope for the future.

In the last twenty years the fruits of PCR's vision have been realized in Southern Africa: Angola, Mozambique, Zimbabwe have achieved independence. Namibia is now independent, and irreversible changes are taking place in South Africa. The churches are perhaps partially responsible for the changes, and they will certainly mobilize to achieve victory over apartheid racism.

The work against racism is far from over. In the period after Canberra PCR must remain on the "cutting edge" and continue to be faithful to the mission of the gospel and the WCC, by engaging in the challenging struggle for racial justice in Asia, the Pacific, and the countries of the North, and for the rights of women and indigenous people. We also need to "shake the foundations" in order to overcome the prevailing inertia, shatter the false dreams about what it takes to satisfy people's quest for justice, and plan how the WCC can continue to be a pioneering and revolutionary force in ecumenical action. In 1994, which marks the 25th anniversary of PCR, the WCC must recommit itself to the vision of a world that practises equality and justice for all.

COMMISSION ON THE CHURCHES' PARTICIPATION
IN DEVELOPMENT (CCPD)

History and mandate

Established in 1970, the Commission on the Churches' Participation in Development represents one of the younger programmes of the WCC. Although the issue of human development was by no means a new concern of the ecumenical family, the 1960s brought renewed attention to its urgency. In those years an optimistic mood prevailed, and the general feeling was that transfer of capital and technology from North to South would generate a development process which would benefit all within the limited time-span of a couple of decades.

However, the structures of poverty and oppression have turned out to be much stronger than was assumed to be the case in the 1960s and early 1970s. CCPD's activities since Vancouver have taken place in an international setting in which the position of the poor has been deteriorating. There are now more hungry people in the world than ever before, and their numbers are increasing — as are the numbers of those who can neither read nor write, who are without safe water or sound homes, and who are short of wood fuel with which to cook and keep themselves warm. In many countries the gap between rich and poor is widening, not narrowing, and there is little prospect that this process will be reversed in the near future. In fact, there are deliberate efforts in both North and South to increase differences in income, thereby strengthening dualistic societal structures and leading to further "marginalization" of vulnerable groups.

Subsequent development decades have failed, but the word "development" continues to be used, often to support the so-called "adjustment programmes" which are in fact forcing the adjustment of the poor to greater poverty and suffering, and which often lead to further ecological degradation. It is therefore highly appropriate and urgent to re-affirm the ecumenical conviction — formulated by CCPD in the early years of its existence — that human development includes social justice, people's participation, self-reliance, qualified economic growth aimed at satisfaction of basic needs and liberation from poverty and oppression.

At the Vancouver assembly in 1983 the following convictions — which undergird the work of CCPD — were (re)affirmed:

— the churches' participation in development means their solidarity with the poor;

— social and economic justice (including the sustainability of creation),
  in conjunction with people's participation, is central to an ecumenical
  understanding of development;
— the empowerment of people, by working through networks of groups
  and people's movements, is essential to CCPD;
— the sharing of experiences and material resources is an integral part of
  the struggle of the poor to become agents of their own development.

The evolution of thinking and practice within CCPD led to a reformula-
tion of its mandate. As approved by the WCC central committee meeting
in Geneva, 1987, this now reads as follows:

a) The Commission on the Churches' Participation in Development (CCPD)
   shall, in co-operation with other sub-units, work with churches in their
   commitment to being in solidarity with the poor, giving special attention to
   the experiences and perspectives of the poor:
   — by promoting biblical, theological and ethical reflection on the church-
     es' action for justice, participation and development, as well as studies
     on economic and social questions in their global dimensions and
     particular aspects;
   — by fostering communication and processes of learning for justice and
     people's participation through forums and networks involving churches
     and groups striving for empowerment of the poor as essential to the
     process of development.
b) CCPD shall animate discussions within the WCC in the field of socio-
   economic justice.
c) CCPD shall be responsible for the administration of the Ecumenical
   Development Fund.

Challenges from Vancouver

The report of Vancouver issue group VI on "Struggling for Justice
and Human Dignity" includes, at various points, the following statements:

A special manifestation of [this] injustice is the prevailing international
economic order. It has institutionalized domination by Northern economies of
trade, finance, manufacturing, food processing and knowledge. Handled
mainly through transnational corporations, this economic order subordinates
and renders dependent the Southern economies...

Power elites concentrate wealth for the control of political and economic
instruments and institutions...

The machine of the prevailing economic order starves millions of people
and increases the number of unemployed every year...

> We interpret this development as idolatry, stemming from human sin, a product of satanic forces. We are in a situation where we must go beyond the normal prophetic and intercessory actions of the churches...
>
> The church is thus challenged not only in what it does, but in its very faith and being...
>
> In confessing Jesus Christ, churches must also confess their sins; they should recognize their complicity in, or tolerance of, the processes of death and be prepared to confront the dangers inherent in exorcizing such evils...

CCPD has taken these statements very seriously, and much of its work since the Vancouver assembly has concentrated on the responsibilities of churches and Christians in economic life and the interaction between theology and economic theory and practice. The challenges of Vancouver have provided a theme around which the various desks in CCPD have integrated their activities.

The organizational structure of CCPD

In addition to a director who gives general leadership to the staff team and co-ordinates its various activities, CCPD has staff persons working on the following specific programmes: socio-economic issues (since 1985), theology and ideologies, development training and advisory services, and network co-ordination. Together with the Sub-unit on Education, CCPD has a joint venture on "Learning and Education for Justice, Peace and the Integrity of Creation". From 1988 to mid-1989, CCPD had a special consultant on the debt crisis.

The WCC has an Advisory Group on Economic Matters (AGEM) consisting of economists, theologians and social scientists, whose activities are lodged administratively in CCPD.

Socio-economic issues: Much of CCPD's work in relation to socio-economic issues has focused on the effects of the international debt crisis on poor and vulnerable groups. Its objective was to assist — and stimulate — action and reflection about the debt crisis and related issues among churches, ecumenical bodies and CCPD-related organizations. Several publications were issued, including case studies and education/information kits for use in parishes. CCPD participated in, and made contributions to, many church-related meetings dealing with the debt crisis.

CCPD helped organize the West European consultation on the debt problem of the African, Caribbean and Pacific countries in Brussels in May 1988. This resulted in a statement with concrete recommendations for church positions on short- and long-term policies on the debt crisis, as well as possible strategies for educating and mobilizing church constituencies on the issues. Follow-up activities resulted in a visit by African church leaders to policy-makers in Brussels and the USA.

CCPD also co-sponsored an ecumenical hearing on the international monetary system and the churches' responsibility which took place in West Berlin, August 1988 (one month prior to the International Monetary Fund-World Bank annual meeting in the same city). Top officials from the World Bank, the IMF and the West German government were questioned by a panel of experts. Witnesses representing popular groups from five different continents articulated alternative approaches to development and called for solutions to the debt crisis which do not penalize the poor or lead to human rights violations.

Building on the experience of the ecumenical hearing in West Berlin, ecumenical groups in Washington organized a series of alternative events timed in relation to the IMF-World Bank annual meeting there in September 1989.

CCPD established collaboration on the debt crisis with other WCC sub-units and programmes, notably the Commission of the Churches on International Affairs (CCIA), "Justice, Peace and the Integrity of Creation" (JPIC), the Commission on Inter-Church Aid, Refugee and World Service (CICARWS) and the Sub-units on Women and Youth as well as with the CCPD-related networks, many of which have programmes on debt issues.

There were also close working relationships with other ecumenical bodies at both international and national levels, for example the Caribbean Conference of Churches, the Latin American Council of Churches, the Christian Conference of Asia, the All Africa Conference of Churches, and many church-related organizations in various parts of the world. The issue of the debt crisis also led to close working relationships with Roman Catholic agencies.

Christian faith and economic life: The Vancouver assembly said that the church is challenged by the prevailing international economic order — and not only in what it does, but in its very faith and being. To follow this up, CCPD organized, together with the Office on Research and Social Action of the Lutheran World Federation, a meeting in Sao Paulo, Brazil in March 1987 with people's movements struggling for economic justice. The participants came from various parts of the world and described themselves as "Christian communities at the edges of society". "A Call to Obedient Discipleship" was drawn up and distributed widely for signatures. The document calls on churches and individual Christians to initiate, encourage and support efforts to create just and fully participatory economic systems that guarantee the right to life for all people as expressed in the rights to food, shelter, work, health, dignity and self-determination. CCPD organized a debate about the call to obedient discipleship, and the results, reflecting different points of view, were published in the *CCPD Documents Series*. (The ecumenical hearing in West Berlin, mentioned above, was an offspring of the Sao Paulo meeting.)

The WCC central committee meeting in Hanover, August 1988, welcomed the proposal that CCPD work towards a draft of an "Ecumenical Statement on Christian Perspectives in Economic Life". The process leading up to such a statement was to be organized under the auspices of AGEM. At its first meeting on this subject, in January 1989, it was emphasized that the process should allow for the broadest participation possible, from both within the WCC itself and the ecumenical movement as a whole.

It was also felt that the WCC should not "rush into" making a statement, and that the preparatory process could therefore well extend beyond the Canberra assembly. The central committee in Moscow, July 1989, endorsed this view and agreed that the text of the ecumenical statement should be brought to the first full central committee meeting after the Canberra assembly. In the meantime CCPD has organized a series of regional consultations to gather inputs and insights for the statement from those perspectives. Consultations were also organized to develop specific themes such as women and economic life, and world religions and economics.

The question of how local congregations can be involved in the action/reflection process is of special concern to CCPD. A meeting to be held in Bossey, July 1990, will address this issue and elaborate models and methodologies in the area of learning for economic justice.

Socio-economic studies: The work by AGEM seeks to inform and support the ecumenical movement by providing detailed policy and action-oriented studies on political-economic issues. Since the Vancouver assembly AGEM has addressed issues such as the international financial system, employment and unemployment, and self-reliant development in Africa. The report on the international financial system (which was translated into German and Spanish) served as the basis for the "Statement on Third-World Debts" issued by the WCC central committee meeting in Buenos Aires, Argentina, in 1985. A popularized summary of all the work done by AGEM since 1979 was published in 1988 under the title *Ecumenical Reflections on Political Economy*.

Theology and ideologies: The principal role of CCPD is not to "create" theology — or ideology — from its office in Geneva, but to be sensitive to the stirrings of the human spirit as it struggles for human dignity and justice. Its role is that of a dialogue partner helping to clarify the theology and ideology implicit in a situation of struggle. On the basis of this understanding of its role, CCPD has engaged in a process leading to the document "Towards a Church in Solidarity with the Poor", which was published prior to the Vancouver assembly and which was widely shared among the churches.

Since the Vancouver assembly CCPD has continued to work along these lines. A church in solidarity with the poor needs to listen to the poor, to their stories about day-to-day life and to the way they do theology. This perspective led to discussions with the WCC secretariat for Bible studies, and it was decided to launch a Bible interpretation programme which will bring a grassroots perspective to bear on the study of the Bible. The programme seeks to enable the perception of the Bible of those who are on the "underside" to come to expression and to gain a hearing within the ecumenical community.

In the area of the study of ideologies, an international consultation was held in Buchow, GDR, in April 1988 on the theme "Ideologies and People's Struggles for Justice, Peace and Freedom". The participants, who came from 15 countries, critically assessed the theory and practice of both capitalist and socialist societies. The results of the consultation were published in CCPD's *Occasional Study Pamphlet Series*.

Development training and advisory services: The programme for development-training and advisory services was launched in 1984. In view of the special needs of the African churches, the programme concentrated until 1988 on Africa; during this period numerous consultations were held in many African countries. The objective was to assist the churches in setting up their own development services, and to train staff through seminars and workshops. Much of the work in this field was done in close collaboration with the African Network on the Churches' Participation in Development and was financially supported by EZE, the Protestant central agency for development aid of the Federal Republic of Germany. Although the special attention for training needs in Africa remained high on the CCPD agenda, the scope of the programme was widened after 1988 to include all regions.

The purpose of training and development education is ultimately the empowerment of persons, groups and sectors of society to participate in processes for social transformation. CCPD aims to promote cross-fertilization between such activities undertaken in various local situations and to seek insights for the mutual support of local and regional programmes. CCPD tries to achieve this by organizing consultations and workshops and by publishing relevant materials. CCPD works in close collaboration with the related networks in various parts of the world, all of which have identified training and education as one of their most important activities.

Networks: Early in its existence (in 1972 in fact), the commission had stated that CCPD is "a movement of people for development, not an organization. What is needed is the appropriate institutional expression which serves the movement but does not fashion or dominate it." Relationships with so-called "counterpart groups" were established. At a later stage the network approach was developed, and regional networks were formed in Asia, Africa and Latin America. A "functional network" was established of organizations in industrialized countries which are working on development education.

CCPD understands the networks as fellowships of autonomous groups committed to a common cause and working in solidarity with one another, sharing insights, experiences and resources, and undertaking common actions to further their cause and grow as a fellowship.

CCPD sees the network approach as a "praxis" model fundamental to its work. Working through networks is a long-term experiment in sharing power, one which provides an essential people's perspective on macro-level realities. Some of the issues on which networks and network partners concentrate are training for development, socio-economic questions, people's theology and Bible studies, popular education, women and youth. Solidarity actions are organized for those suffering from oppression, and South-South exchange of persons takes place among network partners.

Justice, Peace and the Integrity of Creation: The JPIC process has been a priority item of CCPD since the Vancouver assembly. Within the broad JPIC process CCPD's emphasis is on justice as it relates to socio-economic issues and to people's participation. CCPD has sought to contribute, on the basis of its specific mandate, to the JPIC process in many different ways (including financial support to JPIC programmes).

In 1985 CCPD embarked on a joint programme with the WCC Sub-unit on Education on "Learning and Education for JPIC", and a staff person was appointed for this task. The programme tackled the challenge of introducing JPIC concerns and studies in the curriculum of the churches' formal and informal educational activities, and tried to break down the separation between "classical" Christian educators and action groups. To this effect many national and regional seminars were organized. In order to involve children more closely in the JPIC process, a children's creative art festival was organized; this had a tremendous response from children all over the world.

Together with the Programme to Combat Racism and Urban Rural Mission/Commission on World Mission and Evangelism, CCPD organized a small workshop in 1989 which led to the publication of a booklet underlining the importance of justice in the world convocation on JPIC. Representatives of people's movements were invited to a people's forum to take place just before the world convocation on JPIC in Seoul, March 1990, in order to stress the centrality of justice within the broad concern for JPIC.

Ecumenical Development Fund/2% Appeal: The Ecumenical Development Fund (EDF) was established by the WCC executive committee in 1970 as a means of mobilizing the churches for long-term commitments to development. At the same time the executive committee launched an appeal to member churches to contribute "not less than 2% of their total income for development programmes and projects around the world, including those in their own country". The EDF, which is administered by CCPD, is the major instrument for handling money received through the 2% Appeal; but block grants to EDF are also accepted. The EDF is primarily an experiment in creating new types of relationships between donors and receivers. Transferring power to so-called "receivers of grants", EDF is a unique way in which resources can be shared ecumenically, a challenge to churches to share both material and non-material resources and to be in solidarity with the poor and oppressed. It is based on mutual trust rather than on control and submission. In the context of EDF several round-table structures have been established, bringing together "donors" and "receivers" in an effort to create more equitable relationships between them. In the course of time these round tables have been transferred to CICARWS.

On several occasions the governing bodies of the WCC have called for member churches to renew their commitment to the 2% Appeal. In the period 1983-90 approximately US$12,848,830 was disbursed through the EDF.

Orientations for the future

CCPD intends to retain for the future its overall emphasis on socio-economic issues and the responsibilities of churches and Christians in economic life. Within this broad context economic justice for women, and training and education for socio-economic issues, have been identified as priority areas for new work. CCPD will also continue to support strongly and stimulate the ongoing JPIC process, and will contribute to this process on the basis of its mandate.

Another focus of CCPD will be communication for justice as an essential process for sharing experiences, wisdom, analyses, strategic knowledge and vision in the context of the struggle for justice. Communication for justice must be oriented towards actions for justice. Promoting justice for the poor and oppressed remains the vocation of CCPD.

CHRISTIAN MEDICAL COMMISSION (CMC)

The Christian Medical Commission was established in 1968 as a "sponsored agency" under both the Commission on World Mission and Evangelism (CWME) and the Commission on Inter-Church Aid, Refugee and World Service (CICARWS). Its first orientation was as an advisory body to church-related medical programmes and as a consultative agency on health projects and services. In 1977 the CMC became a sub-unit within Programme Unit II.

Mandate and vision

Following the Nairobi assembly in 1975, CMC was mandated to assist churches in their search for an understanding of health and healing, to promote new approaches to health care, and to encourage those involved in church-related health programmes to join in planning and co-ordinating their activities for more effective service. This mandate did not change after Vancouver.

The Vancouver assembly, with its vision of maturity of the church, has called for nurturing the "full expression of the church's ministry of healing and sharing" and developing, as a priority, "a community of healing and sharing within the WCC and the member churches where men, women, young people and children, able and disabled, clergy and laity participate fully and minister to one another".

Programmatic emphases

Completing the study/enquiry on health, healing and wholeness: The Unit II committee, in its report to the first central committee following Vancouver (Geneva, 1984), noted the insights gained in the study of "The Christian Understanding of Health, Healing and Wholeness" and affirmed plans to continue the theological exploration on this topic with an emphasis on the biblical understanding of suffering, sickness and dying, and the role of reconciliation and hope in the healing task of the churches.

Three final regional consultations on health, healing and wholeness were held for North America (1984), Europe (1986) and Northeast Asia (1987). The issues which emerged very clearly from these consultations were the highly technical and impersonal developments in modern medicine, the erosion of traditional values, spiritual emptiness, the hazards of industrialization, and the need for the church to challenge these trends and to build communities which encourage more humane healing practices. The study revealed that health is not primarily "medical", and called upon the church to regain its healing function.

A paper evolving from the study was presented at a plenary session of the central committee in Moscow in July 1989. The central committee asked the WCC member churches to make policy statements on their involvement in health care and healing, re-affirming the healing ministry of the church and stating their commitment to community-building and to justice in health.

Promoting innovative approaches to primary health care: For two decades now CMC has been playing a major role in promoting primary health care (PHC) within church circles and with the World Health Organization (WHO). Church-related institutions have been challenged to redirect medical mission from institution-based care to community-based programmes. Existing hospitals have responded in various ways: some have promoted outreach programmes; others have integrated and/or supported primary health care activities; some have developed into modern tertiary medical centres, while some have closed down due to the sky-rocketing cost of medical care. Some co-ordinating agencies for church-related health work, national councils of churches and member churches of the WCC have developed pilot projects on community health programmes and challenged donor agencies to give preference to primary health care over tertiary care.

A study (which began in 1977) was commissioned to look into the feasibility of self-reliance in PHC; it was completed in 1987 with the publication of *Financing of Primary Health Care Programmes: Can They be Self-sufficient?* The study concluded that it seems unlikely that a PHC programme will ever be 100% self-reliant — and indeed can never be expected to be self-sufficient. However, certain income-producing components of PHC programmes have the potential to generate funds to pay for educational and preventive work.

Community participation is difficult to measure in financial terms. The questions of who pays for services, and how equitable health care can be provided in communities subject to injustice and poverty, remain un-resolved. Examples of multilateral financing of services were pointed out, including co-financing of church services by governments.

It was recommended that CMC advise donor agencies to move towards a more realistic appraisal of the time which PHC programmes need to reach maturity and a degree of self-reliance, and to promote practical methods by which cost issues can be better understood and managed at the project level. The global focus on mechanisms for cost recovery and community-financing of health care makes it increasingly important for the churches to examine their own experiences closely and to participate actively in the debate, speaking for justice and equity.

CMC continues to give varied forms of assistance to WCC member churches and health networks. After the Vancouver assembly field visits of staff and short-term consultants, with the assistance of commissioners, took place in various regions and countries. For example, in response to Vancouver's request for assistance to the Pacific region a team from CMC and Church and Society visited the republic of the Marshall Islands. Team members assessed the ongoing primary health care programmes, as well as plans to improve the understanding of, and advocacy for, efforts towards better health conditions in the Marshall Islands. All such visits were intended to help in the ongoing evaluation of existing PHC program-mes in their relation to strategies and services, curriculum development, the acquisition of necessary equipment and development of new areas of work (e.g., the field of industrial health).

CMC continued to play a supportive role with those struggling against injustice, poverty and ill-health. After more than a decade of promoting PHC, there was a realization from partner agencies and networks that trainers for community-based programmes themselves needed further training and capacity building.

The possibility for exchange of expertise and for developing a regional and global core of trainers led to a "think-tank" workshop (Geneva, 1989) which identified priority areas for training, and defined the curriculum content for training for community-based programmes. This led to the development of more regional workshops on lifelong learning for change (in Zimbabwe, Amsterdam, Benin and Liberia, 1990). These sought to empower people to take responsibility for aspects of their lives which relate to health, and to form a global network of persons involved in community-based health and development work. Such training for transformation should be further expanded, so that churches from all regions will discover the interconnectedness between the "technical aspects of community-based health care" and "healing communities". It must be understood that PHC is not only a third-world concern but also a first-world one.

Consultations and workshops focusing on certain issues and elements within the scope of PHC have been held internationally, regionally and nationally, including the national workshop on non-governmental organizations (NGOs) in PHC (Harare, 1985) aimed at improving the managerial skills of participants working in health stations; a meeting on the use of herbal medicines in PHC (Togo, 1987); an international consultation on addictions (Geneva, 1988); and workshops on family health programmes in PHC (Harare, 1988, and the Gambia, 1989). Joint sponsorship of these meetings with organizations in the area and with some international organizations, such as the League of Red Cross Societies, WHO and the International Christian Federation, aimed at maximizing resource utilization and strengthening networking. All the proceedings of these consultations have been documented and published.

At the 1984 central committee meeting the churches were also encouraged to ask their governments to support the efforts of WHO to combat alcoholism and drug abuse. The consultation on addictions issued a specific call for the churches to become directly involved in combating alcoholism and other substance abuse. Follow-up consultations have taken place in several regions (Rwanda, 1988; Honduras, 1988; and Cyprus, 1989).

Enabling the church to function as a healing community: The Acquired Immune Deficiency Syndrome (AIDS) is an incurable disease that has moved the world to intense engagement since the mid-1980s. CMC was mandated by the WCC central committee (1987) to work closely with the Sub-units on Education and Church and Society in an effort to provide principles for the pastoral ministry of the church as a healing community to AIDS patients, and to make educational guidelines and preventive measures widely known to member churches. In this connection CMC published the manual, *What is AIDS?* A second international consultation on AIDS and pastoral care (Moshi, 1988) and a follow-up counselling and training workshop (Barbados, 1989) have taken place. (In the last workshop a manual on pastoral counselling was produced.) Another "how-to" booklet providing guidelines for pastors, youth leaders and teachers about dealing with the problems of HIV infection and AIDS has been published by CMC.

Indeed the tragedy of human suffering so characteristic of AIDS is the acid test of whether the church properly understands its role to heal, and is ready to act accordingly. The church is also called upon to respond to other forms of suffering. Specific examples of work towards health, healing and wholeness, as this is being pursued in some regions of the world, have revealed ways to alleviate human misery. More such work is needed, not only as models or pilot projects but as a norm for every congregation. Since caring and healing congregations have been recognized as the key to promoting good health and health care, attention has been given to identifying, encouraging, publishing and supporting existing programmes, and enabling the creation of such congregations where they did not yet exist.

Promoting rational drug use: The CMC pharmaceutical programme developed from the concern over problems in the availability, distribution and consumption of drugs. Many people have no access at all to pharmaceuticals, while for others overprescribing and overconsumption are widespread. The CMC continues to be concerned about reliance on drugs when the underlying cause of an illness may be a condition such as malnutrition or obesity. The provision of essential drugs is an element of primary health care; therefore CMC, along with promoting PHC, actively supports an essential drugs programme which places priority on assuring the appropriate use of a limited number of preparations.

Much of the work has been carried out in collaboration with coordinating agencies for church-related health work or with other NGOs. Visits to their programmes, advising on pharmaceutical matters, took place in many (mainly sub-Saharan) countries. These visits were made by a special field consultant until 1985 and since 1987 by CMC's Geneva-based technical adviser on pharmaceuticals. In addition, a workshop on essential drugs in primary health care was organized in Nicaragua with participants coming from Central and South American countries.

Inappropriate drug donations are often an obstacle to implementing rational drug policies, and become a burden rather than a help for the recipients. A major achievement for this period is therefore the development of "Guidelines for Donors and Recipients of Pharmaceutical Donations" which has found the support of many other organizations and, in the long run, will make it more difficult to "dump" inappropriate or useless drugs.

The programme of rational drug use will shift its emphasis to include alternative elements of health care and an integrated approach to health care, as well as the promotion of the "essential drugs" concept.

Strengthening external networking for more effective service: The CMC has maintained close co-ordination with WHO, UNICEF, the League of Red Cross Societies and other international NGOs, such as the International Baby Food Action Network (IBFAN). On the occasion of their meeting on 4 November 1986, WHO director-general Halfdan Mahler and WCC general secretary Emilio Castro issued a joint statement expressing grave concern on three issues fundamental to the development of effective PHC. These were:
1) the gross inequities in health and health care;
2) a vertical, selective approach to health problems; and
3) quite insufficient progress in allowing people to take their own health into their own hands.

Dr Mahler and Dr Castro called on church leaders in all countries "to review critically their current performance in improving the health of people, to focus on long-term health development needs as part of socio-economic development, on the ethical challenge of 'Health for All by the Year 2000', and on primary health care in its fullest meaning as the key to attaining that goal". The central committee at its meeting in Geneva, 1987, commended the joint statement for circulation to WCC member churches for appropriate study and action.

External networking has been based on issues of common concern, such as infant and child health and welfare. One vivid example was the ongoing correspondence with the Interfaith Center on Corporate Responsibility and Action for Corporate Accountability, both based in the USA, as well as dialogue with, and support for, the ongoing activities of IBFAN and its worldwide network. In co-ordination with the Commission on the Churches' Participation in Development (CCPD) CMC visited and met with, at their request, officials of Nestlé at Vevey, Switzerland (1987) and the Nestlé Infant Formula Audit Commission (1989). In the dialogue it was made clear that the well-being of infants and children was foremost in the concern of CMC and CCPD. It was hoped that Nestlé and other manufacturers would comply with the provisions of the international code of marketing of breast milk substitutes (adopted by the WHO assembly in 1981), including the cessation of all free supplies of powdered infant milk to hospitals. Whether to participate in the renewed boycott of Nestlé was left to the WCC member churches to decide.

Relationships with regional and national church bodies were actively pursued. CMC co-sponsored with the Christian Conference of Asia the consultation on "Health, Healing and Wholeness: New Strategies for Asia 2000" (Bangkok, 1989). During field trips, staff members visited member churches and national councils of churches and church-related medical/health programmes.

Collaboration with the Roman Catholic Church has always been a concern of CMC. Regular visits to the Vatican have been made with the aim of once again adding a full-time Roman Catholic consultant to the CMC staff. Issues of common concern which surfaced in the dialogue were reciprocity, developing a common understanding in approaches to health in order to augment each other's efforts and to avoid competition and duplication, and developing common grounds and action for advocacy and experience-sharing. Roman Catholic consultants regularly attended commission meetings.

Communicating CMC to WCC constituencies and networks: The year 1990 marked the 20th year of *Contact*, which is published six times a year in four languages (English, French, Spanish and Portuguese). Selected issues are also being printed in Kiswahili in Kenya and Tanzania, and in Arabic in Egypt. *Contact* articles have carried the mandate, vision and programmatic emphases of CMC, and its efforts in support of activities in the field.

Changes, developments and special challenges

Three major shifts have been noted during the last quarter of the period from Vancouver to Canberra. These were:
1) training trainers to facilitate empowerment of people at the micro level;
2) developing and popularizing integrated health care; and
3) developing educational materials to help congregations regain their place in the health, healing and wholeness ministry.

Thoughts on the future orientation of CMC

After a decade of study and enquiry, theological reflections can be translated into action. CMC will continue to identify and share successful models of healing ministry, utilizing the full potential of congregations. Various modes of communication can be used to share experiences, including story-telling, drama and Bible stories; the media can include radio, film and video.

The issue of community-based health care still requires CMC's main attention. The cultural determinants of health, sickness, disease and healing demand more consideration. Therefore CMC has the opportunity to ensure that the dialogue on health, healing and wholeness continues within the churches, with their different cultural backgrounds. Circumstances creating ill-health and despair (such as wars, militarism, and wrong modern value-systems) can be priority concerns. Issues which can be a starting point for CMC's work are: areas of need in the churches, how to enable the churches' health programmes, and assessment of the churches' role in health care. The main principles in CMC's work are equity (in regard to access to services, to resources, to opportunities, etc.), justice, socio-economic development and sustainability (self-reliance). CMC intends to have people's participation as a major focus in the years to come.

In the light of the Canberra theme, CMC should explore new ways of interpreting spirituality and health for our times — for people are searching for meaning and new symbols.

One way towards the renewal projected in the Canberra theme is learning and practising behaviour that generates hope. Hope-breeding behaviour helps to redefine persons in terms of value and status. Persons being available to each other, and patient community-building, are equally important in generating hope. Diaconal actions in witness and service are expressions of hope which generate new hope. Over the years CMC has struggled truly to integrate the justice dimension of health. This message should continue to challenge church-sponsored health programmes and congregations to act as truly healing communities.

FUTURE CHALLENGES FOR UNIT II

While JPIC as a programme will undoubtedly assume a different form after the Canberra assembly, the need to link struggles for peace, protection of the environment and justice will continue as a main priority in the post-assembly period for the WCC. The experiences gained through working for JPIC have enriched the ecumenical movement's approach to justice and service, and will continue to challenge the churches and their ecumenical structures. Similarly, the experiences of HRROLA can be used to enrich the Council's approach to human rights. HRROLA was created to respond to a particular human rights situation in Latin America; as needs have changed, the programme has evolved in response. But even if HRROLA disappears as a separate Unit II programme, its experience can serve as a basis for further ecumenical involvement with human rights issues.

Since Vancouver all five sub-units in Unit II have undergone changes in direction and emphases as a result of the assembly itself, the changed world situation and the major consultations which have taken place during this period. In many respects the concerns of the sub-units are converging. As a result of the Larnaca consultation, CICARWS is coming to see advocacy as an essential part of its diaconal mission and is finding more common ground with other Unit II sub-units. Growing awareness that economic issues are central to international institutions has meant greater CCIA involvement in areas traditionally associated with CCPD. Similarly, the economic basis of racism and the struggle for sanctions in South Africa has brought PCR closer to other sub-units in Unit II. The culmination of CMC's ten-year study process on health, healing and wholeness is leading to a growing awareness that health issues must be addressed within the context of a healing community.

All the sub-units are making connections between their work and the theology and spirituality of struggle. For example, spirituality and racism" was the theme of a 1989 consultation organized by PCR, while CCPD is working to deepen reflection on the theological basis of economic structures. Changes in the orientation of each of its sub-units offer new possibilities for even closer collaboration within Unit II — a process which is necessary to translate the values of the kingdom into practical action to confront the challenges and needs of the churches as they move into the last decade of the 20th century.

Unit III
Education and Renewal

Building the body: an overall perspective

Two issues which never cease to attract the attention of the WCC central committee are those of participation and representation. These are very often raised by Unit III and are heard as a challenge to the ecclesiologies of the constituent churches of the World Council of Churches. The advocacy which the unit has taken upon itself for inclusive and participatory communities has perhaps become a burden which prevents the WCC member churches from hearing the many issues to which Unit III calls attention. Nevertheless, there is a clear indication that the understanding of "who constitutes the church" is crucial to the role of the Unit within the Council. Unit III has consistently sought the implementation of the Dresden (and, later, the El Escorial) recommendations on the level of the churches' commitment to programmes and concerns of women and young people.

The questions raised are: Who speaks for the church? And who can represent a member church and "carry weight", both in the WCC and in the member church from which he or she comes? This *theological* issue has remained with us in the period from Vancouver to Canberra. What is encouraging is that the WCC is beginning to struggle with the theological significance of a unit on education and renewal.

One of the greatest problems has been the lack of direct support from the churches for the issues and concerns of the Unit. The WCC's member churches can plan to sustain programmes in the "society-related" areas of its work; but the churches' "domestic needs" of education and congregational renewal — which touch directly the people who make up the membership statistics presented to the Council — remain areas which "do not need" special attention. For example, the churches have continued to speak about young people, and differently-abled and other marginalized persons, but have done very little about them: there has been very little intentional support for the needs of the youth of the church, and the needs of differently-abled and other marginalized persons have been even more neglected. Further efforts are needed to empower these persons to participate effectively in the work of the WCC as a whole. With respect to women the situation is a little more hopeful; we look for progress here since in January 1987 the central committee authorized the Ecumenical Decade of the Churches in Solidarity with Women.

The story of the Unit from Vancouver to Canberra includes both advances and impasses. We have continued to see modifications of its constituent parts; this is as it should be, given that at Evanston 1954, its predecessor, called the Division of Ecumenical Action, was conceived to be "provisional, experimental, flexible enough to accommodate fresh needs and respond to emergency issues". We have made significant changes, such as the bringing together of the Programme on Theological Education (PTE) and the Ecumenical Institute, Bossey.

Since Vancouver the Unit III committee has grown in coherence and developed in its relationships. The committee believes that the undergirding concepts of the Unit are those of spirituality, inclusiveness and wholeness, and that these concepts can be offered as working principles to the WCC as a whole and to its member churches. Renewal and spirituality are seen by the committee as the unifying bond which holds the Unit's five sub-units together.

When it comes to working out this identity in practice there have been many problems. The sub-unit structure, with its working groups and commissions, continues to be the operative mode within the WCC. Thinking and acting as a programme unit is ad hoc and is not backed by any continued or sustained support from a unit committee. Not even the Unit executive group can enable the Unit to be a coherent whole. Nonetheless, the Unit has been held together by the emphasis of its constituent parts on people's stories and people's movements, the orientation towards the marginal and the forgotten. This common perspective on the church's mission has been a common source of sustenance, and of mutual learning and encouragement. We trust that the process will continue after the Canberra assembly and that further progress will be made in enabling programmes to work together.

The Unit continues to search for more effective modes of learning and of serving as an educational task force for promoting ecumenical concerns such as the appropriation of the findings of the *Baptism, Eucharist and Ministry* document. It has concentrated a good deal of effort on witnessing to the need for inclusive community, and on stimulating that spirituality which moves us to promote the kingdom values that bring us renewal. Spirituality as a theological factor has guided all our programmes and all our relationships, making "spirituality for justice and peace" its umbrella theme. The intentional recourse to our spiritual resources has meant that worship and liturgical life have taken increasingly larger portions of the time which we have spent together for deliberation, decision-making, and acting to bring about positive change in dehumanizing situations.

Unit III has thereby functioned as the "spirit which troubles the calm waters" of our theologies and styles of relationships. In a word, the Unit keeps alive the necessity for churches to struggle for justice and human dignity. Both these issues have theological bases and implications for the Council's mission of witnessing to a divided world. We have kept the emphasis on the need for more intensive relationships within the ecumenical movement at all levels, and especially at the level of local congregations and ecclesial communities.

We have tried to clarify our self-understanding under the theme of "Renewal and Spirituality", and have undertaken joint studies of this subject. We have worked together as a unit on the Ecumenical Decade of the Churches in Solidarity with Women. It is our hope that as a unit we shall enable the global ecumenical youth gathering to become an effective forum for evaluation and planning.

Mutual sharing in planning and discussion of sub-unit work at the level of the sub-unit directors and within Unit staff meetings on issues such as theological language, have helped us to see the Unit as a whole. But it is also true that — as stated in Vancouver — "unless sub-units share their resources and combine their efforts to work on common projects at national/regional levels, effective integration cannot be realized". We believe that this re-orientation should apply to the whole WCC.

Reviewing our work geographically, we find a heavy concentration in all regions of the world except North America. There is very little involvement with the USA and Canada. More recently we have attempted to correct the imbalance in Europe by seeking the involvement of more churches in Central and Eastern Europe. We have been asking how to become more relevant globally as we seek to share resources and to act in solidarity. The Unit seeks inclusiveness and participation and is therefore always keenly aware of all who are being marginalized, for whatever reason. We hope that the concern for wholeness will also be evident in the accounts of the work of each of our sub-units.

SUB-UNIT ON EDUCATION

Introduction

The two major emphases of the Sub-unit on Education since the Vancouver assembly have been ecumenical learning and learning for justice, peace and the integrity of creation. At its first meeting in 1985, the working group on education decided that these two emphases should provide the focus for all the Sub-unit's programmes; and thanks to this decision, the Sub-unit succeeded, to a significant degree, in overcoming the compartmentalization which had plagued its work in the past.

Besides permeating the work of seven other programme areas, ecumenical learning and learning for justice, peace and the integrity of creation also had distinctive programmatic thrusts. The other seven programme areas were biblical studies, adult basic education, family education, advocacy for children, the church and persons with disabilities, learning in a world of many faiths, cultures and ideologies — a Christian response (Interlink), and ecumenical scholarships and leadership formation. As far as possible, Sub-unit activities in all these areas have been carried out in collaboration with the relevant national and regional ecumenical bodies.

The programme on church-related educational institutions ended in 1985, and the follow-up was entrusted to regional bodies.

Ecumenical learning

This programme, which was set up to encourage ecumenical learning within the churches, was able to build on the findings of two previous Sub-unit consultations on this concern: "Education for Effective Ecumenism" (co-sponsored with the Ecumenical Institute, Bossey, 1982) and the consultation on ecumenical learning (1986) both of which pointed to "the obligation of the churches to educate for life in the oikoumene — for life in the world and in the ecumenical situation which is a part of the life of all our churches today" (Ulrich Becker, "Ecumenical Education is Again on the Spot"). It has been able to reach out to ecumenical bodies in the regions, notably in Africa, where it helped to begin work on an ecumenical curriculum in collaboration with the All Africa Conference of Churches; in the Middle East with the Middle East Council of Churches; and in the USA, India and the Pacific (working with the National Council of Churches, the All India Sunday School Association, the Pacific Conference of Churches and the Pacific Association of Theological Schools respectively). Collaborative work has also been carried out with national ecumenical bodies and with other international Christian organizations such as the World Alliance of Reformed Churches, the YMCA, and various member churches. The programme has made possible inter-regional exchange visits among Christian educators for participation in intentional ecumenical learning events.

This programme was instrumental in co-ordinating plans for regional education conferences (1989-90) and a global consultation (to be held in June 1990) to explore options for the WCC's educational work in the post-Canberra period. *Alive Together! A Practical Guide to Ecumenical Learning* was published by the programme in 1989.

Learning for justice, peace and the integrity of creation

Since the late 1970s, the Sub-unit on Education has collaborated with the Churches' Commission on Participation in Development (CCPD). In 1982 the WCC central committee approved a recommendation to set up a joint programme of the two Sub-units. The move was taken both to streamline the activities of the WCC in the area of education and to try to bridge the growing gap between Christian educators and so-called "development" educators. Following a decision of the central committee in 1984, the joint programme became known as "Learning for Justice, Peace and the Integrity of Creation". It was "to be responsible for bringing together the educational experiences of churches in their involvement in issues of justice, peace and integrity of creation and to be concerned with the educational components and implications of the WCC-wide programme, as part of the preparatory process for the world conference in 1990".

The programme organized numerous national and regional workshops in Latin America, Africa, Asia and the Pacific in conjunction with the ecumenical bodies in the areas. An attempt was made in these workshops to relate JPIC concerns to the general educational activities of the churches. Teachers, animators and curriculum designers were invited to focus on JPIC issues in their own context, and to develop strategies for a co-ordinated approach to these issues. In addition, the programme contributed to the preparation of resource materials for the world convocation on JPIC, and sponsored a children's art festival on JPIC issues in 1988, from which a calendar was produced, as well as a series of slides and a video cassette.

Work is now under way to evaluate the results of the regional and national workshops and to make recommendations for the future of this programme.

Biblical studies

In addition to its role of providing a firm theological basis for the work of the Sub-unit, the paramount task of this programme in the immediate post-Vancouver years was the training of Bible-study enablers. Hans-Ruedi Weber was executive secretary of the programme from its inception in 1972 (when it was part of the General Secretariat, being transferred to the Sub-unit on Education in 1976) to his retirement in March 1988. He brought exceptional gifts to the task, marking with creative energy a whole generation of Bible-study enablers in various regions of the world. One of the last courses carried out by this programme under his direction was a workshop on participatory Bible study (held in collaboration with the Programme on Theological Education and the Ecumenical Institute, Bossey) in June 1987.

Over the past two years the programme has worked closely with other sub-units of the WCC to produce and evaluate Bible-study material both for the Canberra assembly and for other ongoing WCC programmes. Consultation and research in the field of biblical interpretation, as well as the establishment of contacts and working relationships with other international organizations active in the field of Bible studies, constitute other aspects of the programme's work.

One of the challenges this programme has had to face was the lack of involvement by Orthodox churches. This situation has changed over the last two years, however, and there are promising signs that co-operation with churches in the Middle East and the Soviet Union will continue to grow. This development needs to be encouraged and strengthened.

Adult basic education

This programme works with churches and other interested bodies to enable marginalized adults to participate fully in the transformation of society. "Adult basic education" has been defined as a process of lifelong learning which is both conscious and critical, and is rooted in the culture of a specific group. An essential part of the work of the programme is the training of co-ordinators and facilitators to discover, strengthen and expand people's own expertise. Training for literacy is one of the many activities of the programme, which is designed as an integral part of the work of the community on resolving the fundamental problems of persons who are marginalized.

During recent years the locale for this work has shifted from Latin America and the French-, Portuguese- and Spanish-speaking countries of

Africa (where Paulo Freire made such notable impact) to the countries of English-speaking Africa, Southeast Asia and the Pacific.

The programme has sought ways to enable the exchange of experienced collaborators among various regions of the world, and to make a more concerted effort to include women's perspectives in its activities. It has also given particular attention to the training of indigenous peoples. Work was begun on the development of a system of social analysis for use by local organizations, so that people learning basic literacy skills could "build knowledge collectively" as they struggle to survive, to resist oppression and to build a better society. Such knowledge is grounded in their everyday experience and culture and shaped by the national and international contexts.

The programme has made an effort to work with other sub-units of the WCC on problems such as local development, community-based health programmes, and ecumenical learning. It has also been involved with UNESCO in preparing for the International Literacy Year 1990, providing support to concerned groups and promoting the involvement of the churches. In addition to the direct involvement of the staff, the programme has helped women to participate as resource persons in various social analysis workshops held in the Pacific, Africa and Asia.

Family education

The Office of Family Education was created in the 1970s, following a re-organization of the earlier Department on the Co-operation of Men and Women in Church, Family and Society. It has traditionally worked with regional councils, churches and renewal groups in different parts of the world to challenge churches and the society to re-think the role of the family in the struggle for human dignity, equality, justice, liberation, reconciliation and peace.

Over the years the Office has facilitated and participated in numerous international, regional and local consultations related to family life, pastoral counselling, and relationships between women and men. It has also provided "seed money" to various local groups to set up counselling centres, family co-operatives and training programmes. The Office is presently evaluating the various projects it supports in an attempt to discourage donor dependency, and to discontinue projects which no longer correspond to the needs of the local community.

The challenge to the churches posed by the problem of the Acquired Immune Deficiency Syndrome (AIDS) has been a concern of this Office. It has worked closely with the WCC's Christian Medical Commission

(CMC) and the Sub-unit on Church and Society to articulate a programme of pastoral care for persons affected with AIDS and for their families.

The Office of Family Education has also responded to the request of the Vancouver assembly for a study on sexuality and human relations which would stimulate churches in their teaching and care for the whole person. The study "Living in Covenant with God and One Another" has been tested by selected groups around the world and is being made available to the churches.

The articulation of a coherent and contemporary understanding of "family" in its various manifestations and cultural expressions will be a high priority for the coming period. A strong emphasis on women and their struggle for equality and liberation, and concern for children, will also be important parts of the work. This must all be held within the context of the community of women and men; the education of men is surely a necessary element in developing a healthy family life.

Advocacy for children

The Sub-unit's involvement with the issues related to children dates from the 1971 merger into the WCC of the World Council of Christian Education (WCCE) — which itself harks back to the World Sunday School Association of the 19th century. Since Vancouver the place of children in the church has been dealt with in several consultations or workshops in other areas — for example, in the fields of ecumenical learning and learning for justice, peace and the integrity of creation. And the needs of children have been a focal issue in the intercultural education project Interlink. In 1983 the Sub-unit organized children's participation in some of the worship services and Bible study sessions of the Vancouver assembly. As at Vancouver, the presence and participation of children will be highlighted at Canberra in many ways — an affirmation of "the central place of children in the life of the church".

The Sub-unit was one of the founding members of the inter-non-governmental organizations (NGOs) project on street children (1982-84) and its successor organization, CHILDHOPE, which raises awareness about the plight of millions of homeless children around the world and supports and strengthens national and regional movements on this issue, and the efforts of NGOs and individuals who work directly with them.

In view of the awareness of the fact that children the world over will face a difficult future, increased attention will have to be given in the post-Canberra period to the concerns of children, including the implications of these concerns for adult Christian education.

Persons with disabilities

The WCC's involvement with the question of the church and its relationship to persons with disabilities began in 1971 with a Faith and Order consultation on "The Unity of the Church and the Unity of Mankind". The issue was given some prominence at both the Nairobi and Vancouver assemblies, and in 1984 a WCC task force on persons with disabilities recommended to the central committee meeting in the same year that a Council-wide programme on the church and persons with disabilities be established. For administrative reasons the desk was lodged in the Sub-unit on Education. The programme is assisted by a task force made up of staff members from various sub-units of the WCC.

The programme's aims are to facilitate fuller participation of persons with disabilities in the life of the church, thus promoting the mutual enrichment of all its members. It also seeks to analyze and address the relationship of disabilities to the issues of justice, peace and the integrity of creation and to contribute this dimension to the overall work of the WCC and its member churches. As a result of the programme's work with groups of persons with disabilities in Europe, Africa, the Middle East, Asia and the Americas, a new spirituality and challenging theological understandings of disability are emerging which have implications for both church and society. Much of the work of the programme has centred on developing partnership relations and networks among member churches.

In 1990 the programme produced a resource kit containing biblical/theological reflections and other materials for use by the churches.

Two of the most serious challenges which the programme has faced have been its inability to obtain the support of the member churches for its activities, and the lack of integration of its concerns into the programmes of the WCC as a whole.

The assembly task force on persons with disabilities is working closely with the programme to prepare for the participation and programmatic input of persons with disabilities to the Canberra assembly. The Education Sub-unit is also working on an evaluation of the programme and preparing recommendations on its future for the assembly.

Learning in a world of many faiths, cultures and ideologies — a Christian response

The project, known as Interlink, began in September 1985 and continued for a period of four years. Its aim was to help the churches discover educational approaches appropriate for living in a world of many faiths, cultures and ideologies. Work centred around four areas of concern: (1) intercultural religious education in a developed world context (the Netherlands); (2) intercultural education in the areas of science and technology (the Philippines); (3) Christian nurture in an intercultural context (Kenya); (4) a Christian response to secular philosophies of intercultural education (in collaboration with the International Association for Intercultural Education (IAIE), based in the Netherlands).

The results of the work done in the first two areas brought to light specific problems faced by Christian educators in multi-cultural societies. Recommendations were made for follow-up in the various national situations, and provisions were made for sharing the findings with the churches and other interested groups. As a result of work done in the third area, the National Council of Churches of Kenya approved a plan to produce a series of handbooks for pastors and trainers, incorporating the cultural, religious and ideological elements that are a part of daily life in Kenya. Later books will be designed for specific age groups from six years to adulthood.

In light of the enormous potential value of work done in the fourth area of concern — secular philosophies of intercultural education — the project sought to develop guidelines and principles for intercultural education to be made available to national and international bodies engaged in curriculum development and teacher training.

Reports of the project's work were published in the final issue of its magazine. Two additional publications are planned for 1991: a popular book on why Christians should be involved in intercultural education, and a study on the theological and educational issues raised by the project.

The findings indicate that intercultural education will assume increasing importance in the coming years, indeed that it will be the focus of education for the future. The WCC must reflect on how it can deal with this vital area in the post-Canberra period.

Ecumenical scholarships and leadership formation
The programme's ongoing aims are: (1) to encourage churches and church-related organizations to engage in comprehensive personnel planning, so that specific training needs may be identified; (2) to select the maximum number of recommended candidates from different parts of the world, arrange for their placement and financial support, and facilitate their involvement in the life of the host communities; (3) to discover

opportunities which, as far as possible, will combine academic study and practical experience, and enable candidates to benefit from intercultural and ecumenical exposure.

In 1945, when it began as an aspect of interchurch aid, the scholarships programme offered 27 pastors from six European countries the chance to study in five other European countries. Figures from recent years show major developments from these small beginnings and highlight some encouraging trends:

	1975-81 (average number or percentage)	1982-88 (average number or percentage)	Percentage of increase	Maximum number or percentage
Total awards	147	237	61%	316
Sending countries	52	77	48%	93
Receiving countries	27	34	26%	39
Students from developing countries	73%	84%	11%	88%
Non-theological studies	47%	54%	7%	63%
Awards to women	28%	31%	3%	41%

With the greatly increased number of total awards, some previously under-represented regions have improved their percentages during the years since the Vancouver assembly: the Middle East by 6%, Eastern Europe by 4%, the Caribbean by 6%, the Pacific by 7%; the percentage of awards to candidates from Orthodox churches rose to 9% in 1988; and certain countries which had not recently benefited received awards. Over against such progress is the disturbing fact that, on average, only one-third of the awards have been for studies in developing countries.

The programme has been able to expand, in response to more requests, largely because of new funding provided by contributing agencies. Special funding has been negotiated for South-South, practice-oriented, short-term awards.

In recent years larger numbers of WCC-sponsored students have benefited from the opportunities available at such institutions as the Asian Rural Institute in Japan, the Southeast Asia Rural Social Leadership Institute in the Philippines, the Mindolo Ecumenical Foundation in

Zambia, the Coady International Institute in Canada, the Institute of Social Studies in the Netherlands, the Irish School of Ecumenics in Ireland, and the Selly Oak Colleges in England. A number of these offer full or partial scholarships to WCC candidates.

The programme has a network of 140 national correspondents, but collaboration is hindered by the many changes of personnel (25% per year on average) and the small amount of time which most can devote to these responsibilities. Some countries have set up ecumenical scholarships committees which assist with local publicity and the selection of candidates. The scholarships secretary has visited many developing countries to explain the programme and in order better to understand the different situations and needs.

Ongoing evaluation of aspects of the programme takes place through questionnaires to students, study institutions, former scholarship-holders, and requesting bodies. In view of significant developments since the last review of the programme (in 1979-80), the WCC central committee has approved the proposal for a more systematic and thorough evaluation in 1990. The results will be presented to the first meeting of the new central committee after the Canberra assembly.

Special challenge to the Sub-unit on Education

The Sub-unit has been faced with a wide variety of expectations from the churches of the global community — ranging from the need of churches in the third world for basic Christian education and Sunday school materials, to requests in developed countries for new models of Christian education pertinent to particular segments of the congregation. The WCC's option for giving particular attention to the churches of the third world has inevitably led to some frustration on the part of churches in other areas. The need to reflect on priorities and how they are set will therefore remain an ongoing concern of the Sub-unit.

With this in mind, the Sub-unit engaged in a consultative process during 1989 and 1990 with churches and ecumenical bodies involved in education in every region of the world. The purpose was to identify the "burning issues" in education that need to be addressed by the WCC beyond Canberra, and to develop proposals for formulating educational emphases, goals and strategies for the WCC as we face the third millennium. These proposals are to be formulated by the working group on education at its final meeting in June 1990. New emphases must include the strengthening of educational processes in the churches and at the grassroots.

PROGRAMME ON THEOLOGICAL EDUCATION (PTE)

Mandate

According to its mandate the Programme on Theological Education is set up "to assist the churches in the reform and renewal of theological education". This description makes it clear that the principal actors are the churches; theological education, like ministry, which it serves, is the proper task of the church. The WCC, through PTE, stands with the churches to achieve goals set by the churches with regard to ministry and theological education. But of course this includes PTE challenging, questioning and affirming notions of ministry, theology and education. To that extent PTE has sought to be a resource and an instrument of renewal for the churches.

PTE operates with the understanding that ministry belongs to the whole people of God, and the task of the ordained and lay leadership of the church is to enable the whole people of God to fulfill their calling of ministry in the world. PTE has seen its role as the "enabler of enablers" through a variety of programmes.

PTE grew out of the work of the Theological Education Fund (TEF) which was founded by the International Missionary Council in January 1958 "to develop and strengthen indigenous theological education... stimulate local responsibility, encourage creative theological thinking and provide a higher standard of scholarship and training which is suited to the needs of the churches to be served". In its three mandates before it developed into PTE its emphases, in varying degrees and combinations, were described by such words as "excellence", "contextualization", "authenticity" and "creativity" — all in connection with theological education. The emergence of PTE from TEF has meant both continuity and change. For example, the above phrases have not been lost sight of. But instead of a preoccupation with the third world PTE now works for renewal in all regions of the world. It seeks to overcome the dichotomy of emphases on North and South, and especially to shed the image of being concerned only with the third world. The other major change is that PTE, instead of being an enabling fund, is now a programme which seeks the renewal of the churches' ministry and ministerial formation.

Programme activities

Under the general theme of ministerial formation PTE has focused on two issues: theology by the people and spiritual formation. The former grew from the rediscovery that ministry belongs to all God's people because the church, the sign, instrument and sacrament of the kingdom of God, is also the *people* of God. That being the case, PTE's task has been to explore how the people of God are being equipped for the theological task and for their ministry in today's world. In consultations, visits to theological schools, and publications, this theme has been studied and commended to the churches. The report of a consultation on it has been published under the title *Theology by the People: Reflections on Doing Theology in Community*. This was followed by *Stories Make People*, a collection of "stories" of people doing theology. Of course, PTE did not invent "theology by the people". Basic Christian communities and Christian groups all over the world have been involved in it for a long time now. PTE's task was to discover this phenomenon, to remind the theological world of its presence, to learn from it, and to share it as widely as possible.

Theology by the people raises three issues: that those involved in doing theology are all the believing Christians; that the perspective of doing theology is that of justice for all the oppressed people of God; and that the process of doing theology means engagement with the struggles of the poor people of the world. Thus theology by the people is more than a concept; it is a movement of renewal in theology.

Spiritual formation

The subject of theology is God, who is Spirit. Therefore theology, theological education and ministry are necessarily concerned with spirituality and spiritual formation. And it has been PTE's concern to press for the rehabilitation of spirituality in programmes of theological education so that the theological task can be made whole. Furthermore, over the years spirituality has been linked to the perfection of individuals. In the ecumenical context there has been a rediscovery of spirituality as communal, as open to the world, and involving both "combat" and contemplation. Issues of justice and peace are also spiritual matters. Spiritual formation in theological education has been promoted through many regional consultations. The preparatory Iona document (1987) has been studied by many faculties and groups, and the final report has been published as a resource book for fostering spiritual formation in theological education.

In going about our work we have seen more clearly the inter-relatedness of theology by the people, spirituality, and the concerns of justice and peace. For not only is the subject of theology God (and therefore theology is concerned with spirituality), but the kingdom values which theology attempts to translate across time and culture are spiritual values. Ecumenical theological education cannot ignore them. Thus justice and peace, and the concerns of the integrity of creation have also been brought into our programmatic activities in this area.

Women in theology

Taking seriously the insights of the study on the "Community of Women and Men in the Church" (1978-81), PTE has worked for the recognition of the place of women in the areas of theology and ministry. One achievement was to launch with the Women's Sub-unit a special programme on young women doing theology. The purpose was to identify younger women theologians and to empower them so that they might participate more fully in the theological and ministerial tasks of the church. Enabling women in and for ministry will be a continuing emphasis of PTE.

Resource-enabling

PTE has been an instrument for the transfer of resources among the various regions of the world. It has been inspired by the conviction that each region has resources to share, be they human or monetary, spiritual or material.

In the field of human resources, the exchange of persons from different regions was promoted. The most notable area has been Africa-Asia visits (with return visits in 1987 and 1989) through which persons from each region could share their hopes and fears about theology and theological education. The goal was to facilitate ecumenical learning, intercultural encounter, inter-regional co-operation and the sharing of models of innovative theological learning.

As for the area of material resources (partly as a carry-over from its TEF prehistory, and as a response to the need for resources to implement visions), PTE has made resources available, especially to churches in Asia, Africa, the Caribbean, Latin America, the Middle East and the Pacific, in the following categories: (1) creative-innovative programmes; (2) associations of theological schools; (3) faculty development; (4) alternative patterns of theological education; and (5) faculty and student exchange. Some library grants were also made. Since 1984 PTE has made "seed" grants amounting to: in 1984, $303,603; in 1985, $200,255; in 1986, $255,480; in 1987, $298,054; in 1988, $304,308; and in 1989, $315,712.

In addition to its direct funding, PTE also advocates resource-sharing among the churches for theological education. Examples are the special project for theological education in the Pacific, including the starting of the master's programme at the Pacific Theological College, Suva, Fiji, and the solidarity fund for Southeast Asia. A special fund for Latin America has already been developed, and an African ministerial fund is being planned.

World Conference of Associations of Theological Institutions

PTE carries out its work in co-operation and partnership with the associations of theological schools and institutions (of which there are more than 25 worldwide). Recently these associations have come together with the support of PTE to form a World Conference of Associations of Theological Institutions; this is an ecumenical forum for mutual sharing and stimulation and for joint planning and the enabling of theological education.

Consultations and workshops

Consultations have been a key instrument in the pursuit of an ecumenical perspective on theological education and ministerial formation.

Meetings held since Vancouver at the global level include those on "Theology by the People" (Mexico, 1985) and "Spiritual Formation and Theological Education" (Kaliurang, Indonesia, 1989). Many regional-level meetings have been held, for example on issues of theological education in relation to women ("Towards a Network of European Feminist Theologians", Boldern, Switzerland, 1985, in co-operation with the Sub-unit on Women and the Ecumenical Forum of European Christian Women; and "Women in Theological Education", Buenos Aires, Argentina, 1989), and dialogue ("Implications of Interfaith Dialogue for Theological Education", Kuala Lumpur, 1985, with the Dialogue Sub-unit); in relation to the contexts of Africa ("Theological Education in Africa: Quo Vadimus?", Accra, Ghana, in co-operation with the West African Association of Theological Institutions and the Department for the Study of Religions, University of Ghana, Legon), and Latin America ("Popular Theological Education", Quito, Ecuador, 1986); on the issue of contextualization itself ("Doing Theology in Different Contexts", Prague, Czechoslovakia, 1988); and in relation to current ecumenical issues ("Justice, Peace, Integrity of Creation and Theological Education for Asian Theological Students", Hong Kong, 1989). Altogether some 25 consultations have been held or are planned in the regions of Africa, Asia, Central America, Latin America, and Western and Eastern Europe.

In addition several important workshops have been held together with the Ecumenical Institute, Bossey, including those on "The Teaching of Ecumenics" (1986), "Ecumenism for Mission" (1987), "Inclusiveness in Theological and Liturgical Language" (1989), and "Partnership in Ecumenical Leadership Formation" (1989, in co-operation with the Sub-unit on Renewal and Congregational Life).

Visits to regions

The three executive staff travelled and visited schools and programmes in all the regions. On such visits experiences are shared and consultative services are provided. Such visits have generated ecumenical programmes, helped to identify ecumenical leadership, and shared information and insights on ministerial formation. Team visits have been organized especially in connection with PTE consultations.

The "internship" programme

PTE has been aware of the need to develop future ecumenical leaders, and has responded with its internship programme. With the co-operation of the Evangelical Lutheran Church of Oldenburg, FRG, and the Evangelisches Missionswerk of the FRG, PTE has sought to bring ecumenical concerns into the German-speaking student world and to bring the concerns of German-speaking students into the work of PTE. The high point of this programme was the Iserlohn consultation in July 1987 on "Teaching and Learning Theology for the Future of the Church" held in co-operation with Studienwerk Villigst and the Evangelische Akademie, Iserlohn. The consultation, at which some 120 persons were present, produced the study document "Pia Desidera Oecumenica". Internship opportunities for students in Eastern Europe are being planned.

The future

During the Vancouver-Canberra period, and as part of the process for the re-organization of the work of the WCC, PTE and the Ecumenical Institute, Bossey, are being brought together in a new sub-unit which will be concerned with ecumenical theological learning and leadership formation both at the global level and in the local context. This vision is presently in the process of unfolding; it is hoped that this new instrument of service to the ecumenical movement will continue to fulfill the purpose of both PTE (and TEF before that) and Bossey more adequately and more ecumenically.

SUB-UNIT ON RENEWAL AND CONGREGATIONAL LIFE (RCL)

The vocation of the Sub-unit

The WCC fifth assembly (Nairobi 1975) mandated the formation of the Sub-unit on Renewal and Congregational Life, incorporating the former WCC Department of the Laity. The purpose of the Sub-unit is to "develop and implement programmes that assist congregations to be vital centres of Christian worship, life, mission and service. It shall, to this end, assist with the interpretation of WCC programmes as they bear upon congregational life and seek signs of renewal where it is happening" (by-laws). The sixth assembly in Vancouver (1983) recognized the importance of the Sub-unit's role for the whole Council, especially in the fields of worship, spirituality, renewal in local churches and laity formation. The 1985 WCC central committee, meeting in Buenos Aires, stated: "Recognizing Renewal and Congregational Life's role as a co-ordinator for the WCC's work on spirituality, and the importance of this for the Council, the Committee urges that adequate financial undergirding should be provided for this Sub-unit in order to strengthen its work" (*Minutes*, p.54).

Since Vancouver the working group of RCL has held three plenary meetings (Mexico, 1985; Geneva, 1987; Cairo, 1989) and has underlined several programmatic emphases and areas of work to be pursued until the Canberra assembly.

Ongoing reflection on renewal and spirituality

The Sub-unit has been repeatedly asked by the WCC to recognize the wide diversity of understandings of renewal, and the different interpretations of the term "congregation", within the WCC's constituency.

In responding to this, RCL has prepared an ecumenical analysis of the meaning of the terms. This text was discussed and accepted by the Unit III committee at the central committee meeting in Moscow, 1989, which proposed that this theological reflection should be widely circulated and followed up by a compilation of a few concrete models or signs of renewal.

Since the Vancouver assembly RCL has been engaged in a long-term exploration of "A Spirituality for Our Times". This has included RCL's own studies together with the research and experiences of other WCC sub-units in the area of spirituality. The paper on this subject published at the beginning of 1990 represents a brief summary of the rich material available. Because of its complexity, the issue needs closer study. The central committee in 1987 recommended that the overall evaluation on "A Spirituality for Our Times" be published as background material for the pre-assembly reflection.

Main concerns

Worship

The WCC published the first Ecumenical Prayer Cycle (EPC) in 1978, with the title *For All God's People*. Eventually a totally revised edition was felt to be necessary. RCL consultant Rev. John Carden has edited the new EPC, with the title *With All God's People*, in co-operation with Faith and Order. Published in 1989, this is a basic text for promoting ecumenical prayer and mutual recognition among the churches. The central committee in 1988 encouraged "the wide use of the new Ecumenical Prayer Cycle", and has recommended its translation into as many languages as possible. Stated the central committee: "We further encourage the local churches and national councils of churches to adapt the material for various usages."

Since the Vancouver assembly RCL has been promoting ecumenical liturgy and music through its worship workshops, other ecumenical meetings, and the worship resource centre. The worship workshops were designed to enhance the spirit of the Vancouver assembly worship, and they continue to collect and introduce new worship materials and talents around the world. The first such workshop was held in Odense, Denmark, in August 1985, and has been followed by an African workshop in Harare, Zimbabwe (August 1986), an Asian workshop in Manila, Philippines (February 1987), a Latin American workshop in San José, Costa Rica (March 1988), a Caribbean and North American workshop in Toronto, Canada (July 1988), a Pacific workshop in Melbourne, Australia (February 1989), and an Eastern Europe workshop in Belgrade, Yugoslavia (April 1990). A joint workshop on "inclusive worship" was held in Bossey in June 1989 in co-operation with the Sub-unit on Women and the Programme on Theological Education, and the Ecumenical Institute, Bossey.

RCL distributed an offprint from the Vancouver worship book, *Jesus Christ, Life of the World — a Hymnbook*, and circulated it among local congregations and ecumenical music leaders. The fruits of workshops were also published with cassette tapes as "African Songs of Worship", "Asian Songs of Worship", "Todas las Voces" and "Brazilian Songs of Worship".

As a result of the worship workshops regional networks for liturgy and music have been set up, especially the African Association of Liturgy, Music and Arts (which has been holding its own worship workshops since 1986).

RCL, along with other WCC sub-units, is working on the development of an annual month-long seminar on music and liturgy for the training of musicians and liturgists in ecumenical worship.

In 1985 RCL started a worship resource centre in the Ecumenical Centre, Geneva, in order to collect ecumenical worship materials and share them with our member churches, and as a service for other sub-units of the WCC.

To help with the worship workshop programmes and the resource centre, a consultant from the United Methodist Church, USA, has been seconded to RCL for the period 1988 to 1991.

Renewal centres, movements and communities

RCL has been working with renewal centres through the World Collaboration Committee for Christian Lay Centres, Academies and Movements for Social Concern. In 1984 RCL took over the responsibility for co-ordinating the activities of the study centres. The work of study centres is mainly in research and dialogue on mission, religions and culture. During this period the focus has been on strengthening regional associations of lay centres. Its African network started a new office in 1988 and the Caribbean network soon followed. In 1987 a consultation of lay centre staff on "Justice, Peace and the Integrity of Creation" was held in Kyoto, Japan. Regional associations in Africa, Asia and Europe have also held consultations on JPIC, promoting its concern through local lay centres. A report, *On the Road to a New World*, was published. A consultation on "Partnership in Ecumenical Leadership Formation" was held in 1989 at the Ecumenical Institute, Bossey, in co-operation with Bossey and PTE.

RCL has made contacts with religious communities such as Taizé and Iona. In 1988 RCL sent a team of ten people from various parts of the world to visit base Christian communities in Brazil, and the team shared its findings with local communities in Brazil, member churches and the ecumenical constituency through its report "Renewal from the Roots".

This will be translated into Portuguese and French so that it can be shared widely with Brazilian churches and with French-speaking churches in Africa.

Since 1968 the WCC has held the Course for Leadership in Lay Training (CLLT) in order to enable lay centre and movement staff to deal with ecumenical issues within their local and global contexts. Until 1985, the CLLT had been held sporadically and at intervals of several years (see the report, *The World has Human Faces*). The world collaboration committee decided to hold an inter-regional CLLT every year in co-operation with the WCC and the respective regional association of lay centres. Such courses have been held in Manila, the Philippines (1986), Kitwe, Zambia (1988), Erfurt, German Democratic Republic (1989) and San Fernando, Trinidad (1990), under the co-sponsorship of regional associations in Asia, Africa, Europe and the Caribbean. *The New Fisher-folk* was published in 1988 as a manual on how to operate church-related conference centres.

Laity

The discussion has continued on new aspects of, and perspectives on, the role of the laity in the renewal process, with the ecumenical dimension of the subject receiving special attention. An exchange of commentaries and information was established with the Pontifical Commission for Laity in connection with the 1987 Roman Catholic bishops' synod on "The Vocation and Mission of the Laity in the Church and in the World".

RCL has been very much interested in receiving a contribution on this theme from an Orthodox ecclesiological perspective which would deal with the new missionary, social and ecumenical situations in which Orthodoxy, both Eastern and Oriental, lives today. A seminar was held on this subject in Prague, Czechoslovakia.

A small seminar prior to the consultation on "Re-evaluation of Lay Centres" (Crete, Greece, February 1990) examined the issue of new ecumenical perspectives on laity. It affirmed the need to explore the mutual commitment of church ministries in supporting and nourishing community life.

Spirituality

The RCL has initiated a series of seminars and consultations on a spirituality for our times. The initial input was given by a consultation in Annecy, France (December 1984), which addressed the question: What ways of living are demanded of us in today's world? This highlighted some essential points in the ecumenical spirituality which we are seeking. It has been necessary since this meeting to develop the search for a spirituality for our times by drawing on the experiences and the insights of other groups and seminars, through new accents and common affirmations.

The study on "A Spirituality for Our Times" has been enlarged and deepened by reflection on several themes. The first is "Monastic Spirituality", i.e. the consecrated life of nuns and monks in communities. A small consultation on this topic, held in the Orthodox monastery of Lovnica, Yugoslavia (October 1986), brought together nuns and monks from different traditions to share their understanding and practice of religious life today. Second, "Spirituality in Interfaith Dialogue" was the theme of a joint consultation with the WCC Sub-unit on Dialogue in Kyoto, Japan, in 1987. The main purpose of this consultation was to share the experiences of people who make use of the methodologies of spiritual exercises of other religions. Third, a seminar on "Renewal through Iconography" (Chevetogne, Belgium, 1988) has underlined the value of artistic and visual expressions such as icons, symbols and paintings for liturgical renewal and as an essential aspect of ecumenical spirituality.

The congregation

One of the tasks of the Sub-unit is to identify and evaluate new forms of Christian communities (for example base ecclesial communities, house churches, Pentecostal and charismatic groups, renewal movements), as signs of the commitment of the people of God in varied situations for evangelism, service, justice and unity. The structures and practices of the new Christian communities constitute an ecclesiological challenge. What is their impact on the traditional understanding of the nature, integrity and mission of the church?

The RCL working group recommended a pastoral reflection on ecclesial communities from within the context of their own churches, with special reference to the various ministries involved in parish life. In response to this, RCL explored the theme "What is the Role of the Priest/Pastor in a Congregation?" (Aleppo, Syria, April 1990) and the result has been shared with the WCC member churches. In the immediate future RCL will continue to wrestle with the question of the nature of the church.

New emphases and priorities

The local congregation and ecumenical life
The experimental project "Local Congregation and Ecumenical Life" was recommended by the Hanover central committee in 1988 and it began in October of that year in Geneva. The result of the enquiry, *Ecumenical Life in Geneva*, was sent to our ecumenical partners in Geneva. The project continued in Jerusalem (1989), and was extended to Africa (Nairobi) and Asia (Osaka) in 1990, with a report on "The Local Church and its Ecumenical Life" to be submitted to the WCC at the conclusion of the study in 1991.

The emergence of new forms of Christian community
RCL felt the need for an extensive evaluation of the history, mission and present situation of the African Instituted (Independent) Churches (AIC) in order to understand their significance for the renewal of the church today. The documentation received from the organizing secretary of AIC will be enlarged and completed so that RCL can prepare a formal report on this important part of the ecumenical community. This will then be presented to the All Africa Conference of Churches, the WCC central committee and other bodies as a basis for possible future action.

Evaluation
RCL has based itself on a few essential principles. At the heart of its work is *renewal* in its various dimensions; its focus is the *local congregations* and other communities and groups; its major emphasis is on the *laity*, and on relationships with movements and lay centres.

Due to the complexity of RCL's studies, consultations and experiences — particularly in the areas of worship, spirituality, renewal centres and movements, and laity and congregation — closer examination and evaluation is needed in these fields:
— Recognizing and stimulating forms of local ecumenical life and practice. Practical signs of local ecumenism are often ignored and unknown. The WCC should be aware of the means and programmes, experimental or permanent, being developed in local ecumenism.
— Discovering new creative forms of community worship. Singing and rejoicing are prominent themes today; new places of prayer, intercession and pilgrimage emerge, new ecumenical celebrations are called for.

— Serious study of the changes happening at the grassroots level, along with the development of a spirituality related to the sharing of responsibilities and ministries in the building up of the community.
— Exploring contemporary streams of renewal by recognizing the role of charismatic and evangelical communities within our churches and congregations.

RCL therefore hopes to inform and inspire not only the programme of the next assembly, but also the ethos of the ecumenical movement in the coming years. In particular, its work on worship and spirituality should be recognized as an essential component of the major WCC concern for renewal and unity, one which imprints a distinctive mark on the image of the WCC.

SUB-UNIT ON WOMEN IN CHURCH AND SOCIETY

Mandate

The purpose of the Sub-unit is to encourage the participation of women in the total life of the WCC and of the member churches. As an advocate, in collaboration with other units and sub-units in the WCC, member churches and international and ecumenical organizations, it seeks to promote the concerns of and contributions by women in church and society. It serves as a resource for, and link between, traditional and emerging groups to foster the full participation of women for the sake of the unity of the church and humankind.

Vancouver affirmed the Sub-unit's task of advocacy for women, urging it to give more attention to monitoring the churches' participation in the work for change that will promote a true community of women and men. The assembly Programme Guidelines Committee further recommended that "the concerns and perspectives of women should become integral to the work of all WCC units and sub-units".

Since Vancouver a staff task force on women, made up of representatives from the various sub-units, has shared the job of monitoring the response to women's concerns in their respective programmes. It has also supported the personnel office in monitoring staff vacancies in the WCC in its attempts to secure increased recruitment of women staff; a data bank developed by the Sub-unit supplies the names of women qualified to serve on commissions, committees and regional groups, or to participate in regional and international meetings.

With women constituting almost 30% of official delegates (compared to 22% in Nairobi), Vancouver made a significant breakthrough in the area of women's participation. The leadership of women as speakers in plenary sessions, as facilitators in issue groups, as participants in worship, and as contributors to the business plenaries, was both visible and remarkable (in spite of the evident need for women to become more familiar with assembly procedures). It should be noted that the increased number of women delegates was achieved by an increase in the total number of delegates.

On the road towards fulfilment of the WCC policy (agreed upon in Dresden in 1981), the Sub-unit hopes to achieve 40% women's participation in the official delegations to the forthcoming assembly in Canberra. It is vital that churches themselves take this initiative rather than simply yielding to the pressure of official "quotas"; equally important is that they *thereby* ensure that their delegations are truly representative of their memberships. The central committee meeting in Dresden affirmed that the "principle of equal participation between men and women be a goal towards which we move, starting with the composition of the WCC decision-making and consultative bodies during and after the sixth assembly".

Programme emphases

A January 1984 core group meeting in Montreux, Switzerland, set three programme emphases: participation; justice, peace and the integrity of creation; and women doing theology and sharing spirituality. The common thread was the "empowerment" of women and the highlighting of women's perspectives in the communities.

Participation

In order to promote women's participation the Sub-unit has brought women together to share stories of their own experiences, examine obstacles and find ways to strategize for action.

Promoting participation also implies searching for the theological basis of women's involvement. Generally women have been conditioned by, and often do not question, received male interpretations of scripture. A book produced by a workshop in 1984 in India on participation, organized by the Sub-unit, entitled *By Our Lives...: Stories of Women — Today and in the Bible*, links ordinary women's stories to Bible studies. It encourages women to reflect on Bible passages from their own perspectives and to explore passages that affirm women. Translated into German,

French and Arabic, the book has been widely distributed. Parts of the book have been translated into various other languages.

Strengthening leadership training is another means of promoting women's participation. A June 1986 workshop on "Women in Church Leadership", conducted in collaboration with the LWF women's desk and Bossey, focused on the crucial issue of power. Women shared stories of their experiences of working in male structures, discussed how the use of power can empower or disempower others, and made practical recommendations designed to help women become effective leaders. These included encouraging a feminist interpretation of the Bible, networking, training, the introduction of new leadership styles, and the inclusion of women's studies in seminary curricula.

The 1978-81 "Community of Women and Men in the Church" (CWMC) study provided many lessons. In order to test its impact on or relevance to low-income village people, the Sub-unit organized two workshops for village leaders in India and the Philippines in November-December 1988. The original CWMC questionnaire was used for discussion and analysis. In the light of their cultural, socio-economic and political backgrounds, participants determined relevant issues and raised new questions. Justice issues emerged strongly, as did those relating to community life and the role of the church. When they returned home, the village leaders gathered groups to discuss the issues in greater depth; they are to meet again to share findings, and identify common and divergent points. These are then to be shared more widely within Asia and other regions in order to stimulate other groups to engage in similar studies.

The CWMC study revealed a need for further investigation on male-female identity, a re-interpretation of scriptures relating to this area, and a clearer understanding of human sexuality. Many of the WCC participants at the mid-UN Women's Decade conference in Copenhagen in 1980 had expressed interest in the teachings and writings of major world religions concerning women's sexuality and bodily functions. Then in 1983 the Vancouver assembly issued a call for a study on human sexuality and human relations, to be undertaken within the framework of a larger study by the Office of Family Education, and designed to innovate in the area of interfaith dialogue.

The project brought eight women theologians/anthropologists together to examine the basic theological affirmations revealed in primary source material from Buddhism, Christianity, Hinduism, Islam and Judaism. A woman with a physical disability was also invited to participate. The work of these researchers was presented at a forum for non-governmental organizations held parallel to the end of the UN Decade for Women Conference in Nairobi in 1985. It disclosed significant similarities between the way the scriptures of different religions are interpreted and provide the basis for ambiguous attitudes towards women.

Following the Nairobi conference various individuals and groups around the world continued studying and discussing this topic. In 1987, a follow-up project involving another group of women representatives of the same religious traditions began responding to the original study papers; publication of their responses is planned for 1990.

Justice, Peace and the Integrity of Creation (JPIC)

This second programme emphasis has two foci: first the links between militarism and sexism, and the role of women as peace-makers; and second, justice for women, with particular attention to how women are affected by violence, poverty and racism, and as migrants or refugees.

At Forum 85, held alongside the July 1985 conference marking the end of the UN Decade for Women, the Sub-unit, in collaboration with other WCC sub-units, the World YWCA, the Lutheran World Federation (LWF) Women's Desk, and the USA-based Church Women United, gave visibility to Christian women's contributions to the UN Decade.

Together they organized workshops on such issues as women under racism, refugee women, violence against women, women migrant workers, women and transnational corporations, food and water, and the study on "Female Sexuality and Bodily Functions in Different Religious Traditions". The Sub-unit conducted several Bible studies on JPIC, and showed a film series "As Women See It". In collaboration with WCC staff and Church Women United, a local women's committee created a meeting place a little distance away from the hubbub of the conference. Called "Karibu" ("welcome" in Swahili), it resembled in many ways the Vancouver assembly's "Well".

At the 1985 working group meeting in Oaxtepec, Mexico, the Sub-unit was mandated to organize a series of regional JPIC meetings to culminate at the 1990 JPIC world convocation in Seoul. Such meetings were held, in collaboration with regional women's desk offices, in Asia (Bangkok, December 1986), Africa (Ghana, March 1989), the Middle East (Cyprus, September 1988), and the Pacific (Tonga, September 1987). The Ecumenical Forum of European Christian Women organized the European women's JPIC meeting (Switzerland, February 1989). A Latin American JPIC meeting took place in December 1989 in Quito, Ecuador, in collaboration with the women's desk of the Latin American Council of Churches.

Women involved in JPIC issues from both within and outside the churches participated in what, in some regions, was a multifaith encounter. They shared stories of struggles and together sought effective strategies for action. For many it was a genuine awareness-raising experience. The presence of women from other regions highlighted their common struggles, and the need to build and strengthen solidarity with one another. In recognition of this fact, and in order to enhance its impact on the JPIC world convocation, a document showing the links between the various regional issues is being prepared.

The Asia meeting highlighted the effects of militarism on women and raised questions as to the feasibility of setting up an Asian commission for women's human rights, an idea which is currently being explored. In the Pacific women spoke about nuclearization and militarization and how these affect the islanders' health and livelihood. The women of the Middle East made a strong plea for justice and peace in the region; the issues of apartheid, deforestation, refugees, economic crisis, the oppression of women workers, and the dumping of nuclear wastes in the Western part of the continent emerged strongly from the Africa meeting.

Initiated more than a decade ago, the women and rural development programme aims at empowering women who are denied such basic needs as water, food, technology, basic health care, and education, to analyze their problems, identify their own needs and discover their potential to contribute to change in their communities. Awareness-raising is seen as the key to empowerment which, in turn, is the key to development.

Within the framework of the programme the Sub-unit, together with the LWF women's desk, organized a consultation for rural women leaders to help them evaluate and seek alternatives to "development" programmes being done for women. Held in Gweru, Zimbabwe, in September 1986, the consultation began with visits to nine separate local projects. Participants evaluated these and suggested ways of enabling women to develop their *own* programmes.

A rural development fund receives contributions from groups and agencies in support of projects that will enhance women's own development and that of their communities. Projects fall into a number of different categories, including leadership training (with a focus on awareness-raising), income-generation (aiming at self-reliance), the provision of water, food production technology, the production of simple teaching materials for community leaders, South-South exchange/exposure visits, short-term scholarships, provision of creches, literacy/informal education, primary health care and others. All aim at empowering women who have few or no formal educational opportunities.

The rural development programme was evaluated in June 1988. The basic data were project reports sent by local women's groups in response to a Sub-unit questionnaire. The evaluators — a group of village organizers, social analysts, communicators, theologians, teachers and funding agency representatives drawn from the Sub-unit's network — identified some of the main social, cultural, economic and political barriers to women's empowerment. Among these were the lack of basic necessities such as water, food, education, training and information as well as the patriarchal and hierarchical attitudes and structures that reflect and reinforce such deprivation and discrimination.

The report, *We Cannot Dream Alone*, contains case studies, analyses of the issues, theological reflections, stories of empowerment, revised funding criteria and a new set of guidelines for initiating projects.

Women doing theology and sharing spirituality

Women continue to contribute to the renewal of theology, worship and liturgy in the churches. In response to the need of a growing number of women — both students and teachers of theology, and laywomen who read the Bible *as* women — for opportunities to share and debate their new experiences and insights, the Sub-unit (together with the Programme on Theological Education/PTE) published a collection of biblical and theological reflections by third-world women entitled *New Eyes for Reading* (1986).

A December 1987 workshop with a small group of women theologians from five regions contributed to the JPIC process by sharing and analyzing their experiences and theological understandings of the integrity of creation. A special newsletter carried reports from this workshop.

Another international workshop, on "Reading the Bible with Women's Eyes", was held at Bossey in June 1988, co-organized with the LWF women's desk. Forty-five women from eight regions met to reflect on social, economic, cultural and political issues from women's biblical perspectives. Yet another joint venture (with the Ecumenical Institute, Bossey, RCL and PTE) was a June 1989 workshop on inclusive worship.

Young women or lay theologians are asking new questions and providing new perspectives from their varied experiences in churches, church-related groups, networks and institutions. The "Young Women

Doing Theology" project was initiated in 1987 with PTE in order to encourage mutual exchange and networking between young women doing theology and "enablers" from different contexts and cultures, and to highlight feminist theologies and theologies grounded in women's experience. (For this project the term "young women" includes those who have commenced formal study in middle or later life.)

A consultant was appointed in January 1988 to work in Geneva to implement this project. In June 1988, an international workshop in Bossey brought together 17 young women and enablers who shared their struggles and visions, and identified obstacles to, as well as opportunities for, their work. With the aim of sharing the lessons from this workshop, national workshops were then organized in Guatemala, Honduras, El Salvador and Costa Rica. During her visits to India and the Philippines, the consultant made contacts with other young women theologians but unfortunately was unable, for family reasons, to complete this project. It has been recommended by the Unit III committee that PTE, the Sub-unit on Women and the Scholarships Office follow up this project by allocating funds for at least ten women in each region to complete doctoral studies in theology during the Ecumenical Decade (1988-98).

The first WCC consultation for women in interfaith dialogue was organized by the Sub-unit on Dialogue, with some support from the Women's Sub-unit, in June 1988. Buddhist, Hindu, Jewish, Christian, Baha'i and Muslim women as well as women of traditional religions and modern witches met in an atmosphere of dialogue, mutual trust and exchange of experiences.

Immediately before the central committee meeting in Moscow in July 1989, an important consultation on women's spirituality took place. This included a visit to an Orthodox convent near Leningrad. The second international Orthodox women's consultation was held in Crete in January 1990 on the theme "Church and Culture". Here Orthodox churches were urged to "creatively restore" the diaconate for women (as well as for men), thus giving Orthodox women an opportunity to participate in a liturgical as well as a social ministry of the church.

Ecumenical Decade of the Churches in Solidarity with Women (1988-98)

The WCC central committee meeting in January 1987 approved an Ecumenical Decade of the Churches in Solidarity with Women as a long-term framework for actions in solidarity with women.

The 1985 central committee meeting, which took place just after the Nairobi Women's Decade at the conclusion of the UN conference, was convinced that the churches had not been sufficiently aware of the UN Decade, and that in many churches the position of women had not improved over that period. To test this assessment, the Sub-unit conducted a survey in April 1986 of 178 women from 74 countries and 105 churches. Responses confirmed that women still held "traditional" positions and roles in the churches. Although most institutions for theological training admitted women students, few women graduates were ordained. The study concluded that traditional attitudes towards women within the churches both reflected and helped shape patriarchal cultures.

In reporting the results of its survey to the 1987 central committee, the Sub-unit confirmed that churches — which should lead society in relation to justice, the recognition of human values and the provision of equal opportunities — have instead mirrored existing social values, or even lagged behind the progress realized in the secular world. The executive committee proposed an Ecumenical Decade of the Churches in Solidarity with Women, 1988-98, to the central committee, stressing that its focus should be "on the situation of women in the churches as well as churches' participation in improving the conditions for women in society". The central committee endorsed the Ecumenical Decade; it underlined "that this Decade be recognized as a follow-up to the UN Decade for Women (1975-85) which in spite of all its successes did not adequately touch the concerns of church women or challenge the churches to take stock of the position of women in society". The following five objectives were defined by the executive and central committees (March and August 1988):

1) to enable the churches to free themselves from racism, sexism and classism, and from teachings and practices that discriminate against women;
2) to empower women to challenge oppressive structures in the global community, and in their own country and church;
3) to give visibility to women's perspectives and actions in the work and struggle for justice, peace and the integrity of creation;
4) to affirm, through shared leadership and decision-making, in theology and spirituality, the decisive contributions of women in churches and communities;
5) to encourage the churches to take actions in solidarity with women.

In preparation for the launching of the Decade at Easter 1988 the Sub-unit produced materials explaining Decade objectives, background, and priorities, and including a worship resource book, *Churches in Solidarity with Women: Prayers and Poems, Songs and Stories*. Since then, it has produced another resource booklet on *Women, Poverty and the Economy*, the first in a series of publications on Decade issues. The *Decade Link* publishes information on related activities of various local and national churches. National and sub-regional workshops aiming at rooting the Decade in local contexts have been held in Mexico, North America, India, Scandinavia, Burkina Faso, Senegal, Nigeria, Cameroon, Côte d'Ivoire, and elsewhere. It is hoped that the Canberra assembly will offer a focus for evaluating how far the churches have implemented the goals of the Decade in their own situations. Looking beyond Canberra, work has already begun towards enabling the organization of the mid-Decade regional conferences (to be held 1992-93) as approved by central committee in Moscow in July 1989.

Work style
   The Sub-unit collaborates closely with other units and sub-units, women's desks of WCC member churches and of regional and national councils of churches, international and ecumenical organizations such as the World YWCA, the women's desk of the Lutheran World Federation, the Ecumenical Forum of European Christian Women, Church Women United, the Fellowship of the Least Coin, the Asian Church Women's Conference, the Women's Inter-Church Council and others. Such collaboration involves the sharing of human and other resources, and networking.
   Staff visits to churches and other constituencies provide excellent opportunities for listening to concerns, renewing contacts and sharing information. National workshops organized by local counterparts bring together women from different areas within a country to share concerns, and to identify available resources and ways in which they may be shared.
   On the regional and international levels consultations are organized around issues, bringing together women both from within and outside the churches on the basis of their common commitment. Such consultations provide opportunities for cross-fertilization of ideas as well as building bridges of understanding within and among such groups. Creative communication methods and shared leadership are an important feature of such meetings. Whenever possible, the Sub-unit solicits the help of members of its working group in the planning and organization of consultations within their regions; working group members also represent

the Sub-unit at outside meetings and contribute articles to WCC publications.

Future challenges

The following principles were adopted by the commission on women in church and society at its meeting in Tokyo, Japan, 5-11 December 1989.

Reviewing the progress in the Sub-unit's work since Vancouver, and looking beyond the Canberra assembly, the following challenges are seen as crucial to the Sub-unit, to the WCC and to the member churches:

a) Participation:
- — implementation of the Dresden recommendation on women's full participation at all levels of decision-making and in all aspects of work;
- — correction of imbalances in regional representation in the WCC in the areas of staff, programmes, decision-making, and consultation;
- — removal of dominance of the English language in meetings, consultations and publications.

b) Women doing theology and sharing spirituality:
- — programme for women to do theology;
- — new programmes exploring varied expressions of the spirituality of women.

c) Justice, peace and the integrity of creation:
- — continuation of work with rural poor women, and initiation of work with urban poor women;
- — training programmes enabling women to take political action and effect change in their lives;
- — conscientization of the member churches to the issues and plights of poor and oppressed women;
- — advocacy and dialogue with large development agencies in order to increase funding for women's concerns and issues.

d) The Ecumenical Decade of the Churches in Solidarity with Women (1988-98):
- — implementation of the El Escorial recommendation that churches, ecumenical organizations and agencies earmark 50% of their annual funds within the five first years of the Ecumenical Decade for the empowerment of women;
- — necessity to work more closely with Youth to promote the goals and concerns of the Decade;
- — strengthening the Ecumenical Decade as a Council-wide concern, while continuing to strengthen the Decade programme with the

Sub-unit on Women by increasing by two the present two pro-gramme staff positions.

SUB-UNIT ON YOUTH

Young people in the World Council of Churches

The aims of the WCC Sub-unit on Youth are to encourage young people to explore, strengthen and live out their faith, to enable them to participate fully in the life of their churches, in society and in the ecumenical movement, and to build networks of support and understanding between young people for justice and peace. In its programmes the Sub-unit on Youth works, through networking, communication, exchanges and solidarity action, with young people coming together in the ecumenical youth movement. Within this process of ecumenical learning the Sub-unit co-operates with others in the WCC.

The Youth working group formed after the Vancouver assembly has advised the Sub-unit on its various programmes. In an effort to support and co-operate with the regional ecumenical youth movements, regional youth staff have been invited to be part of the Sub-unit's working group. From the several working group meetings, programme priorities emerged for the period under review. These came under the theme "Spirituality, Justice and Peace".

The Sub-unit also continued its important role of monitoring and advocating the participation of youth in the life and work of the WCC. In co-operation with other WCC sub-units, it has offered its services in identifying youth participants and organizing youth pre-events for major WCC meetings. The working group meeting in 1988 expressed concern about the level of youth participation in the programmes of the WCC. In spite of the central committee decision in 1987, the 20% minimum of youth participation is understood rather as a maximum and is therefore seldom attained. The working group also pointed to the El Escorial guidelines on resource sharing, which cite 20% youth participation as a goal, as well as the need to start discussion on the proportion of funds to be allocated to youth programmes as another indication of commitment to youth participation.

The main thrust: spirituality, justice and peace

Young people seek a meaning for life, God's real presence and the revelation of God's will. In the Vancouver assembly, the young people presented a message which highlighted justice and peace as the central concern and plea from all parts of the world: "Among many issues that confront and concern us, one emerges in compelling urgency. We want *peace*: not as the doctrine of national security defines it: repression, covert violence, the absence of war, but as God's shalom built on social justice." Justice therefore forms the basis on which the programmes of the Sub-unit are developed. The quest for genuine spirituality brings forth a commitment to justice and peace. The ecumenical youth movement receives its inspiration and strength from this experience of conversion and new life.

The most serious threats to life are faced by youth everywhere, and the ecumenical youth movements bring together the struggles in which young people are involved to overcome these powers of death. The implications of this global solidarity have been spelt out in the following priorities:

A. The ecumenical youth movement, the church and people's movements:
    — participation in people's struggles and people's organizations (peasants, workers, students, etc.);
    — development of theological reflection and political consciousness in the midst of concrete involvement;
    — prophetic engagement and challenging of our churches based on active involvement in people's struggles.

Solidarity with the struggles of indigenous peoples.

Active and practical support of women's struggle including a commitment to advance it both within and outside the ecumenical youth movement.

B. Ecumenical learning for community building:
    — with young people of other faiths and ideologies;
    — development of skills, leadership formation;
    — critical social consciousness;
    — spirituality for/of people in struggle;
    — combat misuse of Christian faith.

Building up and strengthening links and networks within the regions.

C. Search for a Christ-centred spirituality which is rooted in the life, history and struggle of the people.

The Sub-unit has developed this dimension of its work through its various programmatic concerns, e.g. the World Youth Projects (WYP) programme. This programme underwent an extensive evaluation between 1985 and 1986 in all the regions which have been involved. This has resulted in a radical shift in the orientation of the programme, away from funding and maintaining isolated projects to using the WYP as a creative tool for developing the commitment to building and strengthening the ecumenical youth movement (in keeping with the priorities mentioned above). The new guidelines of the programme emphasize the need for united action and co-operation between all regions on urgent common issues arising from structures of oppression and injustice. The projects and programmes are seen as a learning process requiring sharing, reflection and evaluation by young people themselves. Networking of young people within the regions is crucial for achieving the aims of the programme.

Besides the regional programmes, an inter-regional solidarity forum was created within the WYP programme to which issues are brought from the global ecumenical community. Such solidarity is given programmatic expression through programmes of awareness-building, and through action for solidarity. The following are some examples:

First, a seminar on "Church and Social Transformation" held in Kaub, FRG, in 1987. This was an encounter of young people from churches in very different contexts. The issues of justice and lasting peace in the different situations were discussed from the theological and political points of view in lively and challenging debates, focusing especially on South Africa and Namibia. This seminar was enhanced by the use of creative and participatory liturgies led by the participants themselves.

Second, an ecumenical delegation of youth leaders, organized by the Youth Sub-unit, met with the leadership and members of the Russian Orthodox Church, especially students and young theological teachers in the monasteries, in September 1988. The purpose of this "pilgrimage" was to gain first-hand understanding of the churches in the USSR. This visit was also an act of solidarity and celebration with the Russian Orthodox Church on the occasion of the millennium of the baptism of Rus. The visit culminated in a two-day seminar with youth representatives from the various churches in the USSR, focusing on the situation of the churches in the present restructuring process in Soviet society, and its implications for the role of Christian young people.

Third was the young people's response to the Commission on World Mission and Evangelism (CWME) world mission conference in San Antonio (May 1989), with its theme "Your Will Be Done: Mission in Christ's Way". The theme of the response was "Risking Obedience". All the young participants, including the stewards, participated in a three day youth pre-conference discussing and sharing stories of mission with young people from different parts of the world. The work of mission was affirmed as important both for CWME and for the Sub-unit on Youth.

Fourth, a series of cultural action workshops was planned in the different regions, from 1987 to beyond the Canberra assembly. These have been intended to train youth leaders to use cultural forms systematically as a tool for consciousness-raising and movement-building, as well as a platform for discussions and cultural interaction. The workshops also have explored more creative and participatory forms of liturgy and worship.

The Sub-unit's ecumenical youth action (work camps) and stewards' programme (through which young persons work in support of major ecumenical meetings) continue to be important avenues for ecumenical exposure and leadership formation for many young people from the different regions of the world.

Special feature: International Youth Year (IYY) 1985

One of the important highlights of this period was the celebration of the IYY. The central committee of the WCC recommended that the WCC provide full support to IYY, which should be focused on youth initiatives for peace and justice, and training for action in these fields. The participation of the Sub-unit on Youth, as outlined, was to include the following elements:

— regional and inter-regional programme support and initiatives;
— a poster and calendar contest;
— promoting an effective presence of the WCC and the churches in the United Nations programmes related to IYY.

IYY-related team visits and work camps were organized in several countries. The programme developed with very enthusiastic response from the regions and local host groups. As a result, co-operation between youth groups of different regions was heightened, weak ecumenical networks were strengthened and new ones were brought into being. The whole experience and resources generated by the IYY experience have been documented in a resource booklet entitled *Youth to Youth Team Visits — a Guideline*.

Towards Canberra — and beyond

The Sub-unit continues to develop new strategies to strengthen its work, especially in the area of regional network-building. In this respect the Sub-unit works closely with the ecumenical youth partners in the regions; one example is in the field of ecumenical youth resource development; the other major thrust in strengthening our work is through the global ecumenical youth gathering process.

The idea of a large youth event has been debated in the WCC several times during the past 15 years. Since 1984 the Sub-unit on Youth has been involved in such discussions with the other Geneva-based ecumenical organizations such as the World YWCA, the World Alliance of YMCAs, the International Movement of Catholic Students, and the World Student Christian Federation (WSCF). This idea has been further developed and made part of the Sub-unit's process to rebuild and strengthen the global ecumenical youth movement.

In 1986 the Youth working group emphasized that the basis and strength of the ecumenical youth movement lay with the local groups, and their regional and global linkages with each other. The global ecumenical youth gathering process should therefore reflect this reality; the issues and priorities to be addressed should come from youth movements of the local and national situations. This has been the basis for discussion with the other ecumenical organizations.

A commitment to work together, and to plan the process in equal partnership, was agreed upon by the different ecumenical youth and student organizations, including the World YWCA, the World Alliance of YMCAs, the WSCF, the International Movement of Catholic Students, the International Young Catholic Students and the WCC Sub-unit on Youth. A global youth event is being planned in 1992 as one of the expressions of this process. The main objective of this gathering will be to bring together youth and students active in the ecumenical movement for a common confession of faith, sharing of testimonies, mutual challenge and inspiration, and the development of a strategy for equipping youth and students for renewed discipleship. Well before this global ecumenical youth gathering a series of events will be held to enhance movement-building, to bring young people's issues and concerns on to the common ecumenical agenda, and to strengthen the common witness of the participating organizations.

In the last two years conscious efforts have been made to integrate the global ecumenical youth gathering process within the programmes of the Youth Sub-unit leading towards the assembly and beyond.

SPIRITUALITY FOR JUSTICE AND PEACE:
A COMMON UNIT III EFFORT

In November 1986, all five sub-units of Unit III joined together in holding a consultation with the National Council of Churches in the Philippines (NCCP) on "Spirituality for Justice and Peace". This was significant on several counts. It was the first time the Unit had ever undertaken a common venture. It was grounded in the living experience of a people striving to be faithful to the call to do justice, to love mercy and to walk humbly with God in a situation where oppression, terror and violent death stalked every dissenter from the status quo. It also captured the essence of what Unit III was about, giving flesh to the five emphases of the Unit: ecumenical learning, participation, spirituality, ministerial formation and learning for justice and peace.

The report was published for the consultation by the NCCP. Its title, *Those Who Would Give Light Must Endure Burning*, borrows the prophetic words of Fr Ed de la Torre of the Philippines to underline the conviction that the kind of education and renewal which Unit III wants to foster does not happen without cost, and that there is a way of living that is appropriate to this vision to which the churches are called.

It is doubtless true that everything which the WCC does is concerned in some way with spirituality for justice and peace, and there is a general expectation that this great theme, among others, will touch and transform the lives of member churches at least, if not the wider world. But from Vancouver to Canberra it was the special vocation of Unit III to try to ensure that this transformation really happened by engaging the churches in challenging processes of learning. And it was the Unit's focus on spirituality — what it is, how it is fostered, who it is for — that gave an intentional dimension to its work.

The nature of spirituality

At its first full meeting after Vancouver in July 1984, the central committee welcomed the renewed interest of WCC in spirituality, but warned that "the search for a deeper spirituality pointed more to the way we live as Christians and the way the churches run their affairs and less to the theoretical study of the subject" (*Minutes*, 1984, p.66).

Taking up the challenge to explore these ways of living, the Sub-unit on Renewal and Congregational Life (RCL) organized a consultation in December 1984 on "A Spirituality for Our Times", finding that "the churches are called to a costly spirituality that is Christ-centred and enables us to more effectively witness in the world. This inevitably demands constant conversion and ongoing formation and discipleship, is rooted in a life of prayer and of solidarity with the poor and oppressed, and leads to suffering. Encouraged and challenged by a community that is nourished by word and sacrament, this life is one of joy and hope in the risen Lord" (*A Spirituality for Our Times*, p.23).

The contribution of the Sub-units

The five sub-units in their various ways have sought to foster this understanding of spirituality, returning again and again to its major motifs as an orchestra does to the unifying theme of a symphony.

Even a privatized spirituality has its costs. How much more costly, then, a spirituality that sets its sights on the transformation of structures that imprison us in ways of living that regard barriers of gender, age, race, class, and ministerial or priestly orders as final and irrevocable. It was as if Paul had not said in that high moment of inspiration: "There is neither Jew nor Greek, there is neither slave nor free, there is neither male nor female; for you are all one in Christ Jesus" (Gal. 3:28).

The Sub-units on Women and Youth therefore kept reminding the churches that our oneness will remain incomplete as long as the participation of women and youth is restricted to limits predetermined largely by men.

The Programme on Theological Education (PTE) kept reiterating that, contrary to conventional wisdom, the most efficient and alert theology is done not merely by "scholars", though they make their contribution, but by the whole people of God. In this way PTE has endorsed Martin Luther's contention that "not reading and speculation, but living, dying and experiencing Christ's crucifixion unto condemnation makes a real theologian".

But it is all too easy to speak of "the whole people of God" while giving a merely formal acknowledgment to the place within it of children, persons with disabling conditions, and the marginalized poor — all of whom, if freed to exercise the gifts of grace which God has given them, will bring rich, new dimensions to our understanding of how we are to be one in Christ. Through its programmes on family education, adult basic education, and the church and persons with disabilities, the Sub-unit on Education has worked to bring this concern into clear focus before the eyes of the churches. And RCL, through its work with lay academies and study centres, has exposed members of local congregations to new ideas and ways of fostering a new self-understanding of the people of God, thereby empowering them to take courageous stands on issues of justice and peace.

This call to participation of the whole people of God demands constant conversion and ongoing formation and discipleship. The Unit emphases on ecumenical learning and learning for justice and peace were relevant here. In these approaches to learning there are no "experts" who tell others what it is all about, but everyone is challenged to be open to the riches of other perspectives, to be empowered to join God in God's work in the world.

Because the call is costly, the response must be constantly nourished in a community rooted in a life of prayer, word and sacrament. For this reason RCL has consistently fostered, both in ecumenical gatherings and in local communities of the faithful, a worship springing from the needs, pains and sufferings — as well as the joys, hopes and expectations — of *all* God's people. This brings into focus Unit III's stress on the importance of inclusive worship, a reflection on worship which embraces, but is not restricted to, the question of appropriate language. It arises out of the concern that all God's people should be at home when they worship and should be enabled to bring their diverse gifts as offerings to one altar.

But major challenges remain. Dare we go on speaking about a costly spirituality for justice and peace while refusing each other the nourishment of spirituality that comes from sharing the sacrament of the eucharist at one common table? Can we trust the Spirit to lead us into a new future, one beyond our control?

A Selected List
of Books and Audiovisuals
1983-1990

Assembly related

Come, Holy Spirit — Renew the Whole Creation: Six Bible Studies, 1989

Gathered for Life: the Official Report of the Sixth Assembly of the WCC, ed. David Gill, 1983 (for the USA: Eerdmans, Grand Rapids)

Land of the Spirit? The Australian Religious Experience, Muriel Porter, Risk Book Series No. 44, 1990 (co-publisher: Joint Board of Christian Education, Melbourne, Australia)

General

Directory of Christian Councils, 1985

The Ecumenical Review, quarterly

God is Rice: Asian Culture and Christian Faith, Masao Takenaka, Risk Book Series No. 30, 1986

Handbook of Member Churches, comp. Ans J. van der Bent, 2nd rev. ed. 1985

Hope for Faith: a Conversation, C.F. Beyers Naudé & Dorothee Sölle, Risk Book Series No. 31, 1986 (for the USA: Eerdmans, Grand Rapids)

Icons: Windows on Eternity. Theology and Spirituality in Colour, comp. Gennadios Limouris, Faith and Order Paper No. 147, 1990

Introducing the World Council of Churches, Marlin VanElderen, Risk Book Series No. 46, 1990 (also in French, German and Spanish)

Ireland: Christianity Discredited or Pilgrim's Progress?, Robin Boyd, Risk Book Series No. 37, 1988

Minutes of central committees

The Search for New Community: a Bossey Seminar, ed. Thomas F. Best, 1989

Unfinished Agenda: an Autobiography, Lesslie Newbigin, 1985 (co-publishers: SPCK, London, and Eerdmans, Grand Rapids)

With All God's People: the New Ecumenical Prayer Cycle, 2 vols, comp. John Carden, 1989

Ecumenism

Breakthrough: the Emergence of the Ecumenical Tradition, ed. Robert S. Bilheimer, 1989 (co-publisher: Eerdmans, Grand Rapids)

"Commemorating Amsterdam 1948: 40 Years of the World Council of Churches", eds T.K. Thomas & Thomas F. Best, special issue of *The Ecumenical Review*, 40, 3-4, July-October 1988

Everyday Ecumenism: Can You Take the World Church Home?, John Bluck, Risk Book Series No. 35, 1987

Faith and Faithfulness: Essays on Contemporary Ecumenical Themes — a Tribute to Philip A. Potter, ed. Pauline Webb, 1984

Instruments of Unity: National Councils of Churches Within the One Ecumenical Movement, ed. Thomas F. Best, 1988

Truth and Community: Diversity and its Limits in the Ecumenical Movement, Michael Kinnamon, 1988 (co-publisher: Eerdmans, Grand Rapids)

Vital Ecumenical Concerns: Sixteen Documentary Surveys, Ans J. van der Bent, 1986

Whither Ecumenism? A Dialogue in the Transit Lounge of the Ecumenical Movement, ed. Thomas Wieser, 1986

Ecumenical history

And So Set Up Signs...: the World Council of Churches' First 40 Years, 1988 (also in French and German)

From Generation to Generation: the Story of Youth in the World Council of Churches, Ans van der Bent, 1986

A History of the Ecumenical Movement, vol. I: *1517-1948*, eds Ruth Rouse & Stephen Charles Neill, 3rd ed. 1986

A History of the Ecumenical Movement, vol. II: *1948-1968: the Ecumenical Advance*, ed. Harold E. Fey, 2nd ed. 1986

Memoirs, W.A. Visser 't Hooft, 2nd ed. (unchanged) 1987

The unity of the church

The Apostolic Faith Today: a Handbook for Study, ed. Hans-Georg Link, Faith and Order Paper No. 124, 1985

Baptism, Eucharist and Ministry 1982-1990: Report on the Process and Responses, Faith and Order Paper No. 149, 1990

Baptism and Eucharist: Ecumenical Convergence in Celebration, eds Max Thurian & Geoffrey Wainwright, Faith and Order Paper No. 117, 1984 (for the USA: Eerdmans, Grand Rapids)

Beyond Unity-in-Tension: Unity, Renewal and the Community of Women and Men, ed. Thomas F. Best, Faith and Order Paper No. 138, 1988

Called to be One in Christ: United Churches and the Ecumenical Movement, eds Thomas F. Best & Michael Kinnamon, Faith and Order Paper No. 127, 1985

Church, Kingdom, World: the Church as Mystery and Prophetic Sign, ed. Gennadios Limouris, Faith and Order Paper No. 130, 1986

Churches Respond to BEM, vols I-VI, ed. Max Thurian, Faith and Order Paper Nos 129 and 132 1986, 135 and 137 1987, 143 and 144 1988

Confessing One Faith: Towards an Ecumenical Explication of the Apostolic Faith as Expressed in the Nicene-Constantinopolitan Creed, Faith and Order Paper No. 140, 1987 (also in French and German)

Confessing Our Faith Around the World, vols II, III (Caribbean and Central America), IV (South America), 1984-85

Faith and Order 1985-1989: the Commission Meeting at Budapest 1989, ed. Thomas F. Best, Faith and Order Paper No. 148, 1990

Faith and Renewal: Commission on Faith and Order, Stavanger 1985, ed. Thomas F. Best, Faith and Order Paper No. 131, 1986

Growth in Agreement: Reports and Agreed Statements of Ecumenical Conversations on a World Level, eds Lukas Vischer & Harding Meyer, Faith and Order Paper No. 108, 1984 (co-publisher: Paulist Press, New York)

Living Today Towards Visible Unity: Fifth International Consultation of United and Uniting Churches, ed. Thomas F. Best, Faith and Order Paper No. 142, 1988

One God, One Lord, One Spirit: on the Explication of the Apostolic Faith Today, ed. Hans-Georg Link, Faith and Order Paper No. 139, 1988

Orthodox Perspectives on Baptism, Eucharist and Ministry, eds Gennadios Limouris & Nomikos Michael Vaporis, Faith and Order Paper No. 128, 1986 (co-publisher: Greek Orthodox Theological Journal in the USA)

The Roots of Our Common Faith: Faith in the Scriptures and in the Early Church, ed. Hans-Georg Link, Faith and Order Paper No. 119, 1984

Survey of Church Union Negotiations 1983/1985-86 and *1986-1988*, Faith and Order Papers Nos 133 and 146, 1986 and 1989

Unity and Renewal: a Study Guide for Local Groups, Faith and Order Paper No. 136, 1987

Dialogue

The Bible and People of Other Faiths, S. Wesley Ariarajah, Risk Book Series No. 26, 2nd printing 1987 (co-production with WSCF Asia/Pacific Region; for the USA: Orbis Books, Maryknoll, NY)

Christ and Prometheus? A Quest for Theological Identity, Jan Milic Lochman, 1988

Encounter in the Spirit: Muslim-Christian Meetings in Birmingham, Andrew Wingate, Risk Book Series No. 39, 1988

The Gospel in a Pluralist Society, Lesslie Newbigin, 1989 (co-publisher: Eerdmans, Grand Rapids; for the UK: SPCK, London)

Meeting in Faith: Twenty Years of Christian-Muslim Conversations Sponsored by the WCC, comp. Stuart E. Brown, 1989

My Neighbour's Faith — and Mine. Theological Discoveries Through Interfaith Dialogue: a Study Guide, 2nd printing 1987

New Religious Movements and the Churches, eds Allan R. Brockway & J. Paul Rajashekar, 1987

Risking Christ for Christ's Sake: Towards an Ecumenical Theology of Pluralism, M.M. Thomas, 1987 (out of print)

Spirituality in Interfaith Dialogue, eds Tosh Arai & S. Wesley Ariarajah, 1989 (for the USA: Orbis Books, Maryknoll, NY)

The Theology of the Churches and the Jewish People: Statements by the WCC and its Member Churches, eds Allan Brockway & Rolf Rendtorff, 1988

Mission, evangelism

A Community of Clowns: Testimonies of People in Urban Rural Mission, comp. Hugh Lewin, 1987

Foolishness to the Greeks, Lesslie Newbigin, Mission Series No. 6, 2nd printing 1987 (for the USA: Eerdmans, Grand Rapids; for the UK: SPCK, London)

Go Forth in Peace: Orthodox Perspectives on Mission, ed. Ion Bria, Mission Series No. 7, 1986

International Review of Mission, quarterly

Mission in Christ's Way: Bible Studies, Lesslie Newbigin, 1987 (for the USA: Friendship Press, New York)

Mission and Evangelism: an Ecumenical Affirmation, comp. Jean Stromberg, Mission Series No 4, 2nd printing 1985

The San Antonio Report. Your Will Be Done: Mission in Christ's Way, ed. Frederick R. Wilson, 1990

Your Will Be Done: Orthodoxy in Mission, ed. George Lemopoulos, 1989

Sharing, service and development

Diakonia 2000: Called to be Neighbours, ed. Klaus Poser, 1987

The Economics of Honour: Biblical Reflections on Money and Property, Roelf Haan, 1988

Ecumenical Reflections on Political Economy, comp. Catherine Mulholland, 1988

Enduring Witness: the Churches and the Palestinians, Larry Ekin, 1985

Global Economy: a Confessional Issue for the Churches?, Ulrich Duchrow, 1987

Hope in the Desert: the Churches' United Response to Human Need, ed. Kenneth Slack, 1986

The International Financial System: an Ecumenical Critique, ed. Reginald Green, An Ecumenical Approach to Economics No. 4, 1985

Labour, Employment and Unemployment: an Ecumenical Reappraisal, ed. R.H. Green, An Ecumenical Approach to Economics No. 5, 1987

The Meaning and Nature of Diakonia: Meditations and Reflections on the Twofold Ministry of Diakonia, Paulos Mar Gregorios, Risk Book Series No. 39, 1988

My Neighbour — Myself: Visions of Diakonia, Claudius Ceccon & Kristian Paludan, 1988

The Poor Side of Europe: the Church and the (New) Poor of Western Europe, Coenraad Boerma, Risk Book Series No. 42, 1989

Resource Sharing Book, annual

Sharing Life. Official Report of the World Consultation on Koinonia: Sharing Life in a World Community, ed. Huibert van Beek, 1989

The Stranger Within Your Gates: Uprooted People in the World Today, André Jacques, Risk Book Series No. 29, 1986

Unified in Hope: Arabs and Jews Talk about Peace, interviewer Carol J. Birkland, 1987 (for the USA: Friendship Press, New York)

Church and society

The New Faith Science Debate, ed. John M. Mangum, 1989 (co-publisher: Fortress Press, Philadelphia)

Science Education and Ethical Values: Introducing Ethics and Religion into the Science Classroom and Laboratory, eds David Gosling & Bert Musschenga, 2nd printing 1986 (for the USA: Georgetown University Press, Washington)

Will the Future Work? Values for Emerging Patterns of Work and Employment, eds Howard David & David Gosling, 1985

Churches in international affairs

Christian Response in a World of Crisis: a Brief History of the WCC's Commission of the Churches on International Affairs, Ans van der Bent, 1986

The Churches in International Affairs Reports 1983-1986, 1987

Combating racism

"It's Like Holding the Key to Your Own Jail": Women in Namibia, Caroline Allison, 1986

The Sanctions Mission: Report of the Eminent Church Persons Group, ed. James Mutambirwa, 1989 (co-publisher: Zed Press, London and New Jersey)

Women in church and society

By Our Lives...: Stories of Women — Today and in the Bible, 2nd printing, 1986 (out of print)

Churches in Solidarity with Women: Prayers and Poems, Songs and Stories, 1988

In God's Image: Identity, Scripture and Human Wholeness, eds Janet Crawford & Michael Kinnamon, 1983

Speaking for Ourselves: Bible Studies and Discussion Starters, eds Wendy S. Robins & Musimbi Kanyoro, 1990

We Cannot Dream Alone: a Story of Women in Development, ed. Ranjini Rebera, 1990

We Will Not Hang Our Harps on the Willows: Engagement and Spirituality, Bärbel von Wartenberg-Potter, Risk Book Series No. 34, 1987 (for the USA: Meyer Stone Books, Oak Park, IL)

Education

Families in Transition: the Case for Counselling in Context, eds Masamba ma Mpolo & Cécile De Sweemer, 1987

Family Profiles: Stories of Families in Transition, ed. Masamba ma Mpolo, 1984

Ministerial Formation in a Multifaith Milieu: Implications of Interfaith Dialogue for Theological Education, eds Sam Amirtham & S. Wesley Ariarajah, 1986

The Teaching of Ecumenics, eds Samuel Amirtham & Cyrus H.S. Moon, 1987

Theology by the People: Reflections on Doing Theology in Community, eds Sam Amirtham & John Pobee, 1986 (out of print)

Bible study, meditation, worship

Clearing the Way: En Route to an Ecumenical Spirituality, Gwen Cashmore & Joan Puls, Risk Book Series No. 43, 1990

Immanuel: the Coming of Jesus in Art and the Bible, Hans-Ruedi Weber, 1984 (co-publisher: Eerdmans, Grand Rapids)

Living in the Image of Christ: the Laity in Ministry, Hans-Ruedi Weber, 1986 (for the USA: Judson Press, Valley Forge, PA)

New Eyes for Reading: Biblical and Theological Reflections by Women from the Third World, eds John S. Pobee & Bärbel von Wartenberg-Potter, 1986 (for the USA: Meyer Stone Books, Oak Park, IL)

Power: Focus for a Biblical Theology, Hans-Ruedi Weber, 1989

A Spirituality for Our Times, 1985

Walking on Thorns: the Call to Christian Obedience, Allan Boesak, Risk Book Series No. 22, 2nd printing 1987 (for the USA: Eerdmans, Grand Rapids)

The Way of the Lamb. Christ in the Apocalypse: Lenten Meditations, Hans-Ruedi Weber, Risk Book Series No. 36, 1988

Weep Not For Me: Meditations on the Cross and the Resurrection, John V. Taylor, Risk Book Series No. 27, 3rd printing 1987 (for the USA: Twenty Third Publications, Mystic, CT) (WCC ed. out of print)

When We Pray Together, Emilio Castro, Risk Book Series No. 40, 1988

Who are the Poor? The Beatitudes as a Call to Community, John S. Pobee, Risk Book Series No. 32, 1987

Why, O Lord? Psalms and Sermons from Namibia, Zephania Kameeta, Risk Book Series No. 28, 1986 (in co-operation with LWF; for the USA: Fortress Press, Philadelphia)

Justice, peace, ecology

Christians as Peacemakers: Peace Movements in Europe and the USA, Marc Reuver, 1988 (published for CEC)

Dove on Fire: Poems on Peace, Justice and Ecology, Cecil Rajendra, Risk Book Series No. 33, 1987

Justice, Peace and the Integrity of Creation: Insights from Orthodoxy, ed. Gennadios Limouris, 1990

Resisting the Threats to Life: Covenanting for Justice, Peace and the Integrity of Creation, Preman Niles, Risk Book Series No. 41, 1989

Shalom: Biblical Perspectives on Creation, Justice and Peace, Ulrich Duchrow & Gerhard Liedke, 1989

Communications studies

Beyond Technology: Contexts for Christian Communication, John Bluck, 1984

Christian Communication Reconsidered, John Bluck, 1989

Audiovisuals

Come, Holy Spirit — Renew the Whole Creation, 6 audiovisual prayers, 72 slides with audio cassette, 1990

One World: the World Council of Churches at Work, 29-minute video, 1988; also available in French, German and Spanish

Sharing Life in a World Community: Koinonia, 23-minute video on resource-sharing, 1988

The Triune God: Thoughts Inspired by Rublev's Icon of the Trinity, 11-minute video, 1988

The World Council of Churches in the Ecumenical Movement: an Audiovisual Introduction, 79 slides with audio cassette in English, French, German and Spanish, 25 minutes, 1990

Your Will Be Done: Mission in Christ's Way, 29-minute video on the San Antonio conference, 1989; also available in French, German and Spanish

Members of the Central Committee

*ABAYASEKERA, Ms Annathaie
Church of Ceylon

ABEBAW, Mr Yegzaw
Ethiopian Orthodox Church
replaced by Mr Demtse G. Medhin,
1988

ABEL, Miss Carol
Church in Wales

ADEJOBI, Primate Emmanuel A.
Church of the Lord Aladura, Nigeria

AHREN, Rt Rev. Dr Per-Olov
Church of Sweden

AJAMIAN, Archbishop Shahe
Armenian Apostolic Church
(Etchmiadzin)
replaced by Rev. Fr V. Aykazian,
1988

ALLIN, Rt Rev. John M.
Episcopal Church USA
replaced by
Most Rev. E.L. Browning, 1987

ANDERSON, Rev. Gershon F.H.
Methodist Church, Sierra Leone
replaced Rev. Nelson Charles, 1989

*ANTONIE, H.E. Metropolitan of
Transsylvania
Romanian Orthodox Church

ARNOLD, Okr Walter
Evangelical Church in Germany
(EKD)

*ASHMALL, Mr Harry
Church of Scotland
replaced by Rev. James Rogers, 1988

*ATHANASIOS, H.G. Archbishop
Coptic Orthodox Church, Egypt

AULT, Bishop James M.
United Methodist Church, USA

AYAKAZIAN, Rev. Fr Viken
Armenian Apostolic Church
(Etchmiadzin)
replaced Archbishop S. Ajamian, 1988

BABAI, Bishop Ashur
Apostolic Catholic Assyrian Church
of the East (USA)

*BARROW, Dame R. Nita
Methodist Church in the Caribbean
and the Americas, Barbados
(President)

*BENA-SILU, M.
Church of Jesus Christ on Earth by the
Prophet Simon Kimbangu, Zaire

BHENGRA, Miss Helen
United Evangelical Lutheran
Church in India
replaced Ms Elbina Tudu
(d. March 1984)

---

*   Executive committee member
** Representing an associate member
      church

BICHKOV, Rev. Alexei
Union of Evangelical Christians
Baptists of USSR

BLEI, Dr Karel
Netherlands Reformed Church
replaced Rev. Dr Remko J. Mooi,
1989

BOBROVA, Ms Nina
Russian Orthodox Church

BOROVOY, Protopresbyter Vitaly
Russian Orthodox Church

BOZABALIAN, H.G. Archbishop
Nerses
Armenian Apostolic Church
(Etchmiadzin)

*BRIGGS, Mr John
Baptist Union of Great Britain

BROWNING, Most Rev. Edmond L.
Episcopal Church, USA
replaced Rt Rev. J.M. Allin, 1987

*BÜHRIG, Dr. Marga
Swiss Protestant Church Federation
(President)

BUEVSKI, Mr Alexei
Russian Orthodox Church

BURUA, Rev. Albert
United Church of Papua New Guinea
and the Solomon Islands
replaced by Rev. Edea Kidu, 1990

**CALVO, Rev. Samuel F.
Evangelical Methodist Church
of Costa Rica

CAMPBELL, Rev. Dr Robert C.
American Baptist Churches in the USA

CHARLES, Rev. Nelson
Methodist Church, Sierra Leone
replaced by Rev. G.F.H. Anderson,
1989

CHAVEZ, Pastora Ana Enriqueta
Pentecostal Church of Chile
replaced Ms Marta Palma, 1987

CHRISTIANSEN, Bishop Henrik
Church of Denmark

*CHRYSOSTOMOS OF MYRA,
H.E. Metropolitan
Ecumenical Patriarchate, Turkey
(Vice-Moderator)

CHRYSOSTOMOS, H.E.
Metropolitan of Peristerion
Church of Greece

CROW, Rev. Dr Paul A. Jr
Christian Church (Disciples of Christ),
USA

CRUMLEY, Dr James R. Jr
Evangelical Lutheran Church
in America

CUTHBERT, Rev. Dr Raymond A.
Christian Church (Disciples of Christ),
Canada

DAS, Prof. Dr Vincent A.
Church of Pakistan

DAVID, H.E. Metropolitan of
Suchumi and Abkhazeti
Georgian Orthodox Church

DOLL, Rev. Ulrike
Federation of Evangelical Churches
in the GDR
replaced by Dr C. Woratz, 1985

DOMINGUES, Rev. Jorge
Luiz Ferreira
Methodist Church in Brazil
replaced Mr P.L. de Mello e Silva,
1988

DUKU, Dr Oliver
Province of the Episcopal Church
of the Sudan

DUTTON, Bishop Dr Denis C.
Methodist Church in Malaysia
replaced Datuk Ping-Hua Yao, 1989

DZOBO, Rt Rev. Prof. Noah K.
Evangelical Presbyterian Church,
Ghana

ENEME, Ms Grace
Presbyterian Church in Cameroon

*FAA'ALO, Rev. Puafitu
Church of Tuvalu

**FULIGNO, Pastor Gioele
Evangelical Baptist Union of Italy

**FUNZAMO, Rev. Isaias
Presbyterian Church of Mozambique

GATWA, Mr Tharcisse
Presbyterian Church of Rwanda

GCABASHE, Mrs Virginia
Methodist Church of Southern Africa

GIANNOPOULOS, Archimandrite
Theophilos
Greek Orthodox Patriarchate
of Jerusalem
replaced Metropolitan Vassilios
of Caesarea, 1987

GRAEWE, Dr W.D.
Federation of Evangelical Churches
in the GDR

*GREGORIOS, H.E. Metropolitan
Dr Paulos Mar
Malankara Orthodox Syrian Church,
India *(President)*

GRINDROD, Most Rev. John
Anglican Church of Australia
replaced by Rt Rev. Oliver Heyward,
1989

HABGOOD, Most Rev. John
Church of England, UK

HANNON, Rt Rev. Brian D.A.
Church of Ireland

HARMON, Ms Janice
Evangelical Lutheran Church
in America

*HELD, Rev. Dr Heinz Joachim
Evangelical Church in Germany
(EKD) *(Moderator)*

*HEMPEL, Landesbischof
Dr. Johannes W.
Federation of Evangelical Churches
in the GDR *(President)*

HEYWARD, Rt Rev. Oliver S.
Anglican Church of Australia
replaced Most Rev. J. Grindrod, 1989

HOGGARD, Bishop James C.
African Methodist Episcopal
Zion Church
replaced Dr Rena Karefa Smart, 1990

HOIORE, Ms Celine
Evangelical Church
of French Polynesia

HOOVER, Ms Theressa
United Methodist Church, USA

HUSTON, Rev. Dr Robert W.
United Methodist Church, USA

IBRAHIM, H.E. Metropolitan
G. Yohanna
Syrian Orthodox Patriarchate
of Antioch and All the East

*IGNATIOS IV, Sa Béatitude
Greek Orthodox Patriarchate
of Antioch and All the East
(President)

IMASOGIE, Rev. Dr Osadolor
Nigerian Baptist Convention

JAPHAR, Ms Inge Halim
Indonesian Christian Church

JARJOUR, Mrs Rose
National Evangelical Synod of Syria
and Lebanon

JEFFERSON, Rev. Canon Ruth
Anglican Church of Canada

JEREMIAS, Bishop
Autocephalic Orthodox Church
in Poland

JESUDASAN, Most Rev. I.
Church of South India

JOHN, H.E. Archbishop of Karelia
and All Finland
Orthodox Church of Finland

JORNOD, Pasteur Jean-Pierre
Swiss Protestant Church Federation

JULKIREE, Ms Boonmee
Church of Christ in Thailand

*KADDU, Mrs Joyce
Church of Uganda

KAESSMANN, Rev. Margot
Evangelical Church in Germany
(EKD)

KAREFA SMART, Dr Rena
African Methodist Episcopal
Zion Church
replaced by Bishop James C. Hoggard,
1990

KARPENKO, Mr Alexander
Russian Orthodox Church

KAWABATA, Mr Junshiro
United Church of Christ in Japan

KESHISHIAN, Archbishop Aram
Armenian Apostolic Church (Cilicia)

KHUMALO, Rev. Samson
Presbyterian Church of Africa,
South Africa

KIDU, Rev. Edea
United Church in Papua New Guinea
and the Solomon Islands
replaced Rev. Albert Burua, 1990

KIM, Rev. Dr Choon Young
Korean Methodist Church

KIM, Rev. Dr Hyung-Tae
Presbyterian Church of Korea

*KIRILL, H.E. Archbishop of
Smolensk
Russian Orthodox Church

KISHKOVSKY, Very Rev. Leonid
Orthodox Church in America

KNALL, Bischof Dieter
Evangelical Church of the Augsburg
and Helvetic Confession, Austria

KNOBLAUCH, Rev. Bruno
Evangelical Church of the River
Plate, Argentina

KOK, Justice Dr Govaert C.
Old Catholic Church
of the Netherlands

KONIDARIS, Prof. Dr Gerassimos
Church of Greece, died 1987
replaced by Prof. J.S. Romanides,
1988

KRUSE, Bischof Martin
Evangelical Church in Germany
(EKD)

LARSSON, Mrs Birgitta
Church of Sweden

LASARO, Rev. Manasa
Methodist Church in Fiji
replaced Rev. Inoke Nabulivou, 1988

LEMOPULO, Mr Yorgo
Ecumenical Patriarchate
resigned 1987 (WCC staff)

LETHUNYA, Ms Sebolelo Esther
Lesotho Evangelical Church

LODBERG, Mr Peter
Church of Denmark

*LOVE, Dr Janice
United Methodist Church, USA

LUVANDA, Miss Jeneth
Evangelical Lutheran
Church in Tanzania

*MAKHULU, Most Rev.
W.P. Khotso
Church of the Province of Central
Africa, Botswana *(President)*

**MALAKAR, Dr Upendra N.
Church of Bangladesh, died 1988
(not replaced)

MAYLAND, Mrs Jean
Church of England, UK

MBAN, Rev. Joseph
Evangelical Church of Congo

*McCLOUD, Rev. Dr J. Oscar
Presbyterian Church (USA)

MEDHIN, Mr Demtse Gabre
Ethiopian Orthodox Church
replaced Mr Yegzaw Abebaw, 1988

MEKARIOS, Archbishop
Ethiopian Orthodox Church

DE MELLO E SILVA, Mr Paulo
Lutero
Evangelical Pentecostal Church
"Brazil for Christ", resigned 1986
replaced by Rev. Jorge L.
Ferreira Domingues, 1988

MICHALKO, Gen-Bischof
Prof. Dr John D.
Slovak Evangelical Church of the
Augsburg Confession in the CSSR

MITSIDES, Dr Andreas
Church of Cyprus

MOOI, Rev. Dr Remko J.
Netherlands Reformed Church
replaced by Dr K. Blei, 1989

MUCHENA, Ms Olivia
United Methodist Church, Zimbabwe

*NABABAN, Ephorus Dr S.A.E.
Batak Protestant Christian Church,
Indonesia

NABULIVOU, Rev. Inoke
Methodist Church in Fiji
replaced by Rev. M. Lasaro, 1988

NAGY, Bishop Dr Gyula
Lutheran Church in Hungary

NEFF, Rev. Dr Robert
Church of the Brethren, USA

NEWELL, Kara L.
Friends United Meeting, USA

NIFON, Bishop
Romanian Orthodox Church
replaced Bishop Vasile, 1989

OKULLU, Rt Rev. Dr J. Henry
Church of the Province of Kenya

PAJULA, Archbishop Kuno
Estonian Evangelical Lutheran Church

PALMA, Ms Marta
Pentecostal Mission Church, Chile
replaced by Pastora Ana E. Chavez
(WCC staff), 1987

PANKRATY, H.E. Metropolitan
Bulgarian Orthodox Church

PARTHENIOS III, His Beatitude
Greek Orthodox Patriarchate
of Alexandria, Egypt

PATTIASINA-TOREH, Rev. Mrs
Caroline E.
Protestant Church in the Moluccas,
Indonesia

PETROVA, Mrs Stefanka
Bulgarian Orthodox Church

PHILARET, H.E. Metropolitan
of Minsk
Russian Orthodox Church

*PISKE, Rev. Meinrad
Evangelical Church of Lutheran
Confession in Brazil

POITIER, Mrs Annette
Methodist Church in the Caribbean
and the Americas, Bahamas

POST, Rev. Dr Avery
United Church of Christ, USA

PREUS, Bishop David
Evangelical Lutheran Church
in America

RAVALOMANANA, Mlle Vaosoa F.
Church of Jesus Christ in Madagascar

RICHARDSON, Rev. John E.
Methodist Church, UK

RICHARDSON, Rev. Dr W. Franklyn
National Baptist Convention USA Inc.

ROGERS, Rev. James
Church of Scotland
replaced Mr Harry Ashmall, 1988

ROMANIDES, Prof. John S.
Church of Greece
replaced Prof. Dr G. Konidaris, 1988

ROSS, Dr Mary O.
National Baptist Convention USA Inc.

RUSSELL, Rt Rev. Philip W. R.
Church of the Province of Southern
Africa

SABUG, Mr Fructuoso T. Jr
Philippine Independent Church

SANTRAM, Rev. Pritam B.
Church of North India

SEAH, Rev. Dr Ingram S.
Presbyterian Church in Taiwan

SEKARAN, Mr Premkumar
United Evangelical Lutheran Church
in India

SIMIC, Prof. Dr Pribislav
Serbian Orthodox Church, Yugoslavia

SKARRIE-ELMQUIST, Ms Marie
Mission Covenant Church of Sweden

*SKUSE, Ms Jean
Uniting Church in Australia

SMOLIK, Rev. Prof. Josef
Evangelical Church of Czech Brethren

SOUZA, Rt Rev. Neville de
Church in the Province of the West
Indies, Jamaica

SOWUNMI, Dr Adebisi
Church of the Province of Nigeria

STÅLSETT, Rev. Gunnar
Church of Norway
replaced by Mr Per Voksø, 1985

STYLIANOPOULOS, Rev. Dr
Theodore
Ecumenical Patriarchate (USA)

SUMO, Mr Kpadeson
Lutheran Church in Liberia

SUPIT, Dr Bert A.
Christian Evangelical Church
in Minahasa, Indonesia

SUVARSKY, Protopresbyter
Dr Jaroslav
Orthodox Church of Czechoslovakia

*TALBOT, Dr Sylvia
African Methodist Episcopal Church,
USA *(Vice-Moderator)*

THAN, Prof. Kyaw
Burma Baptist Convention

THOMPSON, Rev. Livingstone
Moravian Church in Jamaica

THOMPSON, Mr William P.
Presbyterian Church (USA)

THOROGOOD, Rev. Bernard
United Reformed Church in the UK

TISDALE, Rev. Leonora Tubbs
Presbyterian Church (USA)

*TOLEN, Dr Aaron
Presbyterian Church of Cameroon

*TOTH, Bishop Dr Karoly
Reformed Church in Hungary

TSHIHAMBA, Dr Mukome Luendu
Church of Christ in Zaïre
(Presbyterian Community)

TUDU, Ms Elbina
United Evangelical Lutheran Church
in India, died 1984
replaced by Ms Helen Bhengra, 1984

UKUR, Dr Fridolin
Kalimantan Evangelical Church,
Indonesia

**VACCARO, Rev. Dr Gabriel O.
Church of God, Argentina

VARUGHESE, Dr K. V.
Mar Thoma Syrian Church
of Malabar, India

VASILE, Bishop
Romanian Orthodox Church
replaced by Bishop Nifon, 1989

VASSILIOS, Metropolitan
of Caesarea, Greek Orthodox
Patriarchate of Jerusalem
replaced by Archimandrite Th.
Giannopoulos, 1987

VEEN-SCHENKEVELD, Rev. Marja
J. van der
Reformed Churches in the Netherlands

VERCOE, Rt Rev. Whakahuihui
Church of the Province
of New Zealand

VIKSTRÖM, Archbishop Dr John
Evangelical Lutheran Church
of Finland

*VOKSØ, Mr Per
Church of Norway
replaced Rev. Gunnar Stålsett

WESTPHAL, Ms Marthe
Reformed Church of France

*WILSON, Very Rev. Dr Lois M.
United Church of Canada
(President)

WORATZ, Dr Christine
Federation of Evangelical Churches
in the GDR
replaced Rev. Ulrike Doll, 1985

YAO, Datuk Ping-Hua
Methodist Church in Malaysia
replaced by Bishop Dr D.C. Dutton,
1989

ZUMACH, Mrs Hildegard
Evangelical Church in Germany
(EKD)

APPENDIX 3

Member Churches
and Associate Councils

(as of May 1990)

ALGERIA

Eglise protestante d'Algérie*
(Protestant Church of Algeria)

ANGOLA

Igreja Evangelica Congregacional en
Angola
(Evangelical Congregational Church in
Angola)

Igreja Evangélica Unida de Angola*
(United Evangelical Church of
Angola)

Missao Evangélica Pentecostal de
Angola*
(Evangelical Pentecostal Church of
Angola)

ANTIGUA

Methodist Church in the Caribbean and
the Americas

Moravian Church, Eastern West Indies
Province

ARGENTINA

La Iglesia de Dios*
(Church of God)

Iglesia de los Discipulos de Cristo*
(Church of the Disciples of Christ)

Iglesia Evangélica Luterana Unida*
(United Evangelical Lutheran Church)

Iglesia Evangélica Metodista
Argentina
(Evangelical Methodist Church of
Argentina)

Iglesia Evangélica del Rio de la Plata
(Evangelical Church of the River
Plate)

AUSTRALIA

Anglican Church of Australia

Australian Council of Churches **

Churches of Christ in Australia

Uniting Church in Australia

AUSTRIA

Alt-katholische Kirche Österreichs
(Old Catholic Church of Austria)

Evangelische Kirche Augsburgischen
u. Helvetischen Bekenntnisses
(AuHB)
(Evangelical Church of the Augsburg
and Helvetic Confession)

---

*   Associate member church
** Associate council

Ökumenischer Rat der Kirchen in Österreich **
(Ecumenical Council of Churches in Austria)

BANGLADESH

Bangladesh Baptist Sangha

Church of Bangladesh*

BARBADOS

Church in the Province of the West Indies

BELGIUM

Eglise protestante unie de Belgique
(United Protestant Church of Belgium)

BENIN

Eglise protestante méthodiste au Bénin et au Togo
(Protestant Methodist Church in Benin and Togo)

BOLIVIA

Iglesia Evangélica Métodista en Bolivia*
(Evangelical Methodist Church in Bolivia)

BOTSWANA

Botswana Christian Council **

Church of the Province of Central Africa

BRAZIL

Conselho Nacional de Igrejas Cristas do Brasil (CONIC) **
(National Council of Christian Churches in Brazil)

Igreja Episcopal do Brasil
(Episcopal Church of Brazil)

Igreja Evangélica de Confissao Luterana no Brasil
(Evangelical Church of Lutheran Confession in Brazil)

Igreja Metodista do Brasil
(Methodist Church in Brazil)

Igreja Presbiteriana Unida do Brasil*
(United Presbyterian Church of Brazil)

Igreja Reformada Latino Americana
(Latin American Reformed Church)

BULGARIA

Bulgarian Orthodox Church

BURMA

See Myanmar

BURUNDI

Church of the Province of Burundi, Rwanda and Zaïre

CAMEROON

Eglise évangélique du Cameroun
(Evangelical Church of Cameroon)

Eglise presbytérienne camérounaise
(Presbyterian Church of Cameroon)

Eglise protestante africaine*
(African Protestant Church)

Presbyterian Church in Cameroon

Union des Eglises baptistes du Cameroun
(Union of Baptist Churches of Cameroon)

CANADA

Anglican Church of Canada

Canadian Council of Churches — Conseil canadien des Eglises **

Canadian Yearly Meeting of the Religious Society of Friends

Christian Church (Disciples of Christ)

Evangelical Lutheran Church in Canada

Latvijas Evangeliski Luteriska baznica eksila
(Evangelical Lutheran Church of Latvia in Exile)

Presbyterian Church in Canada

United Church of Canada

CHILE

Iglesia Evangélica Luterana en Chile
(Evangelical-Lutheran Church in Chile)

Iglesia Metodista de Chile*
(Methodist Church of Chile)

Iglesia Pentecostal de Chile
(Pentecostal Church of Chile)

Misión Iglesia Pentecostal
(Pentecostal Mission Church)

CONGO (People's Republic of the)

Eglise évangélique du Congo
(Evangelical Church of the Congo)

COOK ISLANDS

Cook Islands Christian Church

COSTA RICA

Iglesia Evangélica Metodista de Costa Rica*
(Evangelical Methodist Church of Costa Rica)

CUBA

Consejo Ecumenica de Cuba**
(Ecumenical Council of Cuba)

Iglesia Metodista en Cuba*
(Methodist Church in Cuba)

Iglesia Presbiteriana-Reformada en Cuba*
(Presbyterian Reformed Church in Cuba)

CYPRUS

Church of Cyprus

CZECHOSLOVAKIA

Ceskobratrsk cirkev evangelick
(Evangelical Church of Czech Brethren)

Ceskoslovensk cirkev husitsk
(Czechoslovak Hussite Church)

Ekumenika Rada Cirkvi**
(Czechoslovak Ecumenical Council of Churches)

Pravoslavn cirkev v CSSR
(Orthodox Church of Czechoslovakia)

Ref. krest. cirkev na Slovensku
(Reformed Christian Church in Slovakia)

Slezk cirkev evangelick a.v.
(Silesian Evangelical Church of the Augsburg Confession)

Slovensk evanjelick cirkev a.v. v CSSR
(Slovak Evangelical Church of the Augsburg Confession in the CSSR)

DENMARK

Danske Baptistsamfund
(Baptist Union of Denmark)

Ecumenical Council of Denmark**

Evangelisk-lutherske Folkekirke i Danmark
(Evangelical Lutheran Church of Denmark)

EGYPT

Coptic Orthodox Church

Greek Orthodox Patriarchate of Alexandria and All Africa

Synod of the Nile of the Evangelical Church

EQUATORIAL GUINEA

Iglesia Reformada de Guinea Ecuatorial*
(Reformed Church of Equatorial Guinea)

ETHIOPIA

Ethiopian Evangelical Church Mekane Yesus

Ethiopian Orthodox Church

FIJI

Methodist Church in Fiji

FINLAND

Ecumenical Council of Finland**

Orthodox Church of Finland

Suomen evankelis-luterilainen kirkko
(Evangelical-Lutheran Church of Finland)

FRANCE

Eglise de la Confession d'Augsbourg, d'Alsace et de Lorraine
(Evangelical Church of the Augsburg Confession of Alsace and Lorraine)

Eglise évangélique luthérienne de France
(Evangelical Lutheran Church of France)

Eglise réformée d'Alsace et de Lorraine
(Reformed Church of Alsace and Lorraine)

Eglise réformée de France
(Reformed Church of France)

FRENCH POLYNESIA

Eglise évangélique de Polynésie française
(Evangelical Church of French Polynesia)

GABONESE REPUBLIC

Eglise évangélique du Gabon
(Evangelical Church of Gabon)

THE GAMBIA

Gambia Christian Council**

FEDERAL REPUBLIC OF GERMANY

Arbeitsgemeinschaft Christlicher Kirchen in der Bundesrepublik Deutschland und Berlin (West) e.v.**
(Council of Christian Churches in the Federal Republic of Germany and West Berlin)

Europäisch-Festländische Brüder-Unität, Distrikt Bad Boll
(European Continental Province of the Moravian Church — Western District)

Evangelische Kirche in Deutschland
(Evangelical Church in Germany)

Evangelische Landeskirche in Baden

Evangelisch-Lutherische Kirche in Bayern°

° Individual member of the WCC.
The other churches are members through the EKD (Evangelische Kirche in Deutschland).

Evangelische Kirche in Berlin-
Brandenburg (Berlin-West)

Evangelisch-lutherische
Landeskirche in Braunschweig°

Bremische Evangelische Kirche

Evangelisch-lutherische
Landeskirche Hannovers°

Evangelische Kirche in Hessen und
Nassau

Evangelische Kirche von
Kurhessen-Waldeck

Lippische Landeskirche

Nordelbische Evangelisch-
lutherische Kirche°

Evangelisch-reformierte Kirche
(Synode ev.-ref. Kirchen in
Nordwestdeutschland)

Evangelisch-lutherische Kirche in
Oldenburg

Evangelische Kirche der Pfalz

Evangelische Kirche im Rheinland

Evangelisch-lutherische
Landeskirche Schaumburg-Lippe°

Evangelische Kirche von Westfalen

Evangelische Landeskirche in
Württemberg

Katholisches Bistum der Alt-
Katholiken in Deutschland
(Catholic Diocese of the Old Catholics
in Germany)

Vereinigung der Deutschen
Mennonitengemeinden
(Mennonite Church)

**GERMAN DEMOCRATIC
REPUBLIC**

Arbeitsgemeinschaft Christlicher
Kirchen in der Deutschen
Demokratischen Republik**
(Council of Christian Churches in the
German Democratic Republic)

Bund der Evangelischen Kirchen in der
Deutschen Demokratische Republik
(Federation of the Evangelical
Churches in the GDR)

Evangelische Landeskirche Anhalts

Evangelische Kirche in Berlin-
Brandenburg

Evangelische Kirche des Görlitzer
Kirchengebietes

Evangelische Landeskirche
Greifswald

Evangelisch-lutherische
Landeskirche Mecklenburgs

Evangelische Kirche der
Kirchenprovinz Sachsen

Evangelisch-lutherische
Landeskirche Sachsens

Evangelisch-lutherische Kirche in
Thüringen

Evangelische Brüder-Unität (Distrikt
Herrnhut)
(Moravian Church)

Gemeindeverband der Alt-
Katholischen Kirche in der Deutschen
Demokratischen Republik
(Federation of the Old Catholic Church
in the GDR)

° Individual member of the WCC. The other
churches are members through the EKD
(Evangelische Kirche in Deutschland).

GHANA

Christian Council of Ghana**

Evangelical Presbyterian Church

Methodist Church, Ghana

Presbyterian Church of Ghana

GREECE

Ekklesia tes Ellados
(Church of Greece)

Helleniki Evangeliki Ekklesia
(Greek Evangelical Church)

HONG KONG

Church of Christ in China

Hong Kong Christian Council**

HUNGARY

Magyarorszgi Baptista Egyhz
(Baptist Union of Hungary)

Magyarorszagi Egyhazak Okumenikus
Tanacsa**
(Ecumenical Council of Churches in
Hungary)

Magyarorszgi Evangélikus Egyhz
(Lutheran Church in Hungary)

Magyarorszgi Reformatus Egyhz
(Reformed Church in Hungary)

ICELAND

Evangelical Lutheran Church of
Iceland

INDIA

Bengal Orissa-Bihar Baptist
Convention*

Church of North India

Church of South India

Malankara Orthodox Syrian Church

Mar Thoma Syrian Church of Malabar

Methodist Church in India

National Council of Churches in
India**

Samavesam of Telugu Baptist
Churches

United Evangelical Lutheran Churches
in India

INDONESIA

Banua Niha Keriso Protestan (BNKP)
(Nias Protestant Christian Church)

Communion of Churches in
Indonesia**

Evangelical Christian Church in
Halmahera

Gereja Batak Karo Protestan (GBKP)
(Karo Batak Protestant Church)

Gereja-Gereja Kristen Java (GKJ)
(Javanese Christian Churches)

Gereja Kalimantan Evangelis (GKE)
(Kalimantan Evangelical Church)

Gereja Kristen Indonesia (GKI)
(Indonesian Christian Church)

Gereja Kristen Injili di Irian Jaya
(Evangelical Christian Church in Irian
Jaya)

Gereja Kristen Jawi Wetan (GKJW)
(East Java Christian Church)

Gereja Kristen Pasundan (GKP)
(Pasundan Christian Church)

Gereja Kristen Protestan Angkola
(GKPA)*
(Christian Protestant Angkola Church)

Gereja Kristen Protestan di Bali
(GKPB)*
(Protestant Christian Church in Bali)

Gereja Kristen Protestan Indonesia
(GKPI)
(Christian Protestant Church in
Indonesia)

Gereja Kristen Protestan Simalungun
(GKPS)
(Simalungun Protestant Christian
Church)

Gereja Kristen Sulawesi Tengah
(GKST)
(Christian Church of Central Sulawesi)

Gereja Masehi Injili Minahasa
(GMIM)
(Christian Evangelical Church in
Minahasa)

Gereja Masehi Injili Sangihe Talaud
(GMIST)
(Evangelical Church of Sangir Talaud)

Gereja Masehi Injili di Timor (GMIT)
(Protestant Evangelical Church in
Timor)

Gereja Protestan di Indonesia
(Protestant Church in Indonesia)

Gereja Protestan Maluku (GPM)
(Protestant Church in the Moluccas)

Gereja Punguan Kristen Batak
(GPKB)*
(Batak Christian Community Church)

Gereja Toraja
(Toraja Church)

Huria Kristen Batak Protestan
(Batak Protestant Christian Church)

Huria Kristen Indonesia (HKI)
(Indonesian Christian Church)

IRAN

Synod of the Evangelical Church of
Iran

ITALY

Chiesa Evangelica Metodista d'Italia
(Evangelical Methodist Church of
Italy)

Chiesa Evangelica Valdese
(Waldensian Church)

Evangelical Baptist Union of Italy*

IVORY COAST

Eglise protestante méthodiste de Côte
d'Ivoire
(Protestant Methodist Church, Ivory
Coast)

JAMAICA

Jamaica Council of Churches**

Moravian Church in Jamaica

United Church of Jamaica and Grand
Cayman

JAPAN

Japanese Orthodox Church

Korean Christian Church in Japan*

National Christian Council in Japan**

Nippon Kirisuto Kyodan
(United Church of Christ in Japan)

Nippon Sei Ko Kai
(Anglican-Episcopal Church in Japan)

JERUSALEM

Episcopal Church in Jerusalem and the
Middle East

Greek Orthodox Patriarchate of
Jerusalem

KENYA

African Christian Church and Schools

African Church of the Holy Spirit*

African Israel Church, Nineveh

Church of the Province of Kenya

Methodist Church in Kenya

Presbyterian Church of East Africa

KIRIBATI (Republic of)

Kiribati Protestant Church

KOREA

Korean Methodist Church

Presbyterian Church in the Republic of Korea (PROK)

Presbyterian Church of Korea

LEBANON

Armenian Apostolic Church

National Evangelical Synod of Syria and Lebanon

Union of the Armenian Evangelical Churches in the Near East

LESOTHO

Lesotho Evangelical Church

LIBERIA

Church of the Province of West Africa

Liberian Council of Churches**

Lutheran Church in Liberia

Presbytery of Liberia*

MADAGASCAR

Eglise de Jésus-Christ à Madagascar (Church of Jesus Christ in Madagascar)

Eglise luthérienne malgache (Malagasy Lutheran Church)

MALAYSIA

Council of Churches of Malaysia**

Methodist Church in Malaysia

Protestant Church in Sabah*

MEXICO

Iglesia Metodista de México (Methodist Church of Mexico)

MOZAMBIQUE

Igreja Presbiteriana de Moçambique* (Presbyterian Church of Mozambique)

MYANMAR (Burma)

Church of the Province of Burma

Methodist Church, Upper Burma

Myanmar Baptist Convention

Myanmar Council of Churches**

NAMIBIA

Council of Churches in Namibia**

NETHERLANDS

Algemene Doopsgezinde Sociëteit (General Mennonite Society)

Council of Churches in the Netherlands**

Evangelisch Lutherse Kerk (Evangelical Lutheran Church)

De Gereformeerde Kerken in Nederland (Reformed Churches in the Netherlands)

Nederlandse Hervormde Kerk (Netherlands Reformed Church)

Oud-Katholieke Kerk van Nederland (Old Catholic Church of the Netherlands)

Remonstrantse Broederschap (Remonstrant Brotherhood)

NETHERLANDS ANTILLES

Iglesia Protestant Uni* (United Protestant Church)

NEW CALEDONIA

Eglise évangélique en Nouvelle
Calédonie et aux Iles Loyauté
(Evangelical Church in New Caledonia
and the Loyalty Isles)

NEW ZEALAND

Anglican Church of the Province of
New Zealand

Associated Churches of Christ in New
Zealand

Baptist Union of New Zealand

Conference of Churches in Aotearoa-
New Zealand**

Methodist Church of New Zealand

Presbyterian Church of Aotearoa/New
Zealand

NICARAGUA

Convención Bautista de Nicaragua
(Baptist Convention of Nicaragua)

Iglesia Morava en Nicaragua
(Moravian Church in Nicaragua)

NIGERIA

Church of the Brethren in Nigeria

Church of the Lord Aladura

Church of the Province of Nigeria

Methodist Church, Nigeria

Nigerian Baptist Convention

Presbyterian Church of Nigeria

NORWAY

Den Norske Kirke
(Church of Norway)

PAKISTAN

Church of Pakistan

United Presbyterian Church of
Pakistan

PAPUA NEW GUINEA

Evangelical Lutheran Church of Papua
New Guinea

Melanesian Council of Churches**

United Church in Papua New Guinea
and the Solomon Islands

PERU

Iglesia Metodista del Peru*
(Methodist Church of Peru)

PHILIPPINES

Iglesia Evangélica Metodista en la
Islas Filipinas
(Evangelical Methodist Church in the
Philippines)

Iglesia Filipina Independiente
(Philippine Independent Church)

National Council of Churches in the
Philippines**

United Church of Christ in the
Philippines

POLAND

Autocephalic Orthodox Church in
Poland

Kosciola Ewangelicko-Augsburski w
PRL
(Evangelical Church of the Augsburg
Confession in Poland)

Kosciola Polskokatolickiego w PRL
(Polish Catholic Church in Poland)

Polska Rada Ekumeniczna**
(Polish Ecumenical Council)

Staro-Katolickiego Kosciola
Mariatowitow w PRL
(Old Catholic Mariavite Church in
Poland)

PORTUGAL

Igreja Evangélica Presbiteriana de Portugal*
(Evangelical Presbyterian Church of Portugal)

Igreja Lusitana Catolica Apostolica Evangélica
(Lusitanian Catholic-Apostolic Evangelical Church)

ROMANIA

Biserica Orthodoxa Romana
(Romanian Orthodox Church)

Evangelical Synodal Presbyterial Church of the Augsburg Confession in the Socialist Republic of Romania

Evangelische Kirche A.B. in der Sozialistischen Republik Rumänien
(Evangelical Church of the Augsburg Confession in the Socialist Republic of Romania)

Reformed Church of Romania

RWANDA

Eglise presbytérienne au Rwanda
(Presbyterian Church of Rwanda)

SAMOA

Congregational Christian Church in Samoa

General Assembly, Congregational Christian Church in American Samoa

Methodist Church in Samoa

SEYCHELLES

Church of the Province of the Indian Ocean

SIERRA LEONE

Methodist Church Sierra Leone

United Christian Council of Sierra Leone**

SINGAPORE

Methodist Church in Singapore*

National Council of Churches, Singapore**

SOLOMON ISLANDS

Church of Melanesia

SOUTH AFRICA

Church of the Province of Southern Africa

Evangelical Lutheran Church in Southern Africa

Evangelical Presbyterian Church in South Africa

Methodist Church of Southern Africa

Moravian Church in South Africa

Presbyterian Church of Africa

Presbyterian Church of Southern Africa

Reformed Presbyterian Church of Southern Africa

South African Council of Churches**

United Congregational Church of Southern Africa

SPAIN

Iglesia Española Reformada Episcopal*
(Spanish Reformed Episcopal Church)

Iglesia Evangélica Española
(Spanish Evangelical Church)

SRI LANKA
Church of Ceylon
Methodist Church
National Christian Council of Sri
Lanka**

ST VINCENT
St Vincent Christian Council**

SUDAN
Province of the Episcopal Church of
the Sudan
Presbyterian Church in the Sudan*
Sudan Council of Churches**

SURINAME
Moravian Church in Suriname

SWAZILAND
Council of Swaziland Churches**

SWEDEN
Eesti Evangeeliumi Luteri Usu Kirik
(Estonian Evangelical Lutheran
  Church)
Svenska Kyrkan
(Church of Sweden)
Svenska Missionsförbundet
(Mission Covenant Church of Sweden)
Swedish Ecumenical Council**

SWITZERLAND
Christkatholische Kirche der Schweiz
(Old Catholic Church of Switzerland)
Schweizerischer Evangelischer
Kirchenbund/Fédération des Eglises
protestantes de la Suisse
(Swiss Protestant Church Federation)

SYRIA
Patriarcat grec-orthodoxe d'Antioche
et de tout l'Orient
(Greek Orthodox Patriarchate of
Antioch and All the East)
Syrian Orthodox Patriarchate of
Antioch and All the East

TAIWAN
Presbyterian Church in Taiwan

TANZANIA
Christian Council of Tanzania**
Church of the Province of Tanzania
Evangelical Lutheran Church in
Tanzania
Moravian Church in Tanzania

THAILAND
Church of Christ in Thailand

TOGO
Eglise évangélique du Togo
(Evangelical Church of Togo)

TONGA
Methodist Church in Tonga
(Free Wesleyan Church of Tonga)
Tonga National Council of Churches**

TRINIDAD and TOBAGO
Presbyterian Church in Trinidad

TURKEY
Ecumenical Patriarchate of
Constantinople

TUVALU
Church of Tuvalu

UGANDA
Church of Uganda

UNION OF SOVIET SOCIALIST REPUBLICS
Russian Orthodox Church

All-Union of Evangelical Christians — Baptists of USSR

Armenian SSR
Armenian Apostolic Church

Estonian SSR
Eesti Evangeelne Luterlik Kirik (Estonian Evangelical Lutheran Church)

Georgian SSR
Georgian Orthodox Church

Latvian SSR
Latvijas Evangeliski-Luteriska Baznica (Evangelical Lutheran Church of Latvia)

UNITED KINGDOM and REPUBLIC OF IRELAND
Baptist Union of Great Britain

British Council of Churches**

Church of England

Methodist Church

Moravian Church in Great Britain and Ireland

United Reformed Church in the United Kingdom

Churches with headquarters in Ireland

Church of Ireland

Methodist Church in Ireland

Churches with headquarters in Scotland

Church of Scotland

Congregational Union of Scotland

Scottish Episcopal Church

United Free Church of Scotland

Churches with headquarters in Wales

Church in Wales

Cytun — Churches Together in Wales**

Presbyterian Church of Wales

Union of Welsh Independents

UNITED STATES OF AMERICA
African Methodist Episcopal Church

African Methodist Episcopal Zion Church

American Baptist Churches in the USA

Apostolic Catholic Assyrian Church of the East

Christian Church (Disciples of Christ)

Christian Methodist Episcopal Church

Church of the Brethren

Episcopal Church

Evangelical Lutheran Church in America

Hungarian Reformed Church in America

International Council of Community Churches

International Evangelical Church

Moravian Church in America
(Northern Province)

Moravian Church in America
(Southern Province)

National Baptist Convention of
America

National Baptist Convention, USA,
Inc.

National Council of the Churches of
Christ in the USA**

Orthodox Church in America

Polish National Catholic Church

Presbyterian Church (USA)

Progressive National Baptist
Convention, Inc.

Reformed Church in America

Religious Society of Friends

 Friends General Conference
 Friends United Meeting

United Church of Christ

United Methodist Church

URUGUAY

Iglesia Evangélica Metodista en el
Uruguay*
(Evangelical Methodist Church in
Uruguay)

VANUATU

Presbyterian Church of Vanuatu

YUGOSLAVIA

Ecumenical Council of Churches in
Yugoslavia**

Reformatska Crke u SFRJ
(Reformed Church in Yugoslavia)

Serbian Orthodox Church

Slovenska ev.kr. a.v. cirkev v.
Juhuslavii
(Slovak Evangelical Church of the
Augsburg Confession in Yugoslavia)

ZAIRE (Republic of)

Eglise du Christ au Zaïre
(Communauté baptiste de Zaïre ouest)
(Church of Christ in Zaire — Baptist
Community of Western Zaire)

Eglise du Christ au Zaïre
(Communauté des Disciples du Christ)
(Church of Christ in Zaire —
Community of Disciples of Christ)

Eglise du Christ au Zaïre
(Communauté évangélique)
(Church of Christ in Zaire —
Evangelical Community)

Eglise du Christ au Zaïre
(Communauté lumière)
(Church of Christ in Zaire —
Community of Light)

Eglise du Christ au Zaïre
(Communauté mennonite au Zaïre)
(Church of Christ in Zaire —
Mennonite Community)

Eglise du Christ au Zaïre
(Communauté presbytérienne)
(Church of Christ in Zaire —
Presbyterian Community)

Communauté épiscopale baptiste en
Afrique (CEBA)
(Church of Christ in Zaire —
Episcopal Baptist Community)

Eglise du Jésus-Christ sur la Terre par
le prophète Simon Kimbangu
(Church of Jesus Christ on Earth by the
Prophet Simon Kimbangu)

ZAMBIA

Christian Council of Zambia**
United Church of Zambia

ZIMBABWE

Evangelical Lutheran Church in
Zimbabwe
Methodist Church in Zimbabwe
Reformed Church in Zimbabwe
Zimbabwe Council of Churches**

Abbreviations and Acronyms

AIC	African Instituted (Independent) Churches
AIDS	acquired immune deficiency syndrome
APC	Assembly Planning Committee
BEM	*Baptism, Eucharist and Ministry* (document)
CCA	Christian Conference of Asia
CCC	Caribbean Conference of Churches
CCIA	Commission of the Churches on International Affairs
CCJP	Consultation on the Church and the Jewish People
CCN	Christian Council of Namibia
CCPD	Commission on the Churches' Participation in Development
CDAA	Churches' Drought Action in Africa
CFCs	chlorofluorocarbons
CHCC	China Christian Council
CICARWS	Commission on Inter-Church Aid, Refugee and World Service
CLLT	Course for Leadership in Lay Training
CMC	Christian Medical Commission
CPR	Committee on Programmatic Reorganization
CWCs	Christian World Communions
CWMC	Community of Women and Men in the Church (study)
CWME	Commission on World Mission and Evangelism
ECLOF	Ecumenical Church Loan Fund
ECPG	Eminent Church Persons Group
ECSA	Ecumenical Centre Staff Association
EDCS	Ecumenical Development Cooperative Society
EDF	Ecumenical Development Fund
EDP	electronic data processing
EPC	Ecumenical Prayer Cycle
EWG	Ecumenical Women's Group
FRG	Federal Republic of Germany
GDR	German Democratic Republic
HRAG	Human Rights Advisory Group

HRROLA	Human Rights Resources Office for Latin America
HIV	human immune deficiency virus
IBFAN	International Baby Food Action Network
IMC	International Missionary Council
IMF	International Monetary Fund
IYY	International Youth Year
JPIC	Justice, Peace and the Integrity of Creation
JWG	Joint Working Group
KCF	Korean Christian Federation
LCWE	Lausanne Committee for World Evangelization
LWF	Lutheran World Federation
MECC	Middle East Council of Churches
NCCs	national councils of churches
NCCK	National Council of Churches in Korea
NCCP	National Council of Churches in the Philippines
NGOs	non-governmental organizations
OICD	Office for Income Coordination and Development
PAC	Pan Africanist Congress
PCR	Programme to Combat Racism
PHC	primary health care
PTE	Programme on Theological Education
RCC	Roman Catholic Church
RCL	Renewal and Congregational Life
REOs	regional ecumenical organizations
RTS	round-table structures
SEG	Staff Executive Group
SWAPO	South West Africa People's Organization
TEF	Theological Education Fund
UDI	undesignated income
UNEP	United Nations Environmental Programme
UNESCO	United Nations Educational, Scientific and Cultural Organization
UNHCR	United Nations High Commissioner for Refugees
UNICEF	United Nations Children's Fund
URM	Urban Rural Mission
WCCE	World Council of Christian Education
WEF	World Evangelical Fellowship
WHO	World Health Organization
WSCF	World Student Christian Federation
WUR	Women Under Racism (programme)
WYP	World Youth Projects
YMCA	Young Men's Christian Association